GAA

The Glory Years of Hurling and Football

Ronnie Bellew, a native of Galway,
is a freelance journalist based in Dublin.
He has written extensively on the GAA and
other subjects for publications including the
Sunday Independent and *Ireland on Sunday*.

GAA

The Glory Years of Hurling and Football

RONNIE BELLEW

HODDER
HEADLINE
IRELAND

For my mother
and nephews, Adrian and Ronan

A CIP catalogue record for this title is available from the British Library.

ISBN 0 340 83761 6

Typeset in 11 point Adobe Garamond by Anú Design, Tara
Cover and text design by Anú Design, Tara
Printed and bound in Great Britain by Clays Ltd, St. Ives plc

Hodder Headline Ireland's policy is to use papers that are natural, renewable
and recyclable products and made from wood grown in sustainable forests.
The logging and manufacturing processes are expected to conform to the
environmental regulations of the country of origin.

Hodder Headline Ireland
8 Castlecourt Centre
Castleknock
Dublin 15
Ireland

A division of Hodder Headline, 338 Euston Road, London NW1 3BH, England

Contents

The Changing Face
of the GAA

It could be argued that picking any 15-year period from the GAA's 121-year life cycle to date would provide plenty of material for a book because the organisation has nearly always been at the centre of Irish life and, therefore, has always been newsworthy. But this would not necessarily be an accurate assessment, because there have been periods when the GAA has gone through fairly unruffled times in which it did not impinge on the life of the nation all that much – apart from All-Ireland finals and a few other major games.

This is not true of the period covered in this book by Ronnie Bellew. The start of the book deals with 1991, a season that was dominated by the attention-grabbing, four-game Leinster championship sequence between the footballers of Meath and Dublin that ended on a balmy Saturday afternoon in July in such dramatic fashion when Kevin Foley scored one of the most sensational goals of all time in Croke Park.

It is a good starting point from the perspective of modern GAA history because the three decades before that had seen the GAA, like Ireland itself, battling against the debilitating forces of unemployment and emigration. It was a period in which the GAA did very well to hold its own as thousands of potential club and county hurlers and footballers were forced to leave Ireland to

find employment – many rural clubs, in particular, were deci-
mated in these years. But the strange thing about the GAA then
was that, at the very time when it struggled with the ravages of
emigration, it still stood out as a beacon of hope in many econo-
mically depressed communities. Many GAA clubs, who could
barely find enough players for competitions, still decided to push
ahead with modernising their facilities in the greatest surge of
physical development that the GAA had seen since its foundation.
The result was an extraordinary evolution from often primitive
changing and playing facilities to the most modern resources in
nearly every parish in the land. It was this investment of effort and
money which laid the foundation for the flourishing club and
county scene which the GAA has enjoyed in the period covered
in this book.

While these 15 years will be remembered best for the many
great exploits on the playing fields in both hurling and football,
it has also been a time when the GAA, as a national organisation,
has reinvented itself. The old, conservative, Catholic Church-
dominated image has gradually been dispensed with and has been
replaced by a new image in keeping with the modern Ireland
that has emerged and flourished during this time.

Nothing has epitomised that change more than the decision to
replace the old Croke Park with one of the most modern stadiums
in the world. The sheer magnitude of that task for an amateur
sporting organisation and the incredible efficiency with regard
to financing and expediting the project, showed the GAA in a
whole new light to that large section of Irish society that had
always regarded it as backward, insular and rurally based.

The pace of change in the GAA since 1991 has been amazing.
Then, there was no sponsorship of teams and no names on the
players' jerseys. Rule 21 was in its prime, often being used as a big
stick with which to beat the association whenever other sports

news was slack. And the notion that we would see Irish rugby and soccer teams playing in Croke Park seemed totally unrealistic.

But then everything changed drastically in the Ireland of the last decade of the 20th century and the first of the 21st century. Prosperity came, sneaking in at first and then bursting out in an explosion of affluence that older people could never have envisaged. Commercial sponsorship took off in the GAA at every level from under-14 to All-Ireland finals and suddenly the organisation was awash with money. Inter-county players looked for and got vastly improved 'pay and conditions' in the form of increased mileage allowances, liberal amounts of free playing gear and, in most cases, holidays abroad.

Media coverage of Gaelic games has quadrupled since 1991 with the arrival of local radio stations all over the country being a major contributor.

The previous GAA fear of live television began to evaporate too, as forward-thinking officers realised that the only way to compete for the hearts and minds of young Irish people against the might of televised Premiership matches was to show more hurling and football live on television. Now GAA games are among the leading audience pullers on RTÉ television.

But while the GAA has many facets and infiltrates every aspect of Irish life today, it is the games themselves and the big matches which have been the backbone of the phenomenal progress since 1991.

And what a hectic time we have had! No less than four counties – Donegal, Derry, Armagh and Tyrone – have won their first All-Ireland titles in the past 15 years. By comparison only two counties – Down and Offaly – made the All-Ireland breakthrough in the 25-year period between 1945 and 1990.

At provincial level, we have had remarkable achievements by the footballers of Clare (1992), Leitrim (1994), Kildare (1998),

Laois (2003) and Westmeath (2004) who either won their first titles or won after gaps of more than 40 years. Many of these breakthroughs were inspired by the growth in importance of the cult of the Team Manager, particularly managers who were in charge of county teams other than their own native county – people such as John O'Mahony, Mick O'Dwyer, John Maughan and Páidí Ó Sé.

In hurling, there was the revival of Clare's fortunes which enthralled the whole country as did the return to All-Ireland glory of Wexford and Offaly.

While the arrival of new winners of major titles is always welcome, the confirmation of old traditions is also an integral part of the GAA and, in this book, there are accounts of fabulous clashes between traditional greats such as Tipperary and Cork, Dublin and Meath, Kilkenny and Cork and many others.

I have often noticed a strange dichotomy among GAA supporters which means that success by the great traditional counties in football and hurling is admired and supported at all times but, equally, the arrival of new county teams to sup at the banquet of championship success is also warmly welcomed. In this book, there are several accounts of both scenarios since 1991 which will revive many happy memories.

Today, most people have a very short attention span and, following on that, we can assume that a lot of people quickly forget even substantial moments of recent sporting history. Therefore, *GAA: The Glory Years* will fulfil a very useful purpose in reminding us all, in print, of the great GAA times we have had over the past 15 years.

It is said that journalism is the first draft of history and that aptly applies to this book.

Eugene McGee, September 2005

Foreword

We tuned in to the radio commentary
By the cordial Kerry maestro Micheál Ó Muircheartaigh.
'We send greetings to you all from Djakarta down to Crossmolina
And the ball goes to Kenneth Mortimer having a great game for Mayo
He has a brother doing research work on the Porcupine Bank
But now it goes to Killian Burns of Kerry
The best acordian-playing cornerback in football today.
We hope you're on the astra if you are in outer space.
On my watch it says two minutes and fifty-three seconds left but
We haven't had time to send greetings to our friends in Brazil
Prionsias O'Murchu and Rugierio de Costa e Silva.'

Paul Durcan, *Greetings to Our Friends in Brazil*

On a wet Thursday evening last July, I was standing in a super-market in Stoneybatter when I heard what I thought was the voice of Micheál Ó Muircheartaigh advertising *Hot Press* magazine. I stepped out of the queue and stood closer to the speaker in the corner to confirm that I wasn't imagining it. There was no mistake.

Getting enthusiastic as only he can, it was Ó Muircheartaigh on one of Dublin's commercial radio stations endorsing the maga-zine's GAA special: 'All-Ireland Fever – the GAA's leading stars talk about life at the top. Also in *Hot Press*, track by track on David Gray's new album, The Buzzards, Futurehead, George Clinton and Aimee Mann. *Hot Press*, Out Now!' buzzed the timeless guru of hurling and football. The advertisement only lasted about 30 seconds but the combination of Ó Muircheartaigh and *Hot Press* struck me as a neat epiphany that captures how far the GAA and Ireland have journeyed since the early 1990s.

Fifteen years ago, the notion of *Hot Press* devoting its front cover to the championship and hiring the voice of the GAA to promote the magazine would have been as unthinkable as Bono being asked to sit in as the expert analyst for the All-Ireland hurling final commentary. In the 1980s and early 1990s, *Hot Press* – the unofficial voice of alternative Ireland – was usually fairly hostile towards the GAA. Its sports columnists delighted in humorously gratuitous attacks on 'bogball' (Gaelic football) and 'stickfighting' (hurling). The jibes only mildly rankled with those of us who didn't see any contradiction about playing in a minor hurling match and then going home to unwind to Morrissey, Bowie and The Pogues. Behind the comedy, though, was a serious subtext. Bogball and stickfighting weren't just unfashionable; they were, in the eyes of the *Hot Press* commentators and others, bound up with religious repression, gombeen politics, strait-laced Gaeilgeoirs, and the plain people of Ireland who ate their dinners in the middle of the day.

The reality was far more complex, something that became apparent to even the most caustic critics of the GAA as the 1990s progressed. In July 2005, *Hot Press* was able to declare: 'The GAA is part of what we are. Forget Oxygen or U2 at Croke Park, the biggest shows in town this summer are the All-Ireland championships.'

The leap from the days of bogball and stickfighting to Croke Park 'having the monopoly on must see gigs', is the story of this book. It's the story of the events on and off the field, the breakthroughs, the controversies and the personalities behind a golden era that saw the GAA reinvent itself to become the hottest ticket in town.

Ronnie Bellew, October 2005

1991

The Empire Strikes Back

'You almost wish someone, anyone, would end it. It's gone beyond a joke now.'

Tommy Carr, Dublin senior football captain, 23 June 1991

IT'S DOUBTFUL IF HURLING or football will ever produce anything like it again. Choosing a particular date or event as the beginning of an era is a foolhardy business, but the series of championship games between Dublin and Meath in 1991 was an epochal experience for the GAA. It took four games and a goal from the realms of fantasy to separate the teams and, 14 years on, the series still has the capacity to enthrall.

There had been other great replay cycles in the GAA's 107-year history. The three games it required Kerry to beat Kildare in the 1903 All-Ireland football final are credited with giving birth to Gaelic football as we know it today. Cork and Kilkenny played out an era-defining trilogy for the 1931 All-Ireland hurling title and it took Sligo six games to beat Roscommon in the 1925

Connacht championship; but the Dublin–Meath saga was the first modern epic played out in Croke Park in front of capacity crowds, television cameras and blanket media coverage.

By the time it finished on a sweltering afternoon in July, 237,377 spectators had paid in to see the teams, breaking all previous gate-receipt records. In another first, the authorities gave the go-ahead for live television coverage of the final game and thousands of replica Dublin jerseys were sold to the new Hill 16 army in the weeks leading up to the denouement. At a time when the GAA was beset with uncertainty and anxiety about its future, the footballers of Dublin and Meath gave the association a glorious jolt in the direction of new opportunities and horizons.

The Dublin–Meath series couldn't have occurred at a more opportune time for the GAA. The previous summer, the entire country had been in thrall to the adventures of the Irish soccer team as they progressed to the World Cup quarter-final in Rome. There are academics who will argue that Italia '90 had a profound impact on the national psyche and that the Celtic Tiger was actually conceived during those heady days and nights in Cagliari, Palermo and Rome. Whatever about the socio-economic analysis, the street-level experience of Italia '90 was liberating and joyful at a time when there was an almost fatalistic acceptance of mass unemployment, emigration, and institutionalised hypocrisy in affairs of the Church, state and high finance. It wasn't quite as bad as the 'septic Isle' that Bob Geldolf railed against 10 years earlier in The Boomtown Rats' 'Banana Republic', but there were plenty of demons clattering away in the national closet waiting for release.

For the GAA, Italia '90 presented its own set of dilemmas and challenges. Only the most hardline and bigoted of Gaels resented the Irish team's success but, at the same time, the GAA couldn't but wonder what consequences the experience of an

Irish team competing in the biggest sporting event in the world would have on its own playing numbers and attendances in the years ahead. The drain of emigration meant some rural clubs were already struggling to field teams. Some county boards routinely reported losses and issued warnings about not being able to finance the preparation of county teams. Above all, there was the fear, irrational as it turned out, that, lured by the glamour and sophistication of international and cross-channel soccer, impressionable youngsters would abandon the jersey of their forefathers and defect en masse to the 'Garrison Game'. There was no shortage of pessimists, both within and without the GAA, predicting dark days for the association.

The pessimism was unfounded. The GAA had proven itself immune to all types of upheavals and challenges since its foundation in 1884. It had such hardy roots in the countryside and towns, was so tribal in nature and had such a network of grounds, clubhouses and support that it was unlikely to wilt before competition from Jack's Army – and the FAI, as it proved time and time again during the 1990s, was chronically ill-equipped to exploit any potential dividend that Italia '90 might have produced for domestic soccer. The public response to the Dublin–Meath saga and Cork and Tipperary's joust in Munster proved that there was still a huge appetite for championship football and hurling. Most genuine Irish sports followers were equally at home at a Gaelic, hurling, soccer or rugby match. If the GAA got its act together and cast off the dowdy duds of the past and embraced the modern, there was nothing surer than that a sporting public, who had rediscovered the thrill of live action during Italia '90, would follow.

The President Elect of the GAA, Peter Quinn, cut straight to the nub of the issue during the run-up the 1991 Annual Congress when he stated: 'It [the GAA] is seen as negative, defensive and excessively conservative and backward. I would like to see us have a more positive image.' Quinn, an accountant and businessman from Teemore, County Fermanagh, was a moderniser who recognised that the organisation had unrivalled strengths in its games and the loyalty of hundreds of thousands of people whose lives were enriched by involvement – playing or otherwise – with the GAA.

But he also realised the association was badly in need of an image makeover, the injection of new ideas and vast amounts of cash if the vision for the redevelopment of Croke Park and other projects was to be successful. In Quinn, and Director-General Liam Mulvihill, the GAA had the architects for its equivalent of *glasnost* and *perestroika*. Pragmatism and financial savvy would be the guiding principles during the 1990s and the decision of delegates at the 1991 Congress to finally scrap the ban on teams wearing sponsored jerseys was the first indication of the reforms to come.

Kildare footballers, backed by a high-powered supporters club that had lured Mick O'Dwyer out of retirement to manage the Lilywhites, were the one of the first teams to take to the field in sponsored jerseys when they arrived in Croke Park for a National Football League semi-final against Donegal in April 1991. The Shannon Airport connection saw Clare hurlers find a patron in the Russian national airline Aeroflot and, for a while, the Bannermen sported saffron and blue jerseys with Cyrillic lettering across their chests. Dublin had a brief liaison with the alcohol-free beer Kaliber before Arnott's took over. With the team sponsorship issue finally resolved, the way was clear for the GAA to secure a multimillion pound sponsorship of the championships and begin the reconstruction of Croke Park.

The timing was auspicious. The slow push for reform off the field was overtaken by events on it. By the end of the decade, the one-time 'minnows', 'Cinderellas' and 'weaker counties' – to use the quaint terminology of GAA programmes – had stormed the barricades of tradition and it is their players, managers, officials and supporters who were the making of the modern GAA.

IT WAS RECENT HISTORY, not the future, that preoccupied the minds of Meath and Dublin supporters in the weeks before their Leinster championship first round clash on 2 June. Enmity rather than rivalry would be the best word to describe the dynamic between the counties. Since the mid-1980s, their annual encounters had become increasingly fractious affairs. Meath had been in the ascendant in Leinster since 1986 and had won three provincial titles and two All-Irelands before Dublin halted the sequence in 1989. A year later, Meath regained control before losing to Cork in the All-Ireland final and the 1991 encounter was anticipated as the game that would indicate where the balance of power would swing for the new decade.

Over 51,000 spectators – a record for a first-round championship game – paid into Croke Park, the attendance beefed up by casual observers expecting more than the usual quota of mêlées and punch-ups. Dublin were marginal favourites. New manager Paddy Cullen and his selectors, Dr Pat O'Neill and Jim Brogan, had assembled an athletic and rugged bunch of players. The team had been there-or-thereabouts since winning a National League title in 1987 and players, such as John O'Leary, Gerry Hargan, Tommy Carr, Keith Barr, Jack Sheedy, Paul Curran, Mick Clarke and Charlie Redmond, had the look of potential All-Ireland winners. They were perceived as the coming force in contrast to an ageing Meath team in their ninth year of management under Seán Boylan. No-hopers when he assumed control in 1982, Boylan had worked wonders with the Royals but, by 1991, it appeared as though time was catching up with the

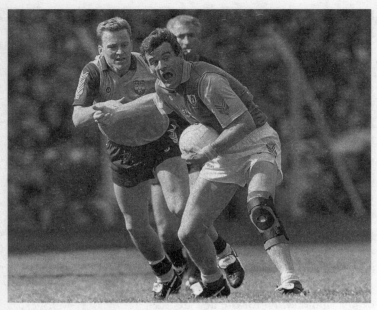

Colm O'Rourke (Meath) and Keith Barr (Dublin) were key figures in the 1991 Leinster saga.

spine of the team: full-back Mick Lyons, centre-back Liam Harnan, midfielder Gerry McEntee and centre-forward Colm O'Rourke. Other stalwarts, such as Martin O'Connell, Liam Hayes and P.J. Gillic, were also deemed to be edging past their best and Dublin's favouritism appeared justified when they totally outplayed their opponents to lead 1–7 to 1–2 at half-time.

The first 35 minutes laid down the pattern for the rest of the saga; Dublin playing the more open, expansive football but were unable to shake off a typically stubborn Meath who tended to drift in and out of matches, snipe for scores from play and leave the rest up to Stafford's accuracy from frees. Meath had a Stafford goal from a disputed penalty to thank for still being within striking distance at half-time but, in the second period with Hayes taking control at midfield, they gradually wore Dublin down. Stafford's accuracy from frees and the industry of newcomer Tommy Dowd saw Meath narrow the gap to a point with time almost up and a stroke of luck was enough to scramble a draw. A desperation kick from Gillic bounced high in the Dublin square and eluded both the goalkeeper John O'Leary and corner-forward Flynn to hop over the bar for the equaliser: 1–12 to 1–12 after a grim game of football.

It was the bounce that launched a thousand stories. More than 60,000 supporters were present for the replay a week later. Dublin started with veteran Barney Rock, a survivor from the 1983 team that beat Galway in the All-Ireland final despite having three players sent off, for the injured Charlie Redmond. Rock hadn't played a competitive game for three months but he was flawless from frees and scored eight points of Dublin's final tally of 1–11. Another veteran, Colm O'Rourke, returned for Meath and subdued the influence of Dublin's attacking centre-back Keith Barr.

This time around Meath led by three points at half-time but Rock's accuracy pushed Dublin ahead in the third quarter before Mick Lyons was sent off after a punch-up with Vinny Murphy. The sides were level in the last minute when Murphy found himself clean through on the Meath goalkeeper Mickey McQuillan but, instead of tapping over or fisting his point, Murphy opted for goal and McQuillan was able to deflect his effort away. David Beggy – who had spent the winter playing rugby in Scotland and was being talked up as a possible Irish international – and Jack Sheedy exchanged goals in the first 10 minutes of injury-time but, incredibly, there were to be no more scores in the remaining 24 minutes that saw a number of Dublin players and referee Tommy Howard succumb to cramp. Final score: Dublin 1–11 Meath 1–11.

'Do These Players Have Anymore To Give?' asked one headline

the next morning. They did and plenty. They were reluctantly given a two-week break by the Leinster Council before the second replay. Meath were boosted by the return of Mick Lyons from suspension while McEntee and Colm Coyle were also back in the squad. McEntee had watched the first two games from the stands but, like Coyle, was to play a critical role in, yet again, hauling Meath back from the precipice.

Whatever personal grudges needed to be sorted out between the combatants had been exhausted in the first two games and the third match was easily the most enjoyable and engaging to date. Dublin were five ahead with 15 minutes to go but it was then that McEntee and Coyle proved their worth. In the 61st minute, Coyle launched the ball goalwards and Flynn was able to punch it home. Two points from Stafford, the last in the 72nd minute, levelled the match for Meath. In the first period of extra-time, McEntee created the opening for a Coyle goal before Dublin responded when Paul Curran poked the ball to the net. Stafford, who kicked 0–10 in total, restored Meath's lead with two frees but Curran had the final say on this occasion when he steered home the Dublin equaliser in the 97th minute. Final score: Dublin 1–14 Meath 2–11.

By now, the saga had taken on a life of its own and the rumour machine in both counties went into overdrive. One day Brian Stynes was on his way back from Australian Rules to rescue the Dubs; the next, former Irish international Kevin Moran – the hero of Dublin's famous 1977 semi-final triumph over Kerry – was about to return from Blackburn Rovers to orchestrate the culchies' downfall. Meath, wisely, upped camp and travelled to Scotland for a weekend's respite from the madness.

While Dublin and Meath prepared for their fourth meeting, the championship gathered momentum elsewhere. Draws were the motif of the summer. Tipperary and Cork played gripping hurling over two games in the Munster final. In the Leinster hurling championship, Dublin, under the management of Lar Foley, shocked Offaly in one semi-final while Kilkenny scraped past Wexford in the other thanks to a last-minute goal from an emerging star called D.J. Carey. Laois and Louth played out another draw in Leinster. A 19-year-old championship debutante called Derek Duggan landed a wunderpoint from a 60-yard free to earn a draw for Roscommon against Mayo in the Connacht football final. Equally spectacular was Ross Carr's injury-time equaliser from a 55-yard free to give Down a lifeline against Derry. As the year unfolded, it proved to be the most decisive kick of all but, for now, the attention of the neutrals was still captivated by the struggle between Meath and Dublin.

The third replay was fixed for Saturday, 7 July and attracted another capacity crowd of 62,000 to Croke Park with hundreds of thousands more in Ireland and abroad watching the game live on television. The game followed the, by now, familiar pattern. Dublin tore into Meath and with captain Tommy Carr, Keith Barr and Eamonn Heery playing brilliant football in the half-back line they were six points ahead by the 50th minute. They suffered a set-back when losing the outstanding Carr to injury but still appeared poised to finally take control of the series. Stafford, though, had other ideas. A seriously underrated player, he scored a goal after 54 minutes to leave Meath trailing by 0–12 to 1–7.

Dublin, though, were able to weather the crisis to go four clear again and they were still three to the good when they won a penalty. Keith Barr drove his shot inches wide but Guiden reopened a four-point gap minutes later before Stafford brought it back to three. Just when the Hill could sense victory, there came one of those moments that haunt a player and team for ever. There were less than three minutes on the clock when substitute Vinny Murphy was presented with an opportunity to

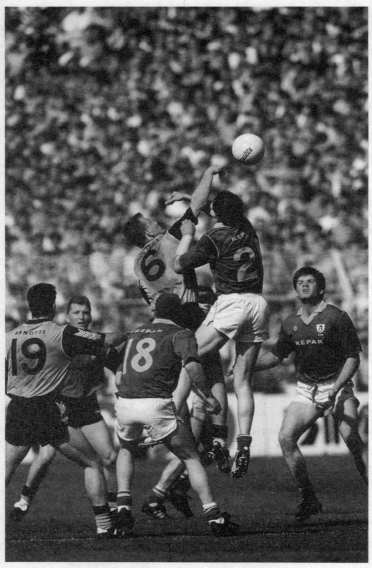

Dublin's Keith Barr rises highest in this clash against Meath.

deliver the fatal blow. It looked a like a good scoring opportunity but, maybe mindful of his last-minute miss in the first replay, Murphy elected to pass the ball to team-mate Declan Sheahan. The ball never reached Sheahan and instead was intercepted close to his own goal by Meath wing-back Martin O'Connell.

Dublin's spirit was finally broken by what happened next. The Meath equaliser has been replayed and dissected countless times in the intervening years but still retains its compelling and climactic quality. Here's how the late Jack Mahon, an All-Ireland medalist with Galway in 1956, describes it in his *History of Gaelic Football*: 'O'Connell found Mick Lyons who gave the ball to Mattie McCabe. On to Liam Harnan, who booted it downfield to Colm O'Rourke. O'Rourke was fouled by Mick Kennedy and he took a quick free, finding David Beggy on his left. One hop and one solo and he transferred to the half-back Kevin Foley. On from him to P.J. Gillic who flicked it on to Tommy Dowd. Dowd took the ball at speed and this injection of pace threw Dublin. Dowd transferred to O'Rourke, but he kept on running and took the return pass also at speed. It seemed as if Tommy himself would score but he passed to Kevin Foley on the edge of the square with the goal at his mercy. The rest is history.'

One can only imagine the collective internal panic that must have afflicted the Dublin team at that moment. After 340 minutes of football, they were still level on the scoreboard but a spent force mentally and they were unable to retain possession from their own kick-out. Meath captain Liam Hayes booted a pinpoint, cross-field pass to Gillic who transferred to Beggy and he casually swung the clincher over the bar. It was endgame at last: Meath 2–10 Dublin 0–15.

Over the four games, Dublin had been the better team but their repeated failure to hold their nerve when the big prize was within touching distance was a flaw that would surface again.

There was no doubting the essential character of the team, though, and they showed immense heart to go on and win three successive Leinster titles before eventually claiming the Sam Maguire in 1995 with eight of the team and subs that played in the 1991 series. Boylan and Meath would be back the following year to take the Leinster and All-Ireland titles from them but just three of the 1991 team would feature in that success. For players such as Harnan, Lyons, McEntee, Hayes, Flynn and Stafford, the four games against Dublin were a defiant reminder of the glory days of 1987 and 1988. Having survived the war with their arch enemy and seen their other bugbear Cork crash out in Munster, they were quickly installed as favourites to round off the first decade of Boylan's stewardship with a third All-Ireland title. Down, the outsiders in Ulster, had other ideas.

Dublin v. Meath, 6 July 1991

Dublin

John O'Leary

Mick Deegan   Gerry Hargan   Mick Kennedy

Tommy Carr   Keith Barr   Eamonn Heery

Jack Sheedy   Paul Bealin

Charlie Redmond   Paul Curran   Niall Guiden

Declan Sheehan   Paul Clarke   Mick Galvin

Subs: Ray Holland for Carr, Joe McNally for Clarke,
Vinny Murphy for Redmond

Meath

Mickey McQuillan

Robbie O'Malley   Mick Lyons   Padraig Lyons

Kevin Foley   Liam Harnan   Martin O'Connell

Liam Hayes   P.J. Gillic

David Beggy   Colm O'Rourke   Tommy Dowd

Colm Coyle   Brian Stafford   Bernard Flynn

SUBS: Finian Murtagh for P. Lyons, Gerry McEntee for
Murtagh, Mattie McCabe for Flynn

BRENDAN McEVOY, secretary of the Down County Board,
wasn't a happy man in January 1991. At 27, he was one of the
youngest officials in the GAA and his analysis of the county's
disappointing exit to Armagh in the previous year's Ulster championship was scathing. 'They were diabolical,' wrote McEvoy in
his report to the county convention. 'For 60 minutes, they played
like a team without method and devoid of ideas. Unless every
single player adopts an attitude of single-minded dedication to
the common goal, then success will continue to pass us by and
we will have nobody to blame but ourselves.'

The omens for 1991 weren't good. The previous autumn, one
third of the players invited to join the Down panel said no. 'Why
has representing the county become unattractive to so many?'

wondered McEvoy. In the New Year, Down were relegated from Division One of the National Football League and there were reports of discord in the camp and poor attendances at training in the run-up to their championship rematch with Armagh.

It was a near-crisis situation for a county that, in 1960, had taken the Sam Maguire across the border for the first time and retained the title the following year before adding a third in 1968. Down weren't just winners – they played uninhibited, attacking football with the emphasis on flair and skill. Their displays in 1960, 1961 and 1968 saw them bracketed along with Kerry and the Galway teams of the 1950s and 1960s as among the purists of the game. They were also tactical innovators and one of the first teams to adopt a modern, professional approach in the preparation of teams for the championship. Players such Paddy Doherty, Sean O'Neill, James McCartan and Dan McCartan were household names throughout the country and such a box-office draw that the 1961 final between the northern side and first-time finalists Offaly drew a record crowd of 90,556 to Croke Park.

By 1991, though, Down had been on the slide from glory for over two decades and just three Ulster titles had been annexed since 1968, the last in 1981. Pete McGrath had taken over as manager in 1990 and while he guided the side to the National League final in his first year in charge, Down's demanding supporters had no great faith in him. McGrath had coached St Colman's Newry to three All-Ireland Colleges titles and had managed the county minors who won the All-Ireland in 1987, but was way down the shortlist of candidates for the senior job and was only appointed after several of the county board's preferred choices said no.

Ross Carr summed up the mood of the players when he said, 'There was no real single-mindedness going into the championship in 1991. I didn't play in the National League. I only came back training for the championship and, three or four weeks before the championship, there was a dozen training at most. People talk about plans that must have been made to win the All-Ireland back in October but by the time the championship came around, we were only concerned about beating Armagh in Newry.'

The one plus Down had was a streak of quality running through the side. Greg Blaney, Paddy O'Rourke and Liam Austen were hardened campaigners and in Mickey Linden, they had one of the game's most gifted forwards. McGrath had unearthed a couple of jewels in James McCartan, the scion of the 1960s dynasty who had played on the 1987 minor side, and Conor Deegan, who had made the transition to senior to claim the full-back position. Ross Carr and Gary Mason in the half-forward line were both dependable deadball strikers and dangerous from general play. McGrath had also discovered another new player, Peter Withnell, who would explode into action later in the summer.

The game against Armagh in Newry was hard, low-scoring first-round fare with a penalty from Linden keeping Down in touch during a first half in which they only managed one other score from play. In the second half, Down kicked six points to Armagh's two and won by 1–7 to 0–8. Derry were next in the semi-final and Down looked a far more potent force in this match and led by 0–9 to 0–4 at half-time, having played some of the best football seen from the county for years. They went seven up early in the second half but the dismissal of centre-forward Greg Blaney unhinged the Mournemen. Derry clawed back the lead and were a point ahead with five minutes left. They still looked like winners heading into injury-time when Barry Breen won a free for Down 55 yards from the Derry goal. Facing the breeze, Carr calmly booted the ball over the bar: All square at 0–13 to 1–10.

Carr scored nine points in the replay as Down swept into the Ulster final with five points to spare, but they were definitely the underdogs when they faced reigning champions Donegal in

Clones on 28 July. It was the day the entire country was served notice of a new force emerging in the north. Playing football reminiscent of the teams from the 1960s, Down ripped Donegal asunder in the first half. With Linden orchestrating the show, they scored 1–6 without reply between the 10th and 25th minutes and led by seven at the break. Their accuracy deserted them in the second half but they still looked a class apart from a Donegal side who learned a hard lesson about the perils of cockiness and complacency that would stand to them the following season.

The meeting of Down and Kerry revived memories of the great clashes between the counties in the 1960s but the 1991 semi-final was a stop–start sort of match between two tense teams. Kerry still had some survivors from the 1975–86 era on board, including Charlie Nelligan, Jack O'Shea, Pat Spillane and Ambrose O'Donovan, but were a team in transition and looked to a new green and gold superstar called Maurice Fitzgerald for inspiration. In a frantic opening 10 minutes, Fitzgerald struck the crossbar twice and Blaney also hit the woodwork for Down while Linden was wide from a penalty.

Down were unlikely semi-finalists and they found an unlikely match winner in the shape of full-forward Peter Withnell. Withnell's story sums up Down's season; unknown at the start of the summer, by the end of September he had become a folk hero after his first season in championship football. The big Drumassin man had been destined for a career in professional soccer with Reading Town until injury disrupted his progress. By 1990, he was working in London and played some Gaelic football in New Eltham to keep himself in shape. He returned home in the autumn of 1990 and was called into the Down squad at the last minute one evening when McGrath was trying to make up the numbers for a challenge match against Meath. Withnell possessed a powerful physique, had a soccer striker's eye for goal and McGrath saw enough that evening to realise he had the makings of an inter-county full-forward.

Withnell had a quiet Ulster championship but came good against Kerry. He blasted a left-footed shot to the net after 20 minutes to steady Down and leave them a point in arrears at half-time. The second half saw more tortuous football with the grand total of three points scored in the 25 minutes after half-time and the sides were level 1–5 to 0–8 with eight minutes left. Mickey Linden eased the tension for Down with a point and Withnell applied the decisive touch when he won a long ball targeted at Linden and scored a second goal, this time off his right. Down added three more points to become 2–9 to 0–8 winners.

Meath waited. The games against Dublin had been the start of a long, long trek to a fourth final in six years. Boylan's men needed two games to beat Wicklow before hammering Offaly in the semi-final and only came good in the second half of the Leinster final against Laois. It had taken them eight games to

Peter Withnell returned from England to play an important part in Down's 1991 campaign.

escape from the province and the strain showed in the All-Ireland semi-final against a fine Roscommon team that led by five points entering the final 20 minutes. The nonchalant Stafford scored five points in the final three minutes as Meath staggered into the final on a 0–15 to 1–11 scoreline.

Despite their topsy-turvy summer, they were warm favourites to beat Down on 15 September, although the loss of Colm O'Rourke because of a throat infection in the week before the game was an acute body blow to a team that some shrewd observers felt was already a busted flush. The outsiders tag was perfect for Down, who avoided the hysteria and overwhelming expectation that had undermined Armagh and Tyrone when they had reached finals in 1977 and 1986.

Down had the tradition of winning in Croke Park and Ross Carr later said tradition acted as reassurance rather than a burden as they prepared for Meath: 'As opposed to having a monkey on your back, we took the attitude that we're back where we belong. That year we were lucky that some of the '60s players came to training and told us what the day would be like. Unlike other Ulster teams, we knew what to expect and we were going to a place we were comfortable in. Our fellas were relaxed. The occasion wasn't going to get to them.' It didn't appear so in the first 20 minutes with Down relying on Gary Mason's frees to stay in the game but they eventually discovered their rhythm and led 0–8 to 0–4 at half-time.

After the break, the Ulster team found another gear and a goal from Barry Breen, along with two more points from McCartan and Blaney eased them 1–14 to 0–5 in front before Meath roused themselves for one last effort. O'Rourke's introduction was the catalyst for another breathtaking comeback and the Leinster side outscored their opponents by 1–9 to 0–2 in the final 16 minutes. A goal from Hayes gave Meath some hope, as did Linden's miss when he was one-on-one with Meath keeper McQuillan. The gap had narrowed to four before Eamonn Burns and Gary Mason calmed Down's nerves with two points to leave the score 1–16 to 1–10 after 61 minutes. Meath pressed on and three points from Bernard Flynn, who had earlier forced a spectacular save from Collins, and another from Stafford, left a kick of the ball in it approaching injury-time. This time, there was to be no repeat of 6 July. Down's captain Paddy O'Rourke broke up one final Meath assault and skied the ball into the Hogan Stand where no Meath player could retrieve it. Final score: Down 1–16 Meath 1–14.

The semi-mutinous crew of the spring had transformed into winners. O'Rourke, Blaney, Carr, Linden and veterans, such as Liam Austen and Ambrose Rodgers, had finally stepped out of the shadows of their legendary predecessors. Sam Maguire was travelling north for the first time in 25 years but, as the cup made its way to Newry on Monday evening, no one could have predicted the iron grip that Ulster football was about to take on the championship.

Down All-Ireland Champions 1991

Neil Collins

Brendan McKiernan   Conor Deegan   Paul Higgins

John Kelly   Paddy O'Rourke   D.J. Kane

Barry Breen   Eamonn Burns

Ross Carr   Greg Blaney   Gary Mason

Mickey Linden   Peter Withnell   James McCartan

Subs: Liam Austin for Breen, Ambrose Rodgers for Withnell

Down captain Paddy O'Rourke acclaims his county's 1991 All-Ireland final victory.

A Bona-Fide Munster Classic

No other competition in the GAA calendar is shrouded with such mystique and self-regard as the Munster hurling championship. Some commentators would have us believe that every Munster final is a crucible for super-human feats, although the hard evidence points to a more prosaic view. Kevin Cashman, Cork's most eminent hurling commentator, wrote in 1995 that only 14 of the 50 Munster finals he had attended were memorable.

The 1991 renewal between Tipperary and Cork, though, was the bona-fide article; between stirring comebacks, great individual displays, disputed scores and an old-style pitch invasion, it had all the ingredients to reassure even the most demanding of *cognoscenti* that the Munster championship could still generate contests of near-mythic proportions. On the same weekend that Dublin and Meath played out the final act of their duel in Leinster, Páirc Uí Chaoimh played host to what Tipperary manager, Babs Keating, described afterwards as 'one of the best games of hurling ever played'.

Keating had masterminded an end to the county's 16-year Munster famine when he led them to the title in 1987. Tipperary made it three-in-a-row in Munster in 1989 when they also brought the All-Ireland title back to the 'home of hurling' for the first time in 18 years. It was an All-Ireland diminished in the eyes of many – including some Tipperary people – because of the controversial circumstances of the ▶

semi-final victory over Galway and the rout of Antrim in the final. Tipperary had been expected to silence the doubters in 1990 but were ambushed in the Munster final by a Cork side riled up by Keating's pre-match analogy between Cork and donkeys being expected to compete against thoroughbreds. Babs kept his counsel in the run-up to the 1991 final but, at nine points behind after 17 minutes, his team looked set for another fall. Tipperary somehow steadied themselves and got to grips with Cork's lethal full-forward line who scored 4–4 between them. John Leahy led the fight back and, in the final quarter, Tipp outscored the home team by 1–6 to 0–2. They levelled the match in the last seconds after Nicky English was denied a possible score when the umpires signalled his kicked effort for a point wide, prompting the injury-stricken legend to muse 'if I had ducks they'd drown'.

English didn't start in the replay in Thurles. The Hennessy–Fitzgerald–Fitzgibbon axis was again on fire and a goal from Hennessy left Cork leading 3–13 to 1–10 with 23 minutes left. Sensing a possible humiliation, Keating and his selectors made a number of critical switches and substitutions, including bringing on Aidan Ryan, who scored the winning goal. When Tipp captain Declan Carr (a brother of Dublin football captain Tommy) doubled the ball to the net to square the match at 3–15 with eight minutes of normal time remaining, the atmosphere in Semple Stadium exploded. In a throwback to the 1940s, Tipperary supporters had already launched a series of pitch invasions from their vantage point on the Killanin End terrace – the initial breach being led by a battler in a wheelchair – to celebrate successive Tipperary scores. An appeal from Babs to the invaders to clear the field went ignored and the last 10 or so minutes were played out with Tipperary supporters massed behind Ger Cunningham in the Cork goal. Tipp were two up when that great Cork poacher Tomás Mulcahy saw a shot ricochet off the post. The play swung quickly towards the Killanin End and Aidan Ryan vindicated the selectors when he soloed through from the wing before blasting the sliotar past Cunningham. Two final points from Cleary secured the title for the home side on a majestic 4–19 to 4–15 scoreline.

Tipperary easily accounted for a fading Galway side in the semi-final (3–13 to 1–9) to book a date with 3/1 outsiders Kilkenny in the final. The Leinster side were in transition and had stumbled through the campaign with narrow wins over Wexford, Dublin and Antrim but the sight of the old foe in the blue and gold roused them to a mighty effort on a dank day in Croke Park. Christy Heffernan and John Power caused chaos in the Tipperary defence during a first half that ended level at 0–9, apiece, although Kilkenny should have been at least three or four ahead given their chances. The game turned on two incidents in the third quarter; Power's influence was diminished when he received a nasty hand injury and, in the 45th minute, Tipperary scored the only goal when a harmless looking 20-metre free was mishit by Cleary but drifted all the way to the Kilkenny net. The Tipperary full-back line played some fine hurling in the final 20 minutes, along with Leahy and the unerring Fox and Cleary to earn Tipp a 1–16 to 0–15 victory. Colm Bonnar also had an outstanding game at the back and along with his brothers, Conal and Cormac, collected a second All-Ireland medal.

Tipperary had regained their title the hard way, but 10 years would pass before the Premier county tasted All-Ireland glory again.

1992

Sam's for the Hills

'Frankly, I don't think we can do it in 15 years and it may take between 20 and 30.'

**GAA Director General Liam Mulvihill,
on the redevelopment of Croke Park, February 1992**

'By their heroic deeds in Croke Park, the Donegal senior football team have done more for the morale of the people of Tir Conaill in 70 minutes than the total efforts of governments and politicians alike since the founding of the State in 1922.'

Michael McHugh, *Donegal Democrat*, September 1992

THE GAA HAS NO OFFICIAL CLOSED SEASON but serious playing action – bar the occasional club championship game – effectively stops between mid-December and the beginning of February. With the pitches all but deserted, it's the administrators who take centre stage and the county conventions usually provide plenty of copy for the newspapers as board officers and club delegates express the concerns of the grassroots.

There's an inventory of hardy annuals that reappear without fail each year: the threat to the GAA from other codes; the opening up of Croke Park to said codes; the decline of hurling; confusion about the rules in Gaelic football; creeping professionalism; the shortage of referees and the inequities in the distribution of tickets for All-Ireland finals. In January 1992, the ticket problem was to the fore in Limerick where a delegate was bothered about the phenomenon of women with knitting needles acquiring tickets for All-Ireland finals: 'What I don't understand is that you see women with knitting needles and others with books and, towards the end, they will turn to you and ask which team is winning. How these people get tickets is beyond me,' said the man from Castletown. Further south at the Kerry convention, a motion from the Tarbert Club that Croke Park be rented out for soccer and rugby drew an exasperated response from one delegate who declared, 'People in the soccer world would drop dead in the morning if we offered them Croke Park. It's the last thing they want because they would have no one to whip anymore!'

Elsewhere, the mood was more serious. As unemployment edged towards the 300,000 mark and with the country effectively in hock to the international banks, the GAA wasn't immune from the deadening economic malaise. The Mayo convention was told that 70 companies nationwide had been approached about sponsoring the county team but that the 'response was extremely disappointing'. Leitrim were in a similar position. The county board there heard 'that there was no hope of getting a major sponsor' and that it was facing bankruptcy. Only the work of the county's supporters' club in Dublin was 'saving [them] from *Stubbs Gazette*'. Whatever about the localised financial problems, at a national level, the GAA was about to take the giant leap into the future and the unknown. Already in negotiations to find multimillion-pound sponsors for the football and hurling champ-ionships, on 2 February, it lodged the final planning application for the redevelopment of Croke Park. A week later, it publicly unveiled the plans for what the papers dubbed 'Space-Age Croker'. Given the prevailing national economic gloom, the vision of a self-financed, 79,000-capacity new stadium was an extraordinary statement of faith in the GAA's future. Little wonder that An t-Uachtarán Peter Quinn was fighting fit when he addressed the association's Annual Congress in April. 'As we assembled here a year ago, we were being warned of the imminent decline of the association, of the irresistible threat from major sporting extravaganzas and the need to change our policies,' he said. 'The usual harbingers of gloom and the critics were having a field day but, on the field of play, an outstanding series of championship games temporarily silenced them.'

Playing to the audience, Quinn continued, 'Again this year we are being warned that we shoot ourselves in the foot with every decision, that our policies fly in the face of progress, that we suffer from suicidal tendencies, that we are out of touch with reality and that the combination of social and governmental pressure will force us to abandon our established ideals. We have heard it all before, and we didn't panic then and there's no need to panic now.'

The most important clause of Quinn's bullish rallying cry to the troops was the reference to the 'outstanding series of championship games'. If 1991 was the year of the draw, 1992 was the year of the breakthrough. By October, a new name had been added to the football roll-of-honour for the first time in 21 years; Clare footballers had ended a 75-year wait for a Munster title; Down hurlers had bridged a 51-year gap in Ulster and Waterford had taken a first All-Ireland under-21 hurling crown.

Down's First All-Star Hurler

Gerard McGrattan was a complete unknown at the start of the 1992 hurling championship but, by the end of the year, he had created his own piece of hurling history by becoming the first Down player to win an All-Star award. The 19-year-old half-forward from Portaferry was a sensation in his first championship season when Down bridged a 51-year gap to claim the Ulster hurling title.

Down hurling is centred round three senior clubs in the Ards Peninsula – Ballygalget, Ballycran and Portaferry – and, while there had been steady signs of progress in the isolated outcrop since the late 1980s, the team's breakthrough in the 1992 championship was unexpected, even though they had been edging closer to Antrim in the previous three seasons. ▶

Having given Kilkenny a serious fight in the 1991 semi-final, Antrim were confident of making it four-in-a-row in Ulster and having another crack at southern opposition. The favourites paid the price for whatever complacency existed when they were comprehensively beaten 2–16 to 0–11 in Casement Park on 19 July. Showing the benefit of having played Division One hurling during the winter and spring, Down, under the management of former Antrim coach Sean McGuiness, hurled Antrim off the field. Senior footballer Greg Blaney, his brother Michael and Noel Sands all played key roles in a famous victory but it was McGrattan who stood out as the class hurler on the day.

He enhanced his reputation with another uninhibited performance against Cork in the All-Ireland semi-final, scoring 5 points from play in just his third senior championship game. Down had given Cork plenty to think about in the first 20 minutes of the match, but the Rebels eventually pulled away to win by 2–17 to 1–11.

It was Down hurlers' finest day in Croke Park since 1932 when the county's minor team – comprised entirely of students from Newry CBS – lost out to a late Kilkenny rally in the All-Ireland semi-final. The Down–Newry CBS outfit were drilled by a Brother Rice from Kilkenny and one of the Kilkenny newspapers expressed astonishment the following week that such a band of skilful hurlers existed in the 'black north'. We don't know what became of Brother Rice and his band of players but Down proved their breakthrough in 1992 was no fluke by winning further titles in the 1990s.

A bad run of injuries meant that McGrattan never again attained the heights of 1992 but, despite the setbacks, he continued to hurl with the county until 2004.

THE FIRST FIRES were spotted in Leitrim and, by the time the
train reached Sligo, 10,000 supporters were waiting for the
Donegal players, their manager Brian McEniff and the Sam
Maguire. It was dark when they escaped Sligo and crawled the
20 or so miles towards the Donegal border by bus, and almost
11 p.m. when the bus, followed by hundreds of cars, reached the
Bundrowes Bridge that separates Sligo from Donegal and
Connacht from Ulster. Then, like two mediaeval chieftains, team
captain Anthony Molloy and McEniff carried the cup across the
border. 'Everybody went fairly quiet – the two boys were going
to walk across Bundrowes Bridge into Donegal. It was dark outside, we could see the bonfires burning on the Donegal side of
the border,' recalled Charlie Collins of Highland Radio later.
'We watched as they walked into Donegal with the cup and
everybody – I mean players, their wives, girlfriends, selectors,
county board people, the physio, the doctor, Seamus Marley the
bus driver – had tears in their eyes.'

Emotional homecomings are an elemental part of the GAA
experience; even a county under-12 C winning team expects a
rowdy cavalcade around the parish complete with bonfires and
a night of celebration. For years, the wild carousals after Galway
won the hurling title in 1980 for the first time in 57 years had
been considered the homecoming of homecomings, but it was
matched and maybe exceeded by Donegal's festivities. By the
time the team completed the long day's journey throughout the
night via McEniff's hometown of Bundoran, Ballyshannon and
Ballintra, there were 30,000 packed into the Diamond in
Donegal town waiting for them.

And on the journey went for a few more nights to Kilcar,
Ardara and the Glenties where some sheep had been dyed green
and gold. In Glenish, someone had attached green and yellow
lights to a ram's horns. 'There was nothing in the county prior to

Donegal supporters celebrate the county's first All-Ireland senior title in 1992.

then with which to compare. A county celebrated in a fashion never dreamt of before,' wrote Donal Campbell and Damien Dowds in *Sam's for the Hills*, their gripping account of Donegal's All-Ireland journey. 'There was no rule book, people did their own thing. The county was alive like never before.'

Brian McEniff had been plotting Donegal's All-Ireland for 30 years. The Bundoran man is the Gandalf of inter-county football, matching Seán Boylan and Mick O'Dwyer in his staying power. The barest outline of his career tells its own story. As a player he won seven county championships with St Joseph's between 1965 and 1981. He managed the county minor team in 1968 and, in 1971 at the age of 28, took over the senior side, leading them to a first-ever Ulster title in 1972 followed by another in 1974. The following year, he was Sligo's trainer when they won a first Connacht title since 1928. He was back again to guide Donegal to two more Anglo Celt cups in 1983 and 1990. (And, in 2001, managed the Irish International Rules squad in

Australia. The trip Down Under was expected to be a valedictory tour for McEniff but back he came again in 2003 to steer Donegal to another All-Ireland semi-final.) All this while being father to a large family and building up a nationwide chain of hotels.

McEniff has had plenty of critics in Donegal over the years who see his refusal to let go as evidence of an unhealthy ego but a more generous reading is that he is in the grip of a magnificent obsession with Donegal football. There's a famous story about McEniff's response to defeat in the 1983 semi-final against Galway. Having seen his side robbed of victory by a late Val Daly goal, McEniff was inconsolable. Instead of taking shelter with the team, family and friends, he spent the night alone on a park bench in Belgrave Square in Rathgar, brooding until dawn before stealing his way back to the team hotel.

By the winter of 1991, McEniff must have begun to question the sanity of his pursuit of the All-Ireland title. The previous summer, his team of all the talents had waltzed through Ulster and were level with Meath in the All-Ireland semi-final before collapsing in the final quarter and allowing Boylan's side rampage home with late goals from Bernard Flynn and Brian Stafford to win by eight. In April, they lost by a point to a raw Kildare team in the National League semi-final. But they were still raging favourites to win Ulster and maybe go all the way to the All-Ireland, until they were destroyed by Down in the Ulster final. Even Cormac McGill, the *Donegal Democrat's* diehard but perceptive footballing seer who wrote under the old-school pseudonym 'The Follower', was close to giving up the ghost. 'Maybe the time has come for a few of our players who have graced the inter-county scene for so long to have a deep self-introspection and conclude "enough is enough" by sliding gracefully from the scene. Hard, harsh words, but football life is hard

Donegal manager Brian McEniff carries the Sam Maguire home.

and harsh and there is no room for sympathy or softness of heart when major honours are at stake,' he wrote the week after the Clones debacle. And when Donegal were hammered by Monaghan in a McKenna Cup match a month before the 1992 championship opener against Cavan, McEniff's team appeared close to meltdown. 'That was the turning point of the season. We went into the dressing room afterwards and the team was on the verge of breaking up,' according to full-forward Tony Boyle. 'We had a very good chat and it was really that day in Ballybay that we decided to give it one more lash.'

To outsiders, Donegal's woes were puzzling. McEniff had

inherited the remnants of two winning All-Ireland under-21 sides and, by 1990 and 1991, Donegal had a formidable blend of toughness and experience sprinkled with plenty of lovely ball players. Martin McHugh – long rated one of the great modern forwards – veteran midfielder Anthony Molloy, Matt Gallagher, Charlie Mulgrew, Donal Reid and Joyce McMullan had won under-21 title medals in 1982. Five years later, Donegal beat Kerry in another under-21 final and Barry Cunningham, Tommy Ryan, John Joe Doherty and Manus Boyle had come through to the seniors from that side. Add in players such as defensive hard men, Martin Gavigan and Martin Shovlin, Brian Murray in the middle, James McHugh on the wing, the young-sters, Declan Bonner and Tony Boyle, and Donegal appeared to have a potential All-Ireland winning combination.

They looked far from All-Ireland material when barely mana-ging a draw with Cavan in Breffni Park in the first round, a game when Martin McHugh rounded off one of his finest days in the county jersey with a point from a 60-yard free into the breeze in injury-time. Seven days later in Ballybofey, a rejuve-nated Donegal won by 0–20 to 1–6 and followed it up with a 2–17 to 0–7 hiding of Fermanagh. After the match, the senior players closed the dressing-room door, called a meeting and told McEniff they weren't fit enough for the high-intensity, short-passing game they were trying to play. With a month to go to the Ulster final against Derry, McEniff and McHugh upped the ante in training and pushed the squad to the limit with a new regime of shock training. 'The All-Ireland was won in the dress-ing room after the Fermanagh game,' McHugh would later claim. 'When the training got harder, the spirit in the camp improved no end.' National League champions Derry had beaten All-Ireland champions Down in the other semi-final, an infa-mous encounter described as 'war without bullets' in the *Irish*

Independent. Proving that the current debate about physicality and cynicism in Ulster football is far from new, the paper commented: 'We knew what to expect. Down and Derry would dip the shoulders and push out the frontiers of lawlessness. It is the way with Ulster football. The law of the jungle prevails.'

There were over 35,000 supporters in Clones on 17 July for the Ulster final, where Derry were expected to sound the death-knell for McEniff and Donegal. Instead, it was the day when Donegal proved that, whatever else they were lacking, it wasn't character. It looked bad for them in the first half, though, when Tony Boyle had to leave the field after a clash with Anthony Tohill, who swung wildly at the Donegal player. The Donegal crowd screamed red and, while Tohill stayed on the field a while longer, they got their pound of flesh when the Swatragh giant was withdrawn from action with a foot injury sustained in the lunge on Boyle.

Far worse was to follow for Donegal when defender John Cunningham was controversially sent off for a second bookable offence before the break. The sides were level at half-time but Donegal turned around a man down and playing into the sun and breeze. Rather than collapsing, they produced what some supporters will claim was the best 35 minutes of football the team ever played. Molloy, the old colossus at midfield, got the better of his long-running personal duel with Brian McGilligan and, with Murray flying in the absence of Tohill, the game turned Donegal's way. Not even a dubious Derry goal from a square-ball after 50 minutes knocked them back. Gavigan, having a Man of Match afternoon, drove them forward from centre-back. McHugh had earlier pointed a monster free from 50 yards to bolster morale and, in the final few minutes, he added one of the most audacious points of his career when he found a way past four Derry defenders for a point off his left from an acute angle to seal a 0–14 to 1–9 victory. The consensus afterwards was that it had been the finest 35 minutes of football seen in Ulster for years.

The compliments didn't flow so readily after the All-Ireland semi-final against Mayo. Most neutrals who even remember the game concur that it was a shocker; a morass of poor shooting, bad passes, bad tackles, and general fumbling and foostering. It was Donegal's worst performance of the year but the nerves, at least, were understandable. Donegal had never won in Croke Park. McEniff was still haunted by 1983 and most of the players didn't have to be reminded of the last quarter against Meath in 1991, so it was no surprise that the élan and belief of the Ulster final had dimmed. Instead, they ground out the result with substitute Manus Boyle kicking some good frees and Tony Boyle landed big scores from play so that at half-time it was six points each.

As the second half dragged on, Mayo were still in contention with Donegal blazing wide after wide before the Mayo management unwittingly sparked the Donegal winning surge by bringing on Padhraic Brogan. A one-time Hogan Cup prodigy with St Jarlath's of Tuam and the scorer of a wondrous goal for Mayo against Dublin in the 1985 semi-final, Brogan had transferred to Donegal in the winter of 1991. He was set up with a job by McEniff but, overnight, walked away unannounced from the team and county in April. At the sight of their former team-mate, Molloy and Gavigan, the heart of the team, wakened from their torpor. The Donegal supporters greeted Brogan with derision and boos and wee Martin McHugh was the first player of many to land digs on the unfortunate Mayo man. The main import of Brogan's introduction was a sudden all-round improvement in general play from Donegal who kicked four points to Mayo's one to close out the match. In the end, the hardworking McHugh tapped over a penalty to ensure the 0–13 to 0–9 passage to the final. Brogan, the wayward star from Knockmore, had, after all, played his part in Donegal's quest for Sam. The semi-final hoodoo had been broken and an added bonus was that Donegal's woeful performance meant they could approach the final as no-hopers with nothing to lose.

'Where's The Queen?' roared Donegal substitute Barry Cunningham when he made it back to the Donegal dressing room underneath the old Hogan Stand long after the final whistle had blown on the 1992 All-Ireland senior football final. Cunningham's rhetorical question was a reference to the old GAA yarn about a conversation between the Paddy Bawn Brosnan, the Kerry great from the 1930s and 1940s, and a Donegal footballer sometime in the 1940s. There are a few different versions but the gist of it is that the Donegal man asked Paddy Bawn about the protocol a winning captain followed when accepting the Sam Maguire. Paddy Bawn went into a lengthy description of where to go, who to greet and concluded 'and then you shake hands with The Queen'.

'But we don't have a queen,' said the Donegal man.

'We will by the time Donegal win an All-Ireland!' responded the Kerryman.

It was a joke finally laid to rest when Anthony Molloy held the Sam Maguire aloft and declared 'Sam's for the hill's', although modern Ireland's answer to a queen, President Mary Robinson, was sitting in the Ard-Comhairle box.

Two hours earlier, Donegal had taken the field as complete outsiders against a Dublin side that had added extra steel to its play since the Meath saga the previous summer. Impartial analysts weren't all that impressed with the Dubs semi-final performance against wide-eyed Clare, but they were still expected to be too slick and athletic for what was perceived by many as a Donegal team a year or so beyond their prime. The Ulster side didn't start well and their nerves weren't helped by the late withdrawal of iconic wing-back Martin Shovlin. Dublin were awarded a penalty after nine minutes but Charlie Redmond blasted it high and wide of the target, a let-off that visibly lifted Donegal. They overran Dublin in the final 15 minutes of the half, the scores coming freely from Manus Boyle, and Declan Bonner who took over free-taking responsibilities on the left side of the field from Martin McHugh. Manus Boyle could have had a goal but saw his shot come off the crossbar after he had beaten Dublin keeper John O'Leary – but Donegal still led 0–10 to 0–7 at half-time.

They preserved the momentum on the restart with Shovlin's replacement John Joe Doherty and the old hands of Gavigan, Molloy and McHugh smothering Dublin in the middle third of the field. Upfront, Manus Boyle – playing only his second championship game of the year – was on fire from frees and play and tormented his marker, Mick Deegan, for the 70 minutes. He finished with nine points – four from play frees – and his accuracy saw Donegal stretch their lead to six points and threaten to overrun Dublin with their pace and short-passing tactics. The previous spring, Donegal had led Dublin by four with two minutes in the league quarter-final, and ended up losing the game when Redmond and Vinny Murphy grabbed late goals. Six down with 10 minutes left in the All-Ireland final, Dublin attempted another salvage mission and when they scored three points in as many minutes, Donegal looked vulnerable. McEniff ran onto the field and reorganised his troops; Barry McGowan, Matt Gallagher and Noel Hegarty held firm at the back and, when Cunningham set up Manus Boyle for another sweet point from play, the game was over. Final score: Donegal 0–18 Dublin 0–14.

Despite the celebrations and late nights, Donegal looked unbeatable in the league campaign of 1992–93 and recorded nine straight wins to set up another meeting with Dublin in a final played in front of 51,000 supporters in Croke Park, a huge crowd for a league decider. A dour game ended in a 0–9 draw with Dublin having Redmond and Keith Barr sent off in the final 10 minutes. Tommy Carr was sent off after five minutes in the replay, but Dublin still dug out a 0–10 to 0–6 revenge victory. Donegal weren't too upset by the defeat but, three months later, they surrendered their All-Ireland and Ulster titles to Derry. Sam had enjoyed his winter in the hills as the baton was passed on to another Ulster team.

Donegal All-Ireland Football Champions 1992

Gary Walsh

Barry McGowan   Matt Gallagher   Noel Hegarty

Donal Reid   Martin Gavigan   John Joe Doherty

Anthony Molloy   Brian Murray

James McHugh   Martin McHugh   Joyce McMullan

Declan Bonner   Tony Boyle   Manus Boyle

Subs: Barry Cunningham for Murray

By 1992 Kilkenny hadn't won an All-Ireland title for nine years, a near crisis situation for the county. There were fears that the county was losing its traditional values and that skill was being sacrificed at the altar of fitness and hand-passing. In an interview in April, team manager Ollie Walsh said that, compared to his day in the 1960s, modern training regimes 'were like training for the Olympics'. 'I think the artistry is a little bit gone out of Kilkenny hurling. I don't like to see that happen.' Anyone who believed for a minute that artistry had deserted Kilkenny was soon put right when they humbled Wexford in the Leinster final on 19 July. The embryonic superstar D.J. Carey, Eamonn Morrissey, Liam Fennelly, Adrian Ronan, Michael Phelan, the O'Connor brothers, Eddie and Willie, and Pat O'Neill hurled up a storm in the first 20 minutes. It was spellbinding stuff and, by the time Wexford, led by former Galway manager Cyril Farrell, found their bearings, the contest was finished. Final score: Kilkenny 3–16 Wexford 2–9.

Kilkenny found it far harder in the semi-final against a resurgent Galway side managed by Jarlath Cloonan. A nucleus of players from the 1980s team – including Joe Cooney, Michael Coleman, Gerry McInerney, Michael McGrath and Pat Malone – were still playing, but the team's preparations weren't helped by a fresh controversy involving centre-back Tony Keady. Three years earlier, Keady's controversial suspension for playing illegally in a club game in New York probably cost Galway a three-in-a-row of All-Ireland titles. This time, he was suspended by the team management for alleged indiscipline in the week prior to the match. A goal from newcomer Liam Burke settled Galway who were level 1–5 to 0–8 at half-time. Malone was winning the midfield battle but suffered a bad eye injury early in the second half and was replaced by Keady. Malone's loss unhinged Galway and Kilkenny took full advantage to win by 2–13 to 1–12, the winning goal scored by Liam McCarthy.

Tipperary had been favourites to retain their All-Ireland title but their form wasn't good approaching the big showdown with Cork in the Munster semi-final. In April, the Premier County had blown an eight-point, half-time lead in the league final

Brian Corcoran (Cork) and Liam Fennelly (Kilkenny) in the 1992 All-Ireland final.

against Limerick who, driven on by another emerging champion Ciarán Carey, sensationally won the match by a point. Tipp and Cork met in Páirc Uí Chaoimh on 7 June, one of the hottest days of the year. Initially, it looked good for Tipp; they held their own in a hard, low-scoring first half and led 0–6 to 0–5 on the turnaround. But Cork cut loose after the break and scored 1–3 without reply and sealed the result with a Thomas Mulcahy goal to win by 2–12 to 1–12. A highlight of the game for Cork was the display of 19-year-old rookie Brian Corcoran, who gave a masterful display at corner-back on Tipp's dangerman Pat Fox. Cork had no trouble with a naïve Limerick team in the Munster final and, after sweeping past Down in the semi-final, set up the traditionalists dream final with Kilkenny.

Just like 1991, it wasn't a memorable decider. Kilkenny were again the outsiders and there wasn't much artistry in evidence in the opening 20 minutes when Cork fired over five unanswered points. A Carey goal from a penalty revived Kilkenny and they trailed by only 0–7 to 1–2 at the break. In the second half, the two artisans, Christy Heffernan and John Power, orchestrated the fight back. The mere presence of Heffernan, brought on as a sub, was enough to spook Cork supporters who remembered his goals in the 1982 and 1983 deciders. At less than 12 stone, Power was one of the lightest players on the field, but, as former

The Mayo Mutineers
and Player Power

Long before the GPA or the Cork hurlers' threatened 'strike' in the winter of 2002, there were isolated rumblings of player power in the GAA. In 1976, the Clare hurling team, led by goalkeeper Seamus Durack, had successfully forced the county board to reinstate Fr Harry Bohan as team manager. It was a straight-forward case in that the players and Clare hurling public were fully behind the offended party and the County Board had badly misjudged local opinion in discarding Fr Harry's services after he had guided the team to a National League final.

What happened in Mayo in September 1992, though, was a far more bizarre affair. Mayo had won a Connacht title that summer but there had been rumours all season that the players were dissatisfied with the management style of Brian McDonald, a Dubliner who had taken charge of the team ▶

the previous autumn. A Connacht title would normally be seen as a reasonable year's work for Mayo, but the side had played dire football when they lost the All-Ireland semi-final to Donegal and the senior players claimed the team's potential had been undermined by McDonald's maverick approach in training and big games.

They dropped a bombshell on the world of GAA administration when they issued a public statement, signed by all 26 senior players, declaring they wouldn't play for Mayo again if McDonald remained on as manager. The players had a 'major fear that the state of Mayo football would become a shambles if Brian McDonald continued in charge'.

Outlining their grievances in graphic detail, the players claimed the manager's training methods were 'embarrassing'. 'For example, the night before a National Football league game, we were demanded to train by the manager in one of the public car parks in Castlebar. Part of the training session consisted of pushing the selectors' cars from one end of the car park to the other. At another stage, we were demanded to do some sort of dance routine.'

There was a tale about an intensive-day's training session consisting of an eight-mile run along the Castlebar–Ballyvarry road, followed by a skills session and rounded off with a weights session in a Castlebar gym.

A week after the players' statement, McDonald stepped down as manager. He was replaced by Jack O'Shea but Mayo's troubles were far from over.

Kilkenny iron-man Frank Cummins said in the run-up the final, 'That man is made of metal. Thank God he was not around in my time!' Cummins would have approved of Power's route one approach early in the second half when he burst through four Cork defenders and booted the ball to the net. Kilkenny never looked back with Eddie O'Connor, Pat Dwyer and Liam Simpson excelling at the back. The switch of Michael Phelan to midfield proved telling with Phelan setting up Liam McCarthy for the winning goal. The grace note was a point from Heffernan, and Liam Fennelly, another survivor from 1983, led Kilkenny for the presentation. Final score: Kilkenny 3–10 Cork 1–12.

It had been a fair to middling championship, but the hurling year was book-ended by two great struggles in the club championship and under-21 competition. In February and March, Cashel King Cormacs led by the Bonnars and coached by Justin McCarthy played Kiltormer of Galway three times in the All-Ireland club championship semi-final. After a series of games that gripped the attention of hurling supporters throughout the country, Kiltormer eventually prevailed by 2–8 in the second replay played in Croke Park on St Patrick's Day. Kiltormer, with former Galway full-back Conor Hayes, the Kilkenny brothers, Ollie and Tony, Justin Campbell, Damien Curley and Martin Staunton in the team, had enough in reserve to beat Birr the following week in the final.

Several of the Birr players, including Johnny Pilkington, Brian Whelehan and Daithi Regan, tasted defeat again in the autumn when they lost the under-21 final replay to Waterford. The first game drew 25,000 spectators to Nowlan Park in Kilkenny and is still rated as one of the best finals played in the grade. The sides finished level on 0–16 to 4–4. Sean Daly had the distinction of scoring three goals for Waterford and Paul

Flynn, who had played on the minor team beaten by Galway in September, looked to have scored the winning goal before Brian Whelehan equalised from a 65. Waterford held Offaly scoreless in the second half of the replay to win by 0–12 to 2–3, Flynn scoring five. Flynn, Tony Browne, Fergal Hartley *et al* reappeared later in the decade, but it was the Birr and Offaly contingent who would dominate headlines and take the ultimate honours either side of the 'golden age of hurling' between 1994 and 1998.

Kilkenny All-Ireland Hurling Champions 1992

Michael Walsh

Eddie O'Connor   Pat Dwyer   Liam Simpson

Liam Walsh   Pat O'Neill   Willie O'Connor

Michael Phelan   Bill Hennessy

Liam McCarthy   John Power   D.J. Carey

Eamonn Morrissey   Liam Fennelly   James Brennan

Subs: Christy Heffernan, Adrian Ronan

A Military Coup in Clare

The Kerry team of the 1970s and 1980s administered some terrible hidings in their day but the most savage had to be the 'Milltown Massacre' of 1979 when Mikey Sheehy, Jack O'Shea, John Egan, Pat Spillane & Co lashed Clare by 9–21 to 1–9 in a Munster championship game in Milltown Malby. Some spectators spent most of the second half wondering how the scoreboard keepers would manage if Kerry scored a 10th goal as there was only room for a three-digit scoreline.

They were a fatalistic bunch, the Clare football supporters, and with good reason. Gaelic football had a hardy tradition in West Clare, where it's played to the almost total exclusion of hurling, but the county hadn't won a Munster title since 1917 nor appeared in a provincial final since 1949. A revolution was required to stop the rot and, in Clare's case, it required military leadership.

Lt Colonel Noel Walsh, a long-serving County Board officer, had long argued for an open draw in Munster rather than the seeding system that, for years, had smoothed the path for the annual Kerry–Cork final. His campaign succeeded in 1991, perfect timing for Clare who, in the autumn of 1990, had appointed another army man, John Maughan, as manager and team trainer.

Still in his twenties when he took the Clare position, Maughan's own football career with Mayo had been ended by injury, but he retained huge enthusiasm for the game and quickly brought his military experience to bear in reorganising and motivating a rudderless Clare team. Maughan laid down a severe training regime and had an on-field leader in ▶

Corporal Noel Roche who had played for Ireland in the Compromise Rules series and had worn the Clare jersey since 1977.

Clare won an All-Ireland B championship in 1991 and gained promotion to Division One of the league, the campaign ending with a creditable two-point exit to Meath in the 1992 league quarter-final. Because of the new open-draw system, Kerry and Cork met in the first round in Munster, with Kerry triumphant. They then went on to beat Limerick in the semi-final. Clare had four to spare against Tipperary in the other semi-final and faced Kerry in Limerick on 19 July. The league quarter-final should have alerted neutrals to Clare's potential but, predictably, the Bannermen were complete underdogs for the Munster final, even though Kerry were of shadow of the imperious teams of the 1970s and 1980s.

A missed penalty in the fifth minute didn't bode well for Clare but they held their nerve and led by 0–7 to 0–6 at half-time and, in the 48th minute, Francis McInerney placed Colm Clancy for a goal to put Clare three clear. Jack O'Shea and Maurice Fitzgerald dragged Kerry back into the game, but the Gaelic Grounds quaked when substitute Martin Daly punched home a second Clare goal in the 60th minute. They may have had the look of a beaten team but Kerry managed to cut the lead to two points before Gerry Killeen pushed it out to four again in the final minutes – to make it Clare 2–10 Kerry 1–12. The final whistle was the cue for bedlam and the type of scenes that hadn't been witnessed west of the Shannon since Galway hurlers made their breakthrough in 1980.

While the Clare supporters celebrated, Kerry's Jack O'Shea confirmed it was his last game for the county after 18 seasons, during which he hadn't missed a single championship game. After the great Kerry midfielder had missed a ball in the second half, the Clare full-back Gerry Kelly is reputed to have said, 'Jacko, it's time to quit!' – and the Kerryman nodded in rueful agreement.

With his eight All-Ireland medals and war chest of All-Stars and other honours, Jacko would have been the last to begrudge Clare their day in the sun and players – such as Francis McInerney, Tom Morrissey, Seamus Clancy, Roche, Aidan Maloney and Killeen – showed their class again in the All-Ireland semi-final against Dublin.

It was the first of many Clare invasions of the capital during the 1990s and their supporters were satisfied with the honour gained in a 3–14 to 2–12 defeat. Clare had Dublin rattled for long stretches and trailed by just two points midway through the second half before Dublin found the winning groove. The Banner's footballers remained competitive in Munster for a few more seasons, drawing with Cork in 1996 and beating them in 1997 with a famous late goal from Martin Daly in Ennis. But the county failed to build on the achievements of 1992 although the 2004 Tommy Murphy Cup victory and Kilmurray-Ibrickane's achievement in winning the same year's Munster club championship, provide some hope that another revival is underway.

Clare supporters celebrate their team's victory of Kerry in the 1992 Munster football final.

1993

After the Deluge

'It's more fun being a Fenian.'

Eamonn McCann, September 1993

'A plague of frogs of almost biblical proportions had descended on the hill, adding a further surreal element to a dreadful day. It was a good job neither side had scored a goal. Had a goal gone in and an inevitable surge of celebration occurred on the hill, the Ulster Council could have had a major tragedy on its hands. It would only have taken a few people to slip to trigger an avalanche of falling bodies. Everyone concerned was fortunate to escape a disaster equivalent to those of Hillsborough or Heysel Stadium.'

Sam's for the Hills by Damien Dowds and Donal Campbell

BY THE END OF THE MATCH, the pitch was an ankle-deep mass of mud and water. Jubilant Derry supporters were unable to make it as far as their retreating heroes without slipping and sliding in the muck and gutter. On the hilly terrace of Clones, spectators – who had literally dug their heels in just to maintain footing during the game – clung on to each other as they made their exit from a potential death-trap. Only the collective good sense and innate decency of the crowd ensured that they were evacuated without serious injuries or even fatalities. The decision to allow the 1993 Ulster final between Derry and Donegal to go ahead in such conditions was a mistake the GAA, and the Ulster Council in particular, preferred not to dwell on for too long.

The newly re-sodded surface at St Tiernach's Park hadn't absorbed the rain that had fallen in the border counties the week before the final. Overnight downpours meant that, by the morning of the match on 18 July, the pitch was unplayable – but Ulster Council officials insisted that the double-header proceed. The monsoons continued all day and, in the first half of the minor decider between Derry and Tyrone, Derry's Cathal Scullion broke a leg when he slipped in pursuit of the ball. In the dressing rooms, the senior players and management teams were convinced their game would be cancelled but referee Tommy McDermott was told by officials to call the teams out and Donegal laid their All-Ireland and Ulster titles on the line in the deluge.

Brian McEniff had to be apprehensive as he watched his team take the field. They had survived the post-All-Ireland mayhem intact and remained unbeaten in the league – including a rancorous one point quarter-final victory over Derry – until losing to Dublin in the replayed final in April. Less than a month later, they were hard pressed to beat Antrim 0–12 to 0–9 in the first defence of the Ulster title. Next up were a rising Armagh side and it looked over for the champions until newcomer John Duffy kicked an injury-time equaliser. Donegal played electrifying football in the replay. With Martin McHugh tormenting Armagh's new centre-back Kieran McGeeney, they led by 2–5 to 0–0 after 15 minutes and won by 2–16 to 1–7. However, the apparent exuberance of that performance was deceptive.

By the time July and Derry in Clones arrived, the wear and tear of the late nights, the extended league campaign and more than 18 months of competition and training without a proper break had taken a cruel toll on McEniff's options. Just 10 of his All-Ireland winning team were fit for the attempt to become the first Ulster champions since Derry in 1976 to retain their title. Martin Gavigan, Anthony Molloy, Donal Reid, Tony Boyle and Noel Hegarty were missing as Donegal slithered to a 0–8 to 0–6 defeat in the mire. Donegal supporters will swear that they would have held on to their Ulster crown if these men had been fit to play. The Donegal hypothesising is understandable but neglects to factor in Derry's proven pedigree and preoccupation with avenging the 1992 final defeat, as well as other losses in the preceding years. Derry announced their intent in the first round by dismantling Down by 3–11 to 0–9 at The Marshes in Newry in May. After some first-half stutters, they eventually cruised past Monaghan in the semi-final to set up the longed-for rematch with their Inishowen neighbours.

If the second half of the 1992 decider had produced some of the best football seen in Ulster for decades, the 1993 decider was about a second-half tour de force from Derry midfielder Anthony Tohill. The loss of Tohill to a self-inflicted injury in the first half was pivotal in the previous year's game and, by the summer of 1993, he was on a one-man mission to make amends.

One of a number of Derry players – including Damien McGusker, Enda Gormley, Henry Downey, Eamonn Burns and Dermot McNicholl – to have graduated from a remarkable crop of St Patrick's Maghera Hogan Cup side in the 1980s, Tohill was almost lost to Australian Rules on leaving school. However, after two years in Oz, he returned home in 1991 and was immediately called into the county panel. Standing 6 feet 4 inches, and built to match, he was a natural midfielder but for a near-giant he also

John Duffy (Donegal) under pressure form Derry defenders in the 1993 Ulster final.

had unusual balance and poise on the ball. He started 1993 as he meant to go on when he powered Queen's University to a Sigerson Cup title and, by the end of the Ulster final, he was the talk of Gaelic football.

Improbable scores from frees were a feature of big Ulster battles in those years but the most improbable of them all had to be Tohill's monster point seconds into the second half of the waterlogged slog in Clones. Donegal led 0–5 to 0–4 when Derry were awarded a free 60 yards from goal – Enda Gormley didn't give Tohill a hope of raising a flag. 'From a forward's point of view, it's disgusting playing in those conditions,' recalled Gormley. 'You've no balance when you're shooting because your standing foot is slipping and you can't control balls that are coming in to you. I had problems hitting free kicks from 25 yards but Anthony Tohill hit a free over from at least 60 yards and it was still rising when it went over the crossbar. That would be 80 yards in perfect conditions. I have never seen a kick like it in my life.'

That *gaisc* sparked a seven-minute spell when Tohill was untouchable around the middle of the field, and he repeatedly drove at Donegal and drew defenders before laying off passes to Damien Cassidy, Damien Barton and Gormley for the points to give Derry a three-point lead. After that burst of creativity, the game regressed into a trench warfare-style stand-off. Donegal managed one more score from John Duffy, but Henry Downey at centre-back, Tony Scullion at full and Gary Coleman repeatedly frustrated the champions efforts to work their short-passing patterns.

It was a desolate way for Donegal to lose their All-Ireland and there was an unpleasant aftermath for McEniff when he was attacked by a group of Derry supporters after the final whistle. Donegal followers had to come to his rescue and form a cordon to ease his passage to the dressing room. It's puzzling why McEniff was such a hate-figure for the Derry fanatics and hot-heads. He didn't cut an incendiary figure on the sideline and was far too diplomatic to have ever offended them in print. Perhaps it was an atavistic reaction to the achievements of Donegal in 1992 and McEniff's own, well-publicised material success.

Whatever the reason, on the surface at least, McEniff and his Derry counterpart, Eamonn Coleman, could hardly have been more different; one the urbane hotelier with plenty of friends in the media and beyond, the other a rural bricklayer and returned emigrant who had the traditional GAA distrust of the scribes. What the men did share – apart from being teetotalers – was the obsession with bringing All-Ireland success to their counties. A few years younger than McEniff, Coleman was born and raised in the townland of Ballymaguigan, which was also home to Jim McKeever who led Derry to an All-Ireland final in 1958 and who is still regarded as one of the all-time Ulster greats. Situated on the northwestern shores of Lough Neagh, Ballymaguigan is one square mile in size and populated by just 80 families. In 1944, a football club – St Trea's – was formed in the area and, by the 1950s, they were challenging for senior honours. There was no tradition of football in Coleman's family yet, by the time he was 14, he was playing senior with St Trea's, scoring a goal in their county senior title victory in 1962. He won an All-Ireland minor medal with Derry in 1965 and, three years later, added an All-Ireland under-21 medal. He played senior inter-county for several years and, in 1983, managed Derry minors to another All-Ireland title.

If anyone was equipped to take Derry one step further than 1958 it was Coleman but, in the mid-1980s, he emigrated to London. He prospered across the water, branching out on his own in the bricklaying trade until he was persuaded to return home and take over the county seniors in 1990. The previous year, his son Gary (along with Tohill, Dermot Heaney and Eamonn Burns) had figured on another All-Ireland winning minor side and the prospect of bringing Gary and his generation through to senior was too much for Coleman to resist. Within two years, he had landed a National League, and now an Ulster had been delivered. The success didn't go to his head. He remained an inscrutable sort of character and his unsullied Derry accent and syntax was difficult for many an untrained southern ear to grasp. But any journalist who did gain access to him came away impressed by his integrity and instinctive understanding of how to tease the best from the most talented group of players the county had ever possessed.

However, they didn't look all that talented in the first half of their All-Ireland semi-final against Dublin, who led 0–9 to 0–4 at the interval. Derry had scored three points by the time Dublin scored their first in the 14th minute but, after that, it was all one-way traffic with Tohill and his senior partner, Brian McGilligan, making little headway around midfield where Jack Sheedy looked a match winner. Coleman was unusually quiet when they entered the dressing room. He had already said his piece and, instead, it was his assistant Mickey Moran who addressed the troops.

In *The Sons of Sam*, Seamus Maloney's account of Ulster football All-Irelands, Enda Gormley recounts that half-time experience: 'As we were going down the tunnel between the Canal End and Hogan Stand, one supporter shouted, "Typical fucking Derry team. They promise so much then go down and shit in the nest." We all heard it. Normally Eamonn Coleman was the vocal man in our dressing room but that day Mickey Moran took over and I have never seen him raised like it in my life. The surprise element of that shocked us and lifted us. He had also heard what the supporter said and he used that as well. I had grown up watching Derry teams in the 1970s in two All-Ireland semi-finals and a National League final. That statement struck a chord with me because I was at those games and I remember the disgust coming home with my parents and my uncle.'

Moran's emotive explosion had the desired affect and, with some tactical switches including the introduction of Dermot McNicholl, Coleman's minor captain in 1983 – it made the difference in the second half, although Derry didn't overtake Dublin until the final 10 minutes. With McGilligan finding his true form and Henry Downey, Johnny McGurk and Gary Coleman running at Dublin from their own half-back line as

Donegal had in the 1992 final, the scores began to flow for the northern side with Gormley and Joe Brolly chipping away until the teams were level 0–14 each. The winner came when McGurk, on another overlap, finished off a move involving Brolly and McNicholl with a left-footed point on the run. Final score: Derry 0–15 Dublin 0–14.

Coleman's side hadn't just qualified for an All-Ireland final, they had shown a new depth in the comeback and proven they had natural ballplayers in Brolly, McNicholl, Gormley, Henry Downey and McGurk. If they hit form at the same time as the big men such as Tohill, McGilligan, Tony Scullion and Seamus Downey, it would take an exceptional team to stop them.

After six minutes of the final, however, it looked distressing for Derry. A stunning Joe Cavanagh goal and points from Tony Davis and Colin Corkery had Cork five ahead before McGurk settled his team with another rousing point. A purple patch that yielded 1–5 without replay – the goal a fisted effort from Seamus Downey – gave Derrry a 1–9 to 1–6 half-time lead. Cork went in a man down after Tony Davis was harshly sent off for a late tackle on Dermot Heaney. It appeared as though referee Tommy Howard was overcompensating for allowing Niall Cahalane to stay on the field after the combative Cork wing-back decked Gormley off the ball. A John O'Driscoll goal after 45 minutes briefly restored the Cork advantage but Derry kept calm and a string of unanswered points from Tohill, McGurk and Gormley pushed their lead out to three. With Gary Coleman and Scullion breaking up attack after attack, they were able to defend the lead until full-time. Final score: Derry 1–14 Cork 2–8.

Watching the damburst of Derry joy and tears was the journalist, socialist and Derry City supporter Eamonn McCann. Sometimes an outsider to the GAA, someone bringing a fresh eye and heart to a seismic occasion, such as a first-time All-Ireland victory, can conjure up the most vivid sense of what's it's all about and McCann was quickly rocked out of his pre-match indifference. 'I hadn't expected to be moved by it. I hadn't expected to be moved by it at all. I'm a Derry city, not a county, man and therefore into soccer rather than Gaelic,' he wrote in the next issue of *Hot Press*. 'Yet when the team took the field and Hill 16 over to our left was instantly engulfed in the colours of the county, I suddenly realised that not only did I want Derry to win but that I wanted it with a sort of desperation which was as foolish in its extravagance as it was strangely sweet to savour. When the final whistle went, I was fighting back the tears. I definitely hadn't expected that. It was a lovely thing to be able to feel part of.'

McCann hightailed back to Derry city that night and was outside the Guildhall on Monday for the team's civic reception. While Maghera is the spiritual hub of Derry football, the city embraced the All-Ireland winners in style, although the loyalist city councillors boycotted the formal civic occasion en masse. 'It isn't just that they [loyalists] perceive the GAA, accurately, as a specifically nationalist phenomenon,' wrote McCann, 'it is also that the air of uncontrolled celebration that has surrounded recent Northern successes in the GAA appears to confirm that Northern nationalists – far from being ground down into misery – might now actually be getting the better of it. Here we had displayed in plain and bright colours one of the most interesting but little remarked on aspects of life in the North: that while all the objective statistics confirm that Catholics in general are worse off than Protestants, it's also true that – in general – Catholics have more crack. It's more fun being a Fenian.'

Derry All-Ireland Football Champions 1993

Damien McCusker

Kieran McKeever   Tony Scullion   Fergal McCusker

Johnny McGurk   Henry Downey   Gary Coleman

Anthony Tohill   Brian McGilligan

Dermot Heaney   Damien Barton   Damien Cassidy

Joe Brolly   Seamus Downey   Enda Gormley

SUBS: Dermot McNicholl for Cassidy,
Eamonn Burns for Seamus Downey

IT WASN'T MUCH FUN being a Wexford hurling supporter in the summer of 1993. It hadn't been much fun since their last Leinster title in 1977, but Wexford hurling supporters are a stoical and durable tribe and hope surfaced again in the springtime when they played out a memorable three-match league decider with Cork.

League titles don't mean much to Cork. It's rare that they get that far such is Rebel hurling's disinterest in the competition, but a league title would have been precious to Wexford and players, such as Ger Cush, John O'Connor, Eamonn Scallon, Tom Dempsey, Martin Storey and most of all George O'Connor. George, whose efforts and sacrifices for Wexford are writ for all to see on his famously gnarled hands and fingers, had played in four Leinster finals and four league finals since joining the county panel in 1981 – and had been on the losing side each time. D.J.'s injury-time goal in 1991 denied him another crack at a Leinster medal and maybe an All-Ireland, but he hung on waiting for the younger players, such Liam Dunne, Larry O'Gorman and Larry Murphy, to come through and provide a fresh impetus.

It appeared that George and Wexford, under the management of Christy Kehoe, might finally get there on 9 May when they were seven points up at one stage in the second half of the league final in Thurles, but then Cork sniped away to level the match. George's brother John had a chance to win the match for Wexford with the last puck of the ball when he was summoned from the back to take a 45-yard free. He had earlier pointed two from twice the distance but the wet conditions didn't help his accuracy at the death and his shot drifted wide. Final score: Cork 2–11 Wexford 2–11. A week later, it was 0–18 for Cork and 3–9 for Wexford, Jim Cashman scoring an equaliser for Cork in extra-time of a match that had repeatedly been there for Wexford's taking.

The following Saturday, the teams lined out again in Semple Stadium. By now the clash had taken on the tempo and intensity of championship hurling. Inevitably, the closer it came to the summer, the sharper Cork would become and so it proved when they pulled away in the final 20 minutes to take the title on a 3–12 to 1–13 scoreline. A nasty surprise awaited the winners in Munster but it was a minor trauma compared to what befell Wexford in Leinster.

11 July, and Wexford are four points in front with less than five minutes left in the Leinster final after playing their best hurling for a decade. Any other team but Kilkenny would have searched for goals in the same situation but corner-forward

Eamonn Morrissey fires over two quick points to shave the lead to two. D.J. lands a third but Kilkenny are still one behind as the game hits injury-time and the ball is deep in Kilkenny territory. If Wexford hold possession, the game is up and a county's 16-year agony is over – but then Kilkenny corner-back Liam Simpson wins the ball. Instead of driving it hopefully down the field, he picks out a roving Adrian Ronan who finds Eamonn Morrissey ranging within scoring distance and he shoots an exquisite equaliser. Final score: Wexford 1–17 Kilkenny 2–14.

It was typical of Wexford's misfortune that, on the one day they successfully shackled their usual tormentor D.J., another Kilkenny player – Eamonn Morrissey – played one of the games of his life. His goals either side of half-time kept Kilkenny in contention when Wexford were hurling with such ferocity and belief that they might have overrun the enemy. Morrissey finished with 2–4 from play and, 11 years later, his equalising point was voted one of RTÉ's 20 Greatest GAA Moments of the Television Age. Apart from the final execution of that score, the build-up was classic Kilkenny in its intelligence and clarity. For Wexford it was a moment that, without exaggeration, could well have finished off the county as a serious hurling contender for a decade or more. They were destroyed 2–12 to 0–11 in the replay and were a forlorn group of players by the autumn of 1994 when a new manager called Liam Griffin was appointed. Within two years, the whole country would know plenty more about Griffin and Wexford.

In Munster, the championship had taken on a curious complexion. At the end of May, Kerry sent mild tremors through the province when they beat Waterford 4–13 to 3–13 in the first round at Walsh Park. Kerry, represented by Ballyduff, had won an All-Ireland in 1898 and Ballyduff was represented on a side that carved out the county's first senior hurling championship victory in 88 years. It wasn't a complete shock as manager John Meyler, a Corkman, had been doing great work for a couple of years with a group of players from the small pocket of dedicated hurling clubs in North Kerry who had somehow kept the game alive in the Kingdom. Meyler and his players enjoyed their rare day in the limelight but, although they fought well, they were predictably outclassed – 4–21 to 2–9 – by Tipperary in the next round.

On the other side of the draw, Clare under the management of Len Gaynor from Tipperary caught Limerick by surprise in the first round. The veteran Cyril Lyons scored 2–4 for an evolving Clare team who were 14 points ahead at one stage. With new names, such as Davy Fitzgerald, Brian Lohan, Anthony Daly and Jamesie O'Connor, nailing down places alongside the likes of Lyons, Tommy Guilfoyle and Ger 'The Sparrow' O'Loughlin, there was an exciting look about the Banner side, but they were still distinct outsiders for their semi-final clash with Cork at the Gaelic Grounds on 13 June. So much so that, on the morning of the game, the veteran hurling writer Raymond Smith suggested in an article on the troubles of hurling that a separate competition be established for the perennial no-hopers such as Clare. 'I give Clare absolutely no chance of beating the Cork team I watched hurling so well in the defeat of Wexford in the League final,' he wrote in the *Sunday Independent*. 'I won't travel to Limerick to witness another slaughter of the innocents.' Clare had other ideas, and beat Cork 2–7 to 0–10 but Smith's premonition about the slaughter of the innocents became reality on 4 July when the Banner uprising was ruthlessly quelled by Tipperary in the Munster final. 'What could we have done? I ask you in God's name, what could anybody have done to stop that?' Gaynor asked after watching his team be wiped out by 3–27 to 2–12. By the end, the Tipperary forwards such as Cleary, Fox and English were firing over scores for fun, although English's grinning affirmation after one score was a gesture another Clare team would mine vengefully for motivation four years later.

Tipperary were immediately installed as clear favourites to beat Galway and set up yet another final tussle with Kilkenny. The rivalry that had developed between Tipperary and Galway in the 1980s was still fiery and, although the pendulum had swung in the Premier County's favour since the 1989 semi-final, Galway were a potent force when the mood took them and the mood was right for the All-Ireland semi-final. They were well primed for an ambush and led by seven points at half-time, a soft goal from Michael McGrath cancelled out Tipp's early

Pat Fox (Tipperary) eludes Brian Lohan (Clare) in the 1993 Munster final.

D.J. Carey (Kilkenny) races away from Ger McInerney (Galway) in the 1993 All-Ireland final.

advantage and a storming performance from Gerry McInerney at centre-back was typical of Galway's endeavour throughout the field. Galway hurled at the same manic pitch for the second half and were worth more than their final 1–6 to 1–14 winning margin. In the other semi-final, Kilkenny – mindful of their late escape in 1991 – were clinical when they beat Antrim by 4–18 to 1–9.

The final was a tough encounter laced with some fluent passages of play and fine individual performances on both sides and it wasn't really decided until the last five minutes when Kilkenny cut loose, confirming the suspicion throughout that they were the marginally better team. They outscored Galway by 1–6 to 0–3 in the final 15 minutes, but the real damage was done in the closing minutes. After staging a spirited second-half comeback, Galway were just a point behind when Kilkenny won a sideline cut close to the halfway line after a hand pass from Joe Cooney to Michael Coleman went astray. P.J. Delaney won possession from the cut and rounded two Galway defenders before finishing past Richard Burke. Within a minute, he had added a point, and another point from D.J. put the title beyond Galway's reach. Final score: Kilkenny 2–17 Galway 1–15.

Kilkenny All-Ireland Champions 1993

Michael Walsh

Eddie O'Connor   Pat Dwyer   Liam Simpson

Liam Keoghan   Pat O'Neill   Willie O'Connor

Bill Hennessy   Michael Phelan

Liam McCarthy   John Power   D.J. Carey

Eamonn Morrissey   P.J. Delaney   Adrian Ronan

SUBS: James Brennan, Christy Heffernan, Tommy Murphy

There was a crumb of consolation for Galway when their wing-back Padhraic Kelly was named Man of the Match by the *Sunday Game*, a rare honour for a losing team in an All-Ireland final. P.J. Delaney, Adrian Ronan and Pat O'Neill would all have been contenders for the winners while there were other eye-catching performances from Galway's Pat Malone and Joe Rabbitte. Another highlight was the compelling battle between Gerry McInerney and John Power on the 40, the two playing out an honourable draw, although Power did score a single big point in the second half. For Kilkenny and their manager Ollie Walsh, the two-in-a-row was an achievement to match that of the 1982–83 side but a hint of how the climate within the GAA was changing came in captain Eddie O'Connor's speech. Along with the usual *cúpla focail* and expressions of gratitude, he hoped that the Kilkenny County Board would reward the players with a team holiday.

The County Board took exception to his remarks and maintained that a trip to Florida – then the destination of choice for GAA teams – was a non-starter and instead offered to pay for a weekend in Killarney for the players and their partners. After a protracted stand-off, a sun holiday in Spain was brokered as a compromise. There was also bad feeling in Derry where the All-Ireland football winners' manager, Eamonn Coleman, indicated that he might return to London. Coleman maintained that he wasn't being adequately compensated by the County Board for the loss of earnings and expenses he incurred while training the team and that financial necessity might again force him to emigrate. He eventually sorted out his differences with the board and was back on the sideline as the champions set out on their league campaign in October.

But the Kilkenny holiday row and Coleman's need to go public to sort out his expenses were symptomatic of growing tensions nationwide between players and managers on one side and officialdom on the other. The players could see that serious amounts of money were beginning to flow in to the GAA. They were already wearing sponsored jerseys and it was a question of when not if the GAA signed major sponsorship deals for the hurling and football championships. Millions were also being exchanged annually for television rights to the big championship matches.

At the Annual Congress in 1992, GAA President Peter Quinn said, 'There would be little threat to the amateur ethos if we are prepared to meet the reasonable demands of our players. Our most valuable assets, they should be treated with respect as mature people.' Quinn was in tune with the gathering militancy of the players, some of whom still had to haggle for the most basic of facilities and expenses. As a 21st-century stadium began to take shape on Jones' Road, 1950s attitudes towards the players still prevailed. The failure to grapple with the disillusion of their most 'valuable assets' would haunt the organisation throughout the 1990s.

Demolition work on the old Cusack Stand began the day after the 1993 All-Ireland football final. The first phase of the complete redevelopment of Croke Park, the €45 million new Cusack Stand was fully completed and open for the 1995 All-Ireland finals.

1994

The Five-Minute Miracle

'The army are still the best recruiting agents the IRA have up there. We have youngsters coming home from training and having rifle butts being stuck in their backs and being thrown onto the ground. What do they think they are at?'

GAA President Jack Boothman, April 1994

'In the last five minutes our players were like magicians. Every time they touched the ball, it seemed to be flying over the bar.'

Offaly hurling manager Eamonn Cregan, September 1994

JACK BOOTHMAN was an unlikely GAA President. The 57-year-old vet from Blessington, County Wicklow, was a Protestant and had been educated in rugby-playing schools, but he was a popular choice with the grassroots when he was voted in as President-Elect at the 1993 Annual Congress. His background mightn't have been that of the typical true Gael, but Boothman was a GAA traditionalist and on election declared, '[The GAA] has ruled my life for 40 years. In fact it is a religion with me. My love of it is surpassed only by the love of my family and the love of God.' The Wicklow man was a safe pair of hands at a time when the GAA was in fundamental transition on several fronts. The wrecking balls had started demolition work on the old Cusack Stand the day after the 1993 football final and, with the reconstruction of Croke Park underway, the GAA was in the mood for a breather and some self-congratulation as its Annual Congress approached in 1994.

There wasn't, however, much appetite for dealing with awkward problems such as Rule 21 – the prohibition on members of the British army or Northern security forces joining the GAA. In January, the Civil Service Club in Dublin unsuccessfully tried to move a motion at the Dublin County Convention calling for the removal of Rule 21, and the issue wasn't even debated at Congress that year. At a time when GAA clubhouses in some parts of the North were still being attacked and members of the association targeted by loyalist assassins, there was a feeling that the security forces weren't doing enough to protect the GAA. Boothman articulated the views of a majority of GAA people on Rule 21 in an interview with the *Sunday Press* the weekend before Congress, declaring that, '1994 would be a little too early [for the removal of Rule 21]. In the GAA we haven't been found wanting for change when it's demanded and we will change in the future but I don't believe in meaningless gestures. That rule is one of the few arguments people have to beat us over the head with. Every other argument down through the years we have defeated with logic. One of the last remaining arguments against us was the sectarian one and I was the answer to that myself.

'The security forces would want to realise first of all that 99 per cent of GAA people are doing their damnest to keep young people out of the IRA and they are not getting any help from the army who are still the best recruiting agent the IRA have up there,' he continued. 'I have opened two clubhouses [in the North] in the last year and one of them was burned down seven times. I was told that it might be burned down again and I told them that I would be straight back up to open it once again if that happened. The security forces do not enjoy the confidence or the trust of an awful lot of people and while that situation remains there is no great point in talking about Rule 21.'

With Rule 21 off the agenda, the other pressing concern for the GAA was negotiating sponsorship deals for the football and hurling championships. In March, a closed meeting of Central Council debated a proposal to drop the prohibition on an alcohol producer sponsoring competitions. The vote on lifting the prohibition was tied and the outgoing President, Peter Quinn, in line with the normal GAA procedure, used his casting vote to maintain the status quo. It was common knowledge that Guinness had been sniffing around the hurling championship for several years but St James's Gate wouldn't have to wait much longer to apply its unique branding expertise to the ancient game. The Bank of Ireland, meanwhile, encountered no ethical objections to its courtship of the GAA and, in June, the old Irish House of Lords building on College Green was the setting for the announcement of the Bank's £3 million sponsorship of the All-Ireland football championship over five years.

While the GAA was slowly forging new alliances with corporate Ireland, there was still the occasional echo of times past, such as Cavan delegate Peter Brady's call at Congress for a ban on the leasing out of GAA grounds to undesirable acts or performers, 'Groups which behave in a violent or vulgar way, or those who demean women should not be allowed to use our grounds for concerts,' he said. 'We should not be involved in anything that harms impressionable young minds.'

Kilkenny County Board chairman Nicky Brennan was more concerned about impressionable young people abandoning hurling, even in the game's traditional strongholds. Brennan was part of a working group charged with reporting on the state of the game, and its pessimistic conclusions were unpalatable reading for the GAA's top brass. Hurling activists felt the working group had been sidelined and Brennan warned Congress delegates that hurling was dying on its feet, declaring that 'the time has come to take action if we want hurling to thrive into the next century'. Hand-wringing about the state of hurling has been a recurring theme down through the decades in GAA debates but, as the latest grave warnings were issued, the game was to again confirm the assertion of the old time GAA writer P.H. Mehigan ('Carbery') that hurling survives and is indestructible because of its 'stern, naked grandeur'.

THERE ARE FEW PLACES where hurling has more resilient roots than Offaly but, at the start of 1994, the talk there was of crisis rather than possible All-Ireland honours. The initial All-Ireland senior successes of 1981 and 1985 led to a flourishing of the game at underage level in the county, with Birr Community School the centre of excellence and Brother Dennis from Kilkenny the svengali. Offaly won three All-Ireland minor titles in 1986, 1987 and 1989 followed by Leinster under-21 titles in 1991 and 1992 but, at senior level, the statistics suggested troubled times. Offaly hadn't won a senior championship game since the 1990 Leinster final and went two years without winning a game in the league.

The statistics, though, didn't tell the full story. An Offaly side packed with players from the all-conquering minor teams was poised to strip Kilkenny of their Leinster and All-Ireland titles in the 1993 Leinster semi-final, until D.J. Carey scored 1–1 in a typical late raid. D.J.'s goal, from a penalty engineered by John Power, was enough to see Kilkenny steal through by 2–10 to 0–14.

The young Offaly players, and by extension their manager Eamonn Cregan who had coached most of them as under-21s, shipped a lot of criticism after that defeat. The Offaly teams of the 1980s had played a traditional, uncompromising brand of hurling and there were suggestions that, while the new generation was undoubtedly more skilful and elegant, they lacked the mettle for senior success. They were spoilt by early success and more fond of the bar stool than the training ground claimed their critics. One dissenting voice was team selector Andy Gallagher. 'As far as I am concerned, Offaly's future starts today,' he said as the 1993–94 league campaign got underway. 'Our hurlers are as good as anybody's and it's really a question of getting down and proving that.' Despite Gallagher's optimism, Offaly displayed their usual aversion to the rigours of winter hurling but exploded into action against Kilkenny in the Leinster championship on 27 June. The three Dooleys – Johnny, Billy and Joe – scored 2–10 between them in a stunning 2–16 to 3–9 dismissal of the champions. Offaly were seven points ahead at half-time and Kilkenny scored two goals in the final minutes to put a decent gloss on the scoreline.

Wexford looked unbeatable against Laois in the other semi-final but then proceeded to do the, by now, customary Wexford thing and fall flat in the Leinster decider on 11 July. They shot 18 wides and were outclassed as Offaly came of age on a 1–18 to 0–14 scoreline. Ten of Offaly's starting players and subs used had come through the three 1980s minor teams: Brendan Kelly,

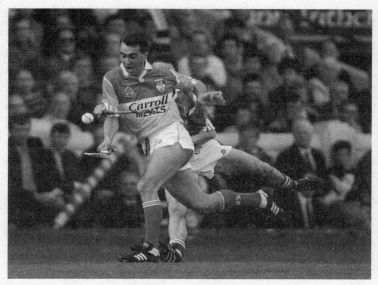

Johnny Dooley of Offaly in the 1994 All-Ireland final against Limerick.

Daithi Regan, Michael Duignan from 1986; Brian Whelehan, Johnny Dooley, Billy Dooley and Johnny Pilkington from 1987, along with John Troy and Hubert Rigney from 1987. They played a brand of hurling that was more Kilkenny than Kilkenny themselves. The emphasis was on moving the ball at speed on the ground, finding a man where possible, and clever and swift co-ordination between the forwards. Billy Dooley's goal in the Wexford game was a gem and the way his brother Johnny described it afterwards hinted at the fresh thinking Offaly brought to the game: 'John Troy did a beautiful reverse flick that took out two defenders and I just hurled it on to Billy and he did the rest.' It was far from reverse flicks they were reared! After watching them beat Galway by six points in the All-Ireland semi-final, Joachim Kelly – a 1980s Offaly icon not given to the dramatic statement – hailed the new generation's style as 'total hurling'.

As Offaly marched through Leinster, a new order was germinating in Munster. Clare extracted revenge for 1993 by beating Tipperary in the first round. It was a sensational result given their 18-point mauling the previous year. Tipperary had strolled through the league and taken the title with eight points to spare over Galway, but they were missing English, Fox, Leahy, Joe Hayes and Paul Delaney for the championship and Clare took full advantage to win by four points. Once they recovered from the shock of beating their tormentors, Clare had no trouble with Kerry in the semi-final.

On the other side of the draw, Limerick finally delivered on their promise when they beat Cork by 4–14 to 4–11 in their opening game. Gary Kirby scored 2–4 and two goals from Pat Heffernan – along with great displays from Dave Clarke, Ger Hegarty, Declan Nash and goalkeeper Tommy Quaid – ensured their passage to the semi-final against Waterford. They survived another high-scoring encounter by two points to advance to the final with Clare. Hegarty was outstanding again at centre-back and, along with Ciarán Carey and Mike Houlihan at midfield and Kirby at centre-forward, Limerick appeared to have struck upon a formidable diamond of players in the middle third of the field.

Clare's collapse in the 1993 Munster final had been attributed to inexperience, and the misfortune of running into a great Tipperary team delivering one their best performances. Clare supporters were sickened in 1993, but they were inconsolable after the 1994 final. The occasion again seemed to spook the Banner and they were simply blown away: 0–25 to 2–10. Brian Lohan, Anthony Daly and Liam Doyle put up gutsy resistance but Clare trailed by 0–20 to 0–9 after 50 minutes and only scored their two goals in the last eight minutes. Kirby again led the Limerick charge from play and frees and the scores continued to flow in the All-Ireland semi-final where the Munster champions overwhelmed Antrim by 18 points. In the other semi-final, Offaly defeated Galway 2–13 to 1–10, a late goal from Billy Dooley settling the issue.

The early exit of 'The Big Three' injected an element of surprise and glamour into the hurling championship. Neither Offaly nor Limerick had featured on anyone's list of possible All-Ireland winners at the beginning of the year and no matter who won it, it would be refreshing after five years of the usual suspects. Offaly were slight favourites on the basis of their wins over Kilkenny, but most neutrals were inclined towards Limerick who were seeking a first title since 1973 when Offaly's manager Eamonn Cregan was one of the stars on the team that beat Kilkenny. Like Clare, Waterford, Offaly, Laois and Dublin, Limerick battled on year after year against the dreary hegemony of Kilkenny, Cork and Tipperary and an All-Ireland victory was long overdue to maintain the spark of enthusiasm for hurling in the county.

Limerick blazed into action from the throw-in and, at times, appeared only a score or two away from routing the Leinster champions. Ger Hegarty, Ciarán Carey, Mike Houlihan and Dave Clarke controlled the middle of the field. Unsung full-forward Damien Quigley scored 2–2 to leave his side 2–8 to 1–5 ahead at the half-time. In the circumstances, Limerick's 12 first-half wides could be forgiven and Offaly needed a Billy Dooley goal from a controversial penalty to cling on to their title ambitions. Cregan made switches at the break, bringing on Michael Duignan for Regan and Pat O'Connor for Joe Dooley and, while the reshuffle brought about some improvement, Limerick were still coasting by 2–13 to 1–11 with little more than five minutes left.

What happened next was a mesmerising Offaly salvo that remains the definitive proof of the uncertainty principle in hurling. Hurling supporters far beyond the borders of Offaly can recite

Johnny Pilkington is mobbed by jubilant supporters after Offaly win the 1994 All-Ireland.

the sequence like a mantra, such was the impact it made on the collective consciousness of the game. To recap, here's how it went. In the 65th minute, Billy Dooley was fouled and his brother, Johnny, addressed the 20-yard free. Without any of the standard 'he's going to try and blast a goal' histrionics, Dooley drove a powerful low shot past the Limerick wall. Goal. Panic rippled through the Limerick team and the ensuing puck-out was driven straight back into the danger area by Johnny Pilkington. The sliotar took two perfect bounces for a predatory forward and Offaly substitute Pat O'Connor finished it to the net. Limerick needed to hold possession to halt the Offaly thrust but, having been in control for so long, the men in green and white were unable to readjust to the sudden switch in the pace of the game. Instead, they were transfixed by panic and every ball seemed predestined for an Offaly hand or stick. The crowd had barely recovered from the two goals when Johnny Dooley and John Troy rifled over two points in a minute. When Billy Dooley delivered a triptych of points in 67 seconds from almost the same patch on the Cusack Stand side of the field, it really did feel as though an unseen hand had intervened.

Offaly were famed and feared for their comebacks. Seamus Darby had done it for the footballers against Kerry in 1982 and Johnny Flaherty plundered a first All-Ireland for the county's hurlers with his hand-passed goal against Galway in 1981. Cregan and his players had watched a video of the 1981 final the Thursday night before the Limerick match but 1981 and 1982 should be re-classified as minor thefts compared to the artistic larceny of 1994. For a start, Offaly were well in contention in the second halves of both the 1980s' games and the winning goals were singular knockout blows; in 1994, four different Offaly players shot seven scores as an entire team went from near lassitude in the first 65 minutes to virtual perfection in the final five. 'There was a stage when we could have taken off 10 players because they were just not playing,' said Cregan afterwards. 'I can say with hand on heart that I thought the game was gone. Then Johnny Dooley's free hits the back of the net and suddenly we can't do anything wrong. I can't explain it. They [Limerick] were the better team for 65 minutes but in the last five minutes our players were like magicians. Every time they touched they ball it seemed to be flying over the bar.'

It was an odd emotional experience for Cregan as he watched Offaly celebrate and his countrymen slope away in despair. Cregan had played on losing All-Ireland final teams with Limerick in 1974 and 1980, when he scored 2–7 against Galway, but at least he had his medal from 1973 as a reward for more than 15 very distinguished years in the county jersey. Limerick manager Tom Ryan and his players would resurface in 1996, but the fates ordained that they were to finish second best to another unstoppable force in the form of Wexford.

Offaly All-Ireland Hurling Champions 1994

Jim Troy

Shane McGuckian   Kevin Kinahan   Martin Hanamy

Brian Whelehan   Hubert Rigney   Kevin Martin

Johnny Pilkington   Daithi Regan

Johnny Dooley   John Troy   Joe Dooley

Billy Dooley   Brendan Kelly   Declan Pilkington

Subs: Joe Errity, Pat O'Connor, Michael Duignan

OFFALY HURLERS' TROUBLES at the beginning of 1994 were mere squabbles in comparison to the open discord and feuding in Down. The Sam Maguire again looked as remote as it had in the mutinous days of spring 1991. Pete McGrath's team had veered badly off course since they won the 1991 All-Ireland title. They enjoyed the post-All-Ireland euphoria well, but not wisely. Serious preparations for the title defence only started after a team holiday in Tenerife, six weeks before the first-round game against Armagh. Down survived that game but were out-muscled by Derry in the semi-final. It got worse in 1993 when they lost by

3–11 to 0–9 to Derry in Newry, the county's worst championship defeat since 1952. Manager McGrath was apoplectic after the game and publicly criticised his players as a 'shambles'. 'I think Down fans are owed an apology by everyone concerned with the team.'

McGrath's comments worsened the existing friction between the management and some star players, although half-forward Ross Carr believed he was 'quite entitled to say that. We let the supporters down and we let ourselves down. We were in the comfort zone after 1991. We were annihilated on the scoreboard that day but we contributed to our own downfall and we weren't as fit as we should have been.' McGrath was an obvious scapegoat for disenchanted Down supporters and he came under more pressure in the autumn when Greg Blaney and James McCartan withdrew from the panel. Blaney, the inspirational veteran, and McCartan, the prodigy, were essential to the Down cause, but there was still no sign of them returning to the fold in the New Year when another veteran, Liam Austin, went public with his concerns for the team. 'Provided we can get everybody back on the same wavelength then we have a chance,' he said. 'But it saddens me to be continually asked what is going on in Down. Down football is bigger than any of us in the county. It is hardly asking too much from us that we pull together.'

The reconciliation between McGrath and his absent stars occurred in February when the manager appointed D.J. Kane – Greg Blaney's cousin – as team captain. Blaney and McCartan returned shortly afterwards and, for the first time in years, Down knuckled down to intensive spring training under Pat O'Hare who had been brought in by McGrath to oversee the physical preparations.

O'Hare's efforts were rewarded on 29 May when Down went toe-to-toe with All-Ireland champions Derry in Celtic Park. It was a game that ranks with Down–Donegal in 1991 and

Donegal–Derry in 1992 as one of the best of the early 1990s northern cycle. Like Donegal the previous season, Derry had kept the
winning surge going after the All-Ireland final when a more
casual attitude to the league might have served their defence of
the All-Ireland title better. They were unbeaten in the competition
until they were ambushed by Westmeath in the quarter-final, a
defeat that clearly spooked Eamonn Coleman. 'We went from
being a super team, right down the ladder to being a laughing
stock,' he said in an interview before the Down game. 'Ever since
then, there are big questions being asked about Derry. They are
good questions and we've got to answer every single one of them.'

Down posed a question too many in an unexpectedly free-
flowing game that was ranked by some commentators alongside
the 1977 All-Ireland semi-final between Kerry and Dublin as one
of the best matches in living memory. Mickey Linden and James
McCartan had rediscovered the form of 1991 for Down, but the
Mournemen, who had led by two points at half-time, trailed by
two with 10 minutes left when they produced a trademark flourish
of genius. The old hands Blaney and Linden managed to thread
the ball through the Derry defence with Linden laying it off to
substitute Ciaran McCabe and he kept his cool to beat Damien
McCusker. Gregory McCartan landed a free to seal the victory
and Derry's summer and reign as champions was over. Final score:
Down 1–14 Derry 1–12. 'There was never any doubt after we beat
Derry that we would win the All-Ireland,' Ross Carr would claim
later. 'Whoever won that game was going to win the All-Ireland.
The Monaghan game would be just another step on the way.'

The night of Saturday, 18 June saw impromptu street parties
all across the South as the country celebrated the Republic's 1–0

victory over Italy at the Giants Stadium, New Jersey, in their first game of the USA '94 World Cup finals. Ray Houghton's third-minute goal and a majestic defensive performance from Paul McGrath stunned the Italians and the country's sporting stock had never been higher. As the South whooped it up, in the North, the celebrations were halted by a savage sectarian attack in Loughinisland, County Down. At 10.20 p.m., a gang of UVF gunmen entered The Heights Bar, opened fire and killed six people including 87-year-old Barney Green. Their only crime was that they were Catholic in the wrong pub at the wrong time. The death toll would probably have been far higher only for the departure the previous week of 11 regulars and the pub's owner Hugh O'Toole to Romania where they had started voluntary construction work on an orphanage. The day after the UVF attack, Gary Mason from Loughinisland lined out for Down and scored six points in his county's 0–14 to 0–8 win in the Ulster semi-final against Monaghan. 'Gary Mason showed the mark of greatness not only to play but to put on the display of free taking that he did, having come from home where his community had been destroyed,' said Ross Carr in *The Sons of Sam*. 'I don't know how he did it and I still can't believe it.'

The win over Derry had reinvigorated Down, and the events of 18 June galvanised their spirits. Tyrone opted for a physical approach in the Ulster final but Down were far too streetwise to be dragged into a maul and could afford the luxury of a missed Mickey Linden penalty and still lead 0–9 to 0–5 at the break. They were awarded another penalty five minutes after half-time when James McCartan was dragged down by Plunkett Donaghy and Chris Lawn. Carr took this one and scored to leave his team eight in front and while Tyrone rallied, Down eased their way to a 1–17 to 1–11 win and the Ulster title.

Another comfortable victory looked likely in the semi-final

against Cork until Down reverted back to bad old habits. A goal from Aidan Farrell saw them lead by two points at half-time and, on the restart, they kicked six points without reply to move eight clear by the 53rd minute, 1–13 to 0–8. They had been in a similar position against Meath in the 1991 All-Ireland final and almost blew it and again they lapsed into *ennui* and allowed Cork and Colin Corkey to eat into the lead. D.J. Kane and Conor Deegan grafted away around the middle of the field, though, and denied Cork the possession they needed to launch a meaningful comeback and Down were through to another final. Final score: Down 1–13 Cork 0–11.

Dublin awaited in the final and while, deep down, the Dublin players can't have relished the prospect of another Ulster onslaught, they were still favourites to prevent the Sam Maguire going north for a fourth successive year. In hindsight, Dublin's painless semi-final outing against Leitrim did them no favours as they were without testing competitive action since the Leinster final. In the opening quarter of a game spoiled by continuous rain, they matched Down score for score, but it was noticeable that their play was more laboured and scores harder won in comparison to Down's economy and cuteness. The Dubs were well aware of the threat posed by Linden and McCartan but were powerless to stop the master and student combining in the 17th minute when Linden drew the cover and slipped the ball to McCartan for a tap-in goal.

Down led by six points approaching the 50th minute but again retreated into themselves with the finish in sight. Dublin sensed weakness and launched another comeback and two frees from Redmond and a point from Sean Cahill brought them within a goal. With seven minutes left, Dessie Farrell won a penalty for Dublin and Charlie Redmond got ready to atone for his spot kick misses against Meath in 1991 and Donegal in 1992.

Facing the Hill, he struck it well, but Down keeper Neil Collins guessed correctly and parried the shot. Redmond raced in to finish the rebound but, under pressure from D.J. Kane, his shot went wide. Deflated, Dublin had no more to give and Down held out for their fifth All-Ireland title. Greg Blaney admitted the next day that Dublin would probably have won if Redmond's shot had been on target. 'We couldn't get the ball past our own half-back line. James McCartan was coming back to win the ball but was bringing his man with him. We were out on our feet.'

Whatever about the missed penalty, it was a victory to cherish for Down manager Pete McGrath. He had survived the heaves against him and cajoled his players to the heights of 1994. Appointing D.J. Kane as captain was a masterstroke in healing the divisions in the camp, and coaxing Conor Deegan home from Chicago was also key to Down's success. Full-back in 1991,

Mickey Linden (Down) celebrates his county's 1994 All-Ireland victory.

Deegan had emigrated to Chicago because he couldn't find a suitable job at home and had been inclined to forget about Down until McGrath's persistence paid off. He was given a new role at midfield and prospered there. The 1994 All-Ireland final, though, will be remembered most for another virtuoso performance from Mickey Linden. Apart from setting up the goal for McCartan, he scored 4 points from play and his contribution throughout the championship was rewarded with another All-Star and the Footballer of the Year. Long after most of his teammates had retired, the Mayobridge player soldiered on, before finally calling it a day at inter-county level after the 2003 Ulster final against Tyrone, just short of his 40th birthday.

Down All-Ireland Football Champions 1994

Neil Collins

Michael Magill   Brian Burns   Paul Higgins

Eamonn Burns   Barry Breen   D.J. Kane

Gregory McCartan   Conor Deegan

Ross Carr   Greg Blaney   James McCartan

Mickey Linden   Aidan Farrell   Gary Mason

Subs: Gerard Colgan for Deegan

Deliverance Day for Leitrim

Every couple of generations, the 'weaker' counties stumble upon a winning combination of players and, in Leitrim's case, deliverance arrived on 24 July 1994 when the county finally added a second Connacht football title to the lone provincial success of 1927.

Outside of Connacht, it was perceived as a shock, but the winning Leitrim team had been coming through since the early 1990s when an outside manager, P.J. Carroll from Cavan, had revitalised a talented squad and guided them to promotion in the league and an All-Ireland 'B' title in 1990. In the following two seasons, they narrowly missed on promotion to Division One of the league and Roscommon, their fiercest rivals, proved an obstacle too far for three successive championships. Even in 1993, after they had travelled to Tuam and beaten Galway for the first time in 44 years, the Roscommon jinx still held sway and Carroll stepped down. He was replaced by Mayo's John O'Mahony who had steered his own county to an All-Ireland final in 1989.

O'Mahony made all the difference. He ensured that this generation of Leitrim footballers wouldn't end their days empty-handed like the team who, inspired by the county's greatest player Pakie McGarty, had reached a National League final in 1958 but lost four successive Connacht finals between 1957 and 1960.

'If I hadn't felt there was a strong possibility of Leitrim winning a Connacht Championship, I wouldn't have touched ▶

the job,' said O'Mahony before the All-Ireland semi-final against Dublin. 'I took the job based on their enthusiasm, their want but, above anything, their passion for the game and their willingness to work harder.'

Leitrim had gone close to beating Galway in 1983 and 1987 and survivors from those teams included Mickey Quinn who was awarded an All-Star for his contribution in 1994. Quinn, his namesake Seamus at full-back, Joe Honeyman, Declan Darcy, Gerry Flanagan, Pat Donohue and Gerry Reynolds formed a tough spine and were complemented by classy ball-players, such as Paul Kiernan, George Dugdale, Liam Conlon, Padraig Kenny and Jason Ward.

Dugdale scored the all-important goal against Roscommon in the first round of the 1994 championship and, even though Leitrim went 28 minutes without scoring in the second half, Declan Darcy pointed a 45 to give them a one-point victory – the first in 27 years over 'the Rossies'.

Kenny scored the winning point against Galway in the replay in Tuam to confirm that the previous year's result was no fluke and Mayo provided the opposition in the Connacht final in Carrick-on-Shannon. Leitrim gifted a goal to Mayo after 20 seconds but Mayo didn't score again for the rest of the half. After recovering from the early shock, Leitrim were clearly the better team and ran out convincing 0–12 to 2–4 winners to spark off scenes as wild and joyous as those that heralded Clare's breakthrough in 1992.

'When the final whistle went, those of us present witnessed the most emotive scenes ever witnessed in a Connacht sports-field,' wrote the late Jack Mahon. 'It was my 50th Connacht senior final occasion in different capacities – player, official, spectator and sportswriter – but nothing ever surpassed the after-match scenes at Leitrim's second Connacht senior success. When Tom Gannon, captain and lone survivor of 1927, went onto the presentation podium to embrace the winning captain Declan Darcy and the long-serving hero Mickey Quinn, not a Leitrim eye was dry and even those of us with no attachment were affected.'

Dublin proved too strong in the semi-final, winning comfortably on a 3–15 to 1–9 scoreline although Seamus Quinn clinched his All-Star with his display in front of a 53,000 attendance boosted by the return of thousands of Leitrim emigrants. Afterwards most commentators reverted back to the 'gallant Leitrim' school of analysis, although Páidí Ó Sé in his *Irish Independent* column remarked that 'Connacht football will have to be examined at every level to see if there is a lifeline there'.

O'Mahony said that he didn't want his team's defeat 'to seem like the same old story for Connacht football, I am certain the gap can be bridged but I am just not certain how'. The solution to O'Mahony's puzzle lay in the minor semi-final in which Galway beat Dublin by 1–12 to 0–12. Pádhraic Joyce, Michael Donnellan, Declan Meehan, Tomás Meehan, Richie Fahey, John Divilly and Paul Clancy all starred for the winners.

O'Mahony would soon make the acquaintance of these young players but, for now, Leitrim were his mission and the following year, he brought them to another Connacht semi-final, in Carrick, where they were cruelly beaten in injury-time by Galway. Hardened by the previous year's trial in Croke Park, who knows what might have happened in the All-Ireland semi-final against Tyrone had Leitrim emerged again from Connacht. As it was, a callow Galway team ran the Ulster champions to three points signalling the beginning of a western revival.

1995

Nobody Said It Was Going To Be Easy

'Oh Jesus, Mary and Joseph, will we ever last?'

Matthew McMahon, Clare FM match commentator, half-time, Muster final, 9 July 1995

'When Clare players went out on that field they were not self-conscious. They didn't care what the crowd thought about them... it was the banishment of self-consciousness on the field that was crucial to our success. It meant that, on the big day, we could produce the big performance. The best way I can explain it is that you have to dance like there is nobody watching. That was at the heart of our success. It was all about casting off the inhibitions of the past.'

Ger Loughnane, *Raising the Banner*

FOR MORE THAN SIX DECADES, Clare were the children of a lesser hurling God. They were the archetypal doomed romantics locked into a cycle of self-doubt and defeat. Somebody had to shout stop and it had to be an insider, someone who had experienced the tantalising proximity of true success only to see the prize wrested clear by ordinary mortals unburdened by expectation and fatalism. Ger Loughnane was born for the mission. No matter what angle you approach it from or how you choose to analyse it, the story of Clare and the 1995 All-Ireland hurling championship begins and ends with Loughnane. There were plenty of other people and factors involved, but Loughnane was the lightning rod man for it all.

Clare hurling manager, Ger Loughnane.

The scene at the end of the 1978 Munster hurling final in Semple Stadium had an almost biblical resonance to it. Cork had beaten Clare by 2 points in as tense a game of hurling you are ever likely to see. With the final whistle went the hopes of another generation of Clare hurlers who were within a few pucks of reversing a losing sequence stretching back to 1932. In the foreground, the cameras captured Loughnane, the Clare left half-back, on his knees, banging his fists off the ground, like some sort of Dalcassian Job bemoaning his outcast fate. The intensity of the Feakle man's reaction was extraordinary. 'When the real challenge came, the confidence wasn't there and we shrivelled up completely. I'd say only one or two of us played up to scratch. That was the end,' he wrote in his autobiography. 'Nobody said it was the end, but we all knew. The day had come for us to make the breakthrough but we hadn't…We were as strong and tough and willing and dedicated as the rest of them.

But Cork and Kilkenny always believed they would win. We never fully did. I was never as good a player again. I was only 25.'

This wasn't a disappointment that would fade within a few days or weeks. There was something burning within Loughnane that would have to find expression through success with a Clare hurling team and the opportunity finally arrived in September 1994. Loughnane had reluctantly helped Gaynor as a selector in that year's championship, only taking the position on condition that he be appointed manager when Gaynor quit. It was a shrewd piece of manoeuvring. Two years earlier, the County Board had sacked him as manager of the under-21s when Clare lost the Munster final by two points to the subsequent All-Ireland champions Waterford. There were officials and administrators who resented Loughnane's disregard for the petty conventions of GAA politics but they couldn't be seen to renege on the deal they struck with Gaynor the previous autumn, and Loughnane took control.

One of the best pieces of writing on hurling is a chapter in the book *Last Night's Fun* by the Belfast fiddler, poet and author Ciaran Carson. In it, he describes his days as a young hurler on the streets of Belfast and his experience of playing for the Antrim minors against Cork in the 1965 All-Ireland minor semi-final: 'Back at home, I could gauge to a nicety when to hold back and then accelerate in order to get my hand to the low ball down the wing. I soon discovered that the Cork boys worked to a different tempo: I confidently reached out for the first such ball that came my way and found my knuckles nearly taken off by the blade of my marker's hurley; they played to different rules as well, it seemed, and this was fair game.' Carson's hurling career didn't last long after the Cork experience but wrote that he still dreams 'recurrently of hurling... It is usually a nightmare of incompetence. I fumble, stumble, I am half-blind.' Ger Loughnane would surely have empathised with Carson's observations after the

National Hurling League final between Clare and Kilkenny in May 1995. Clare had again been found wanting on a fine day and fast sod against a traditional power's tempo and lost 2–12 to 0–9. It wasn't quite a 'nightmare of incompetence' but too many Clare players looked clumsy and ill at ease on the ball compared with their opponents.

'Let's be honest. It wasn't just the two goals that beat us. Kilkenny's craft was the difference. Our hurling is still basically not fast enough. It's desperately hard to match them for natural craft when the day is dry and the ground fast,' Loughnane admitted to the reporters before delivering an astonishing rallying cry given the result: 'We are going to win the Munster title. I think we have the right fellows here and I don't think there is any team in Munster as good as Kilkenny. Maybe it was the nerves today but I think we can play a lot better.'

Upping the pace of Clare's striking and approach to the ball was a pillar of Loughnane's philosophy but, in their first serious trial under his guidance, too many players had reverted to old habits and others had seemed lacking in the basic skills. However, whatever about the skill levels, Loughnane was convinced that he had at least assembled a group of players who wouldn't crack mentally when the pressure came on later in the summer. Character and mental toughness were ultimately more important in his revolution than fancy skills and natural talent. 'When you think of Tipperary, you think of their tradition. When you think of the great Cork and Kilkenny teams of the past, they all had identity. We wanted men who would stand up and be counted – men who would make things happen,' he said later. 'That's why we chose players like Baker, Fergie Tuohy, Conor Clancy, Colin Lynch and Michael O'Halloran who had been left out by other people. We knew they would stand up. Talent is not everything. The only thing that really endures is character.

The only way you can test that out is on the training field in order to see who will survive and who will buckle. When you see anybody buckling in training, you know they will buckle when the big day comes. It's as simple as that. That's as true a law as the law of gravity.'

Players who had been given a raw deal at underage level or ignored all together, prospered under Loughnane, his trainer Mike McNamara and selector Tony Considine. Brian Lohan hadn't made the colleges team or the county minor squad but, once he was given the break, he matured into one of the great full-backs. Seanie McMahon had been dropped from the under-21 team in 1993 but recovered from that setback and, like Lohan, is an automatic selection on any team of the decade. Ollie Baker was a 'made hurler' but had other strengths that became priceless to Loughnane and Clare.

Lohan and McMahon were natural leaders but Anthony Daly was the rock on which Loughnane built his team. Daly had been a Clare regular since 1991 and was a perceptive character with the sort of controlled fervour and intelligence that marked him out as an obvious captain. And along with his captain, lieutenants and 'made hurlers', Loughnane had an additional smattering of class to work with in players such as Liam Doyle, Jamesie O'Connor and Gerard 'Sparrow' O'Loughlin. The 1995 loss to Kilkenny was seen as a disaster for Clare by most commentators, but if you look at it again Clare were actually not all that far off the pace. They needed working on, but the will and spirit was there and the luck would follow. To borrow the slogan used by Guinness in its first summer of sponsoring the hurling championship, 'Nobody Said It Was Going To Be Easy' but Clare people had long abandoned any notions of winning anything the easy way.

The GAA had lifted its prohibition on the sponsorship of competitions by alcohol companies the week after the league

Clare captain, Anthony Daly.

final. A year after Peter Quinn's casting vote had kept Guinness and other drinks conglomerates at bay, Central Council voted 36–3 to scrap the ban and Guinness unveiled a £500,000 sponsorship package for the championship. There was a surprisingly subdued response to the u-turn, although former President Mick Loftus, the Mayo County Coroner, said he would no longer be attending All-Ireland hurling finals while an alcohol company was involved in financing the championship. Within weeks of the Central Council vote, the first billboard and television advertisements began to appear of a helmeted warrior-like figure, hurl in hand ready for battle. The not-so-subliminal association of the national game and the national drink was a heady concoction, but neither party to the deal could have envisaged how their cup would run over that summer.

Clare were a 20/1 chance for the All-Ireland title when they faced Cork in the first round of the championship at the Gaelic Grounds before a paltry 14,000 spectators. Loughnane's prophecy about a Munster title appeared hollow at the interval when his side trailed by three points after playing with the breeze. Clare were in self-destruct mode as shot after reckless shot veered wide and Cork, although playing poorly, moved five ahead shortly after half-time. Then Clare began to fight back. The switch of Liam Doyle to the wing after Frank Lohan was brought on a sub in the corner steadied the defence but Cork still led by three points with seven minutes remaining when O'Loughlin found the net and P.J. O'Connell pointed to give Clare the lead. Cork struck back when Kevin Murray beat Fitzgerald in the 69th minute. More laments and keening looked likely until Clare conjured the most improbable of goals.

Clare had used up all their subs and Seanie McMahon, who injured his collarbone with 15 minutes left, had been pitched into the corner-forward position to do whatever he could with his one functioning arm. He bravely won a cut as the seconds counted down. Fergal Tuohy struck it well and Baker got a touch for a goal. Cork attacked again but Alan Browne's shot came off the post and Frank Lohan showed the instincts that would make him such a valuable player when he raced across the goal to block Ger Manley's attempt for an equaliser or winner from the rebound. Final score: Clare 2–13 Cork 3–9.

An after-match visitor to the dressing room was John Joe 'Goggles' Doyle, the last surviving member of the 1932 team. 'I am a very proud man. They showed great heart today,' said the hale octogenarian. No one doubted their heart, but it wasn't a Munster-title winning performance. Twenty wides was an abysmal tally and Cork had grievances about a second half 65 that never was and even claimed the long grass on the Gaelic Grounds sod hampered their style.

Luck is one of the essential yet often unremarked-upon factors in hurling and whatever luck was in it had been with Clare. Hurling may be one of the most skilful of field games but with a ball darting around at speeds of up to 100 mph between 30 players, a single bounce, accidental deflection or couple centimetres of post or crossbar can swing a twitchy game regardless of the skill levels and physical endeavour or character of the combatants. The events of so many past games against Cork meant that no one could begrudge Clare their minute or so of good Karma when it was most needed. They would more than repay the price for their good fortune in the years ahead.

It was typical of Clare's summer that one of the most berated players on the team was the Man of the Match when the tyranny of 63 losing years ended in Thurles on 9 July. P.J. O'Connell had struggled so badly in the league final that one commentator suggested that his wrist work was more suitable for forking bales of hay than finding the target in top-class hurling, but he still held on to his place for the Cork game and scored two important points without ever suggesting he was a potential match winner. With his loping stride, tan, long hair and 'tache, he was an everyman throwback to the 1980s and a favourite with the Clare supporters, but he was expected to have a fruitless afternoon in the Munster final against Ciarán Carey, Limerick's centre-back and fulcrum.

Another dynamic display from Carey that had been vital in Limerick's 0–16 to 0–15 victory over Tipp in the semi-final and, after that performance, they were favourites to again advance from Munster and atone for the previous September's collapse against Offaly. Too much suffering had made sceptics of many Clare supporters who feared another repeat of the 1993 and 1994 finals. The Banner barometer read cautious to gloomy, a mood reflected in the 1,000 match tickets returned by the County Board to the Munster Council the week before the game.

Clare supporters were outnumbered by at least two to one in Semple Stadium on the sort of summer day Munster purists deem essential for the *echt* hurling experience. There wasn't a cloud in the sky, temperatures were in the high 20s, the breeze wasn't strong enough to have a decisive influence and the Semple sod was perfect. The suffocating anxiety of the last two Munster finals was absent from Clare's play and, while Limerick started well, the underdogs stuck with them score for score. Jamesie O'Connor continued where he left off against Cork and buzzed with purpose at midfield. Fitzgerald, O'Halloran, the Lohans, McMahon, Daly and Doyle coped with anything Limerick could muster in attack and O'Connell was a revelation on the 40.

P.J. scored Clare's first point and ended the match with five to his name as well as numerous assists in a full-on performance that demoralised Limerick. Davy Fitzgerald's goal from a 26th-minute penalty, and his subsequent breakneck retreat down the field, was how Clare's breakthrough was remembered on RTÉ's Greatest GAA Moments of the Television Age but O'Connell's performance encapsulated everything that was good about Clare. Not even a player as wiry and athletic as Carey could cope with the old-fashioned dash and endless energy of the hombre from O'Callaghan's Mills.

O'Connell was one of the players who benefited most from Loughnane's insistence on speeding up the rudiments of the Clare style. Apart from his improved touch, O'Connell – a natural athlete – was as fit as he had ever been after a winter of training with Mike McNamara. A publican from Scarrif, McNamara had some original ideas about hurling and fitness and he pushed O'Connell and his team-mates to the edge in pursuit of fitness levels that would be unmatched by any team for several years. The severity of McNamara's regime on the sand dunes and the hill in Crusheen was as important for Clare as Loughnane's judicious pursuit of players with a stubborn and fearless streak in their make-up. By July 1995, Clare could take the field knowing they were fitter than any team in the country and that they could survive in any physical battle. Loughnane ensured that they were equally as well tuned mentally.

Limerick stuck with Clare for 40 minutes but the floodgates opened with a long-range score from McMahon and, after that, a liberated Clare team drove over point after glorious point, proving that there was a lot more pure hurling in the team than they had been credited for. Towards the end, Loughnane was able to give old timers Cyril Lyons and Jim McInerney a run as all the sorrow of 11 losing Munster finals since 1932 was swept away by a 1–17 to 0–11 victory. A sort of joyful disbelief gripped the Clare supporters who hadn't lost the faith. At last, there was some balm for 1955 when Clare beat Cork and Tipperary only to lose to Mick Mackey's Limerick 'greyhounds' in the Munster final, for 1977 and 1978 when Clare were league champions but froze against Cork in two finals, and for 1986 when they again looked set to beat Cork but didn't possess the belief to do so. The 1993 and 1994 finals had been the end of the affair for some genuine Clare supporters, but it all became ancient history as the team and county enjoyed a week-long hooley that saw the Munster Cup taken to every parish in the county.

It would have been easy for Loughnane and Clare to bask in the after-glow of victory well into the winter and following spring. Winning Munster was an end in itself but, after the triumph, there was a sense within the camp that the journey was just beginning. The minds and bodies were right and if the physical and mental strength was matched by improved accuracy and finer touches, anything was possible. They were young – all 15 starting players in the Munster final were still bachelors – fearless and they wanted more. 'My theory was that it wasn't possible for us to stop the celebrations for the first few days anyway, so I decided to let them have a week of this. By the Friday the players were nearly begging to get back to training,' recalled Loughnane in his autobiography. 'They just had enough of it. We went back to Clarecastle on Friday night just for a run and on the Sunday we started full training again. I think that tour was hugely significant and I think it was a brilliant idea to bring the cup to every village. We brought as many players as we could. When the Clare fans realised the kind of people that we had on the team, that was the start of the great bond that developed between the team and the fans.'

An estimated 30,000 Clare supporters were in Croke Park on 6 August when Galway provided the opposition in the All-Ireland semi-final. The familiar Galway faces of Joe Cooney, Gerry McInerney, Sean Treacy, Joe Rabbitte and Michael Coleman had been joined by newcomers such as Nigel Shaughnessey, Justin Campbell, Conor O'Donovan, Francis Forde and Brendan Keogh from successful underage teams. In theory, they were a match for anyone but they were playing under another new manager, Mattie Murphy, and serious preparations had only begun in earnest in April after a poor league campaign.

It was another day heaven sent for hurling, too warm if anything. Clare's winter training told in the first half when any nerves they may have had were more than compensated by their pace and appetite. Goals from Ger O'Loughlin and Stephen McNamara gave them a deserved 2–6 to 0–7 lead at half-time. Galway looked finished when O'Loughlin added a third goal within two minutes of the restart. The old hands of Cooney and Coleman led the Galway comeback. Cooney set up Forde for a Galway goal and with Coleman driving them on from midfield the Clare lead had narrowed to a single point when O'Connell scored the most important point of his career. He was unmarked when he received possession in midfield in the 56th minute and, from a standing position, drove a huge point into the Canal End. The confidence that had drained away from Clare returned instantly and they overran Galway in the closing minutes. Final score: Clare 3–12 Galway 1–13.

THE CONDITIONS couldn't have been more different on 25 June when Offaly faced Kilkenny in the Leinster final. Kilkenny were favourites even though they had only beaten Laois by two points in the semi-final and needed a last-minute save from sub goalkeeper Joe Dermody to escape from Dr Cullen Park with the win. The pre-match consensus favouring Kilkenny irked an Offaly side that had seven points to spare in a dismal game match with Wexford. The lower deck of the new Cusack Stand was opened for the clash of the teams who had taken the last three All-Ireland titles, but a crowd of just over 25,000 paid in and the game was delayed by a spectacular thunderstorm. The skies opened again as the teams took the field. Kilkenny sought what shelter they could in the dug-outs but Offaly raced back to the safety of the dressing room and emerged dry when the deluge had cleared.

The next 35 minutes were unforgettable. The Croke Park surface had withstood the storms and the teams clattered into each other with a fierceness that still managed to stay the right side of acceptable aggression. This was the sort of hip-to-hip, bone-crunching ground hurling that was only supposed to exist in old-men's stories. Scores were scarce, yet the crowd was hypnotised by the exchanges. Offaly buried any lingering suspicions that they were carefree dilettantes who had fluked an All-Ireland against Limerick. They revealed an inner hardness to their play that hadn't been seen before and, in the second half, gave full expression to their exquisite hurling instincts and touches.

It was 0–5 to 0–3 in their favour at half-time and Kilkenny were suckered seven minutes into the second half when Daithi Regan belted a ball goalwards. The slippery sliotar bounced off Kilkenny goalkeeper Michael Walsh's chest and bounced over the line. It was controversial goal and, given the tension, a critical score. Kilkenny buckled and Offaly took complete control with Billy Dooley, Johnny Dooley, John Troy and Michael Duignan scoring some wonderful points. Final score: Offaly 2–16 Kilkenny 2–5.

Midfielder Johnny Pilkington was typically direct and witty afterwards, 'It's as simple as this. We were insulted at not being made favourites this year,' he said. 'Everyone seemed to be putting Kilkenny ahead of us, even as far back as last September, and we heard some things being said in Kilkenny that annoyed us. We heard one of their players said they'd give us a lesson this time. Fortunately for us, we were fairly thick at school.' Down provided game opposition in the semi-final but Offaly coasted their way into the final, 2–19 to 2–8, Johnny Dooley landing 11 points and brother Billy and Michael Duignan scoring the goals.

Fifteen minutes before the throw-in for the All-Ireland final on 3 September, the touts were flogging the last stray tickets for the Hill at treble the face value. It was a game that anyone with even the vaguest interest in hurling wanted to be at; Offaly and Clare, the sublime versus the insatiable. Offaly, as usual, travelled to Dublin on the morning of the game but Loughnane ensured that his players also had the reassurance and comfort of sleeping in their own beds by flying the team from Shannon to the capital on Sunday morning. In the dressing room beforehand 'there was no discernible air of tension. There were very few words spoken,' recalled Loughnane years later. 'We told them that Clare people were there in their thousands and that people had come from all over the globe and that a massive effort was needed. Above all, we stressed that all the plans we had for Offaly were to be implemented and stressed the importance of work-rate, discipline and taking any opportunities that came our way. We also emphasised that if they suffered any disappointment or setback, they were to put it behind them. When they left the room, they nearly took the doors off the hinges they were so charged up.'

From the start it was obvious that, as in most All-Ireland finals, it was going to be a battle, rather than an open game of hurling. Clare's defence was exemplary, smothering Offaly's forwards without conceding needless frees. Those who believe in portents may have suspected it was Clare's day when Ollie Baker, the 'made hurler', sent a sideline cut over the bar, with Loughnane – the 16th man – standing a few yards behind him as he struck the ball, almost willing the sliotar over the bar at the Hill 16 end. But when Davy Fitzgerald leaked a goal just before half-time – a shot to nothing from Michael Duignan skidding off his hurl – the rational consensus was that Offaly were heading for victory. It was unbearably tense hurling, but Clare scrapped their way back in the second half and were level by the 48th minute when Offaly, against the run of play, pounced for a second goal, Johnny Pilkington scrambling the ball to the net from 10 yards out. For all their resistance at the back, Clare's forwards were making little headway and Jamesie O'Connor couldn't find his usual rhythm but, as often happens in finals, it was the less feted players who decided the outcome. Fergus Tuohy stepped into the breach and his four points were critical in maintaining the Clare challenge.

Buoyed by his early point, Baker wore down Offaly in the middle of the field and the Doyle, McMahon and Daly half-back line effectively shut up shop on the Offaly forwards. It was effectively a battle of the defences but with four minutes left, Clare still trailed by two points. If Offaly scored another point, the game was gone.

It had to be a goal for Clare and the provider was substitute Eamonn Taafe who had been struggling so badly since his intro-duction that he was about to be hauled off before he struck. A long free from Daly floated in towards the Offaly goalmouth, broke loose and Taafe pulled first time. The green flag was raised but, within seconds, Offaly had recovered. They won a free from the puck-out and Johnny Dooley pointed. Level again. Clare applied more pressure and won a 65 which captain Daly opted to take instead of the usual long-ball striker McMahon. Daly's

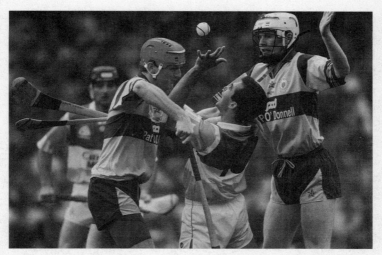

Johnny Dooley (Offaly) under pressure from Brian Lohan and Frank Lohan (Clare) in the 1995 All-Ireland final.

stroke was true and Clare took the lead with less than a minute remaining. Offaly came back at them again and it's often forgotten how close Johnny Pilkington went to stealing the game but his effort was cleared by Frank Lohan. Jamesie O'Connor added another point from a free and Clare survived. Final score: Clare 1–13 Offaly 2–8.

The lost tribe had found their way home. For a few months in the summer of 1995, it felt as if half the country had fallen in love with the Clare hurlers. There was a brash assertiveness and energy about them mixed in with a very Irish cussedness and sense of tradition epitomised by John Joe 'Goggles' Doyle. They may have banished their ghosts and inhibitions in 1995 but Clare's quest for glory would engage and trouble hurling for a decade.

One of the abiding memories of the 2005 championship was Brian Lohan and Seanie McMahon almost managing to turn back the clock 10 years and make it to another All-Ireland final.

At the end of Clare's one-point loss to Cork in the semi-final, Davy Fitz beat the Croke Park sod with his outsized hurl and the tears weren't far away. There were shades of Loughnane and 1978 about Fitzgerald's reaction – the difference this time was that the man giving vent to his fury had two All-Ireland medals and three Munster medals in his trophy cabinet.

Clare All-Ireland Champions 1995

David Fitzgerald

Michael O'Halloran   Brian Lohan   Frank Lohan

Liam Doyle   Sean McMahon   Anthony Daly

Jamesie O'Connor   Ollie Baker

Fergus Tuohy   P.J. O'Connell   Fergal Hegarty

Stephen McNamara   Conor Clancy   Ger O'Loughlin

Subs: Eamonn Taafe for McNamara, Cyril Lyons for Clancy, Alan Neville for Taaffe

Jayo and the Dubs
Come Good

By the end of the 1995 football semi-final between Dublin and Cork, a new word had entered the GAA lexicon: 'Jayomania' – the mass adulation of Dublin supporters for teenager Jason Sherlock who sparked new life into a mentally scarred team. After losing two All-Ireland finals and one semi-final over the previous four years – not to mention the 1991 saga against Meath – Dublin could have lapsed into indifference as 1995 approached. Instead, manager Pat O'Neill and his players resolved on one last heave and Jayo became the elusive ace lacking in previous campaigns.

Sherlock was Irish Youth's Basketball Player of the Year in 1994, a Dublin minor the same year and had been for trials at Liverpool before being drafted onto the senior panel for the Leinster championship. His impact was immediate. He was probably the difference between winning and a dismally early exit for Pat O'Neill's team in the provincial semi-final against Laois. The post denied him in the first half but, 22 minutes into the second, he found the net and sealed the result for the nervy Dubs. Sherlock's brand of creative mischief and trickery added a new edge to Dublin's attacking play. If he wasn't going to score himself, he looked certain to win close-in frees or create openings for the likes of Dessie Farrell, Mick Galvin, Charlie Redmond and Paul Curran. He scored two and had ▶

numerous 'assists' in the Leinster final as Dublin exorcised all sorts of hobgoblins by destroying Meath 1–18 to 1–8. In the All-Ireland semi-final against Cork he scored a 23rd-minute goal that ignited Dublin's challenge when Cork looked the more likely winners. The goal had all the Sherlock trademarks: speed of reaction, pace and a lightning turn followed by a classy finish. He required a garda escort off the pitch after the game as the young Dublin supporters mobbed him from all sides.

Ireland was becoming the land of boybands. The international chart success of Louis Walsh's Boyzone was almost a source of national pride and in Sherlock, Gaelic football had found a pin-up boy in tune with the times. It wasn't long before sponsors were queuing up for his endorsement, and it wasn't longer either before his soccer-star status would earn him the wrath of GAA old-timers, including association President, Jack Boothman. In the meantime, though, the good times rolled and Dublin faced another northern challenger, Tyrone, in the decider.

Tyrone had their own, more understated, hero in the shape of Peter Canavan. He had announced his arrival by scoring 2–5 against Kerry in the 1991 under-21 All-Ireland final against Kerry and had learned his craft in far harsher climes than Jayo. He hit the first of several career peaks in the summer of 1995 when his genius dragged Tyrone through a typically torrid Ulster campaign. His county needed him as never before in the provincial semi-final against Derry. They trailed by 0–8 to 0–5 after having two players sent off, but some good tactical decisions by managers Art McRory and Eugene McKenna kept the team's shape intact and Canavan, whose marker Fergal McCusker was dismissed for an off-the-ball incident, scored eight in a 0–11 to 0–10 victory.

Team-mates such as 'Big Mattie' McGlennan, Adrian Cush,

Ciarán McBride and Stephen Lawn took some of the pressure off Canavan in the Ulster final when they finished strongly to beat Cavan by 2–13 to 0–10 but Canavan was, once again, the inspiration in the All-Ireland semi-final against Galway.

The two new Gaelic *galacticos*, Sherlock and Canavan, had wildly contrasting experiences in the final. Tyrone's full-backs were more mobile than any defence Jayo had faced all summer, but his persistence was rewarded in the 26th minute when he set up Charlie Redmond for the game's only goal, enough to see Dublin 1–8 to 0–5 at half-time. Canavan was the only Tyrone player to score in the first half and, as injury-time began, he had kicked Tyrone within a point of Dublin.

Referee Paddy Russell then made a controversial All-Ireland final decisions: substitute Sean McLoughlin appeared to have scored the equaliser for Tyrone but Russell blew play back, claiming that Canavan had handled the ball on the ground before passing to his team-mate. The decision was enough see Dublin win a very poor final by 1–10 to 0–12. Not that absence of quality mattered to Dublin. Charlie, the man who had missed penalties in 1991, 1992 and 1994 must have believed he was born under a bad sign when he was sent off 14 minutes into the second half of the 1995 final. It took him two minutes to leave the field and, when he did, Dublin lost their composure and struggled from frees. If they had lost, Redmond – so integral a part of their Leinster and All-Ireland journeys since 1991 – would probably have been tempted to catch that night's boat train. Instead, he and his team-mates finally got to lay their hands on Sam.

Peter 'The Great' Canavan would have his turn eight years later, but all sorts of vicissitudes lay ahead for Jayo and Dubs.

1996

Keeping the Faith

'I have heard a lot of questions asked about Wexford these last few years and I don't mind saying that I am proud to have Wexford blood in my veins. I want you to be proud to be Wexford people. History tells you who you are. We are from Wexford, from the Blackstairs Mountains to Fethard, back to Rosslare and all the way as far as Gorey and Arklow in the north.'

Liam Griffin, Wexford hurling manager, July 1996

THE LIAM MCCARTHY CUP hadn't even reached Ennis before the next phase of the hurling revolution was set in motion. Coincidence or not, the evening after Clare won their first All-Ireland title in 83 years, a meeting of disillusioned Wexford hurling supporters concluded with an appeal to the County Board to sack team manager Liam Griffin and his selectors. That summer's Leinster championship defeat to Offaly represented a new low even for Wexford's defeat-inured legions and the sight of lowly Clare galloping to an All-Ireland title was another reminder of how far Wexford had fallen.

The infighting before the Offaly game, that saw veteran defender Liam Dunne stripped of the captaincy for playing in a routine club game, added to the popular consensus that it was time for Griffin, the fast-talking hotelier from Rosslare, to concentrate on his business and leave the hurling to someone else. While the noose was being tightened, Griffin was on his way west to Clare to observe the Banner's homecoming. He had old connections with the county. His father was from Newmarket-on-Fergus and, in the 1960s, Griffin played senior for that club and under-21 for Clare while training as a hotel manager in Shannon. Clare had even flown him back from hotel school in Zurich to play a few league games with the seniors, but the demands on both sides were too much for a long-term commitment. Knowing the terrain so well, Griffin could grasp the enormity of what Loughnane and his players had achieved, so the journey to Ennis and beyond was more than just a gesture of friendship to family and friends and team-mates from the past – it was a quest for knowledge.

In time, Griffin would prove to be as evangelical about Wexford hurling as Loughnane was about Clare. Evangelical is the apposite word. The intensity of their interest in the game, even the language they used when talking about it, indicated that, for both, hurling and the striving for success was about a lot more than just cups and medals and a line in the record books; it was – extreme as it may sound – about the well being of their tribes' very soul. The equation of sport and religious faith is a dangerous road to go down, there's too much opportunity for ersatz spirituality and shallow emotion, but in his famous book, *The Game*, on Canadian ice-hockey in the 1970s, Ken Dryden showed a direct correlation between declining church attendances and rising attendances at ice-hockey games. The conclusion was that as people lost faith in one, they sought the same meaning and sense of place in the other. GAA attendances had been rising steadily since the early 1990s as observance of Sunday masses went into free fall. Hurling, more so than most sports, with all its traditions and hoodoos and veneration of past legends, had never been that far removed from being some sort of alternative faith in some parts of the country and Loughnane and Griffin were the new high priests. If Loughnane was the citadel-storming warrior priest, Griffin was a more pensive character, possessed of a Jesuitical attention to detail and the oratory to match.

And he would need it all and more as he faced into his second year in charge of Wexford. The post-All-Ireland putsch fizzled out within a week when the County Board ratified Griffin and his selectors, Rory Kinsella and Seamus Barron, for a second year in charge. As he reflected on Clare's achievement, Griffin also considered his first year in charge of Wexford and how he had probably underestimated the culture of defeat ingrained in what was a talented but rudderless group of players. They were spiralling towards bottom long before the 1995 Leinster championship. In March, a very moderate Meath team beat them in a league game in Enniscorthy. A spectator spat at Griffin on the way out of that match and the hate mail and late-night phone calls weren't far behind. He was doing his best to introduce a new regime of excellence, but the players weren't responding and they played out the Offaly game in June like men in the grip of lassitude.

Liam Dunne, in his autobiography *I Crossed the Line*, written with Damien Lawlor, admits that he and his team-mates were still living in the 1980s when it came to their philosophy on hurling: 'Liam [Griffin] also tried to take a psychological approach with us but it went in one ear and quickly flowed out the other. We were a macho lot at the time and had no business listening to this philosophy crap and reading the handouts he gave us. Most of the lads thought Griffin was a lunatic and it would take a full year to cop on there was method in his madness.'

After losing to Meath, Dunne says, 'A few of us even chuckled at the result. It would have hurt more if we had cared enough, but then we would have had to do something about it. As the championship loomed, we hoped for a change but failed to look within where change was most needed. Griffin continued preaching, but we would not be converted. While he wanted us reading articles on sports science and sports psychology, most of the lads wouldn't even bother reading a menu. We wanted to hurl alright but weren't prepared to put the work in before games. Griffin would give us handouts on diet and nutrition but most lads threw them out the windows of their cars on the way home... we were the fools though. Our new manager was trying to make changes but we had been around for a few years and thought we knew it all. We were set in our ways but they were not winning ways.'

It all changed on Griffin's return from Clare. He reassembled the team in the second week of September and they began a regime that matched Mike McNamara's 'road to hell' approach with Clare. The months leading up to Christmas were spent in the gym. The handouts on everything from hydration to visualisation were back – and this time they weren't scattered to ditches on the way home from training. Griffin has often said that the turning point for him, the day he believed something was finally stirring again, was in February 1996 when Wexford beat Offaly in the Walsh Cup. Any competitive victory over Offaly was welcome, and it was followed by an emphatic victory over the same opposition in the league quarter-final to set up a league semi-final clash with Galway at the Gaelic Grounds in April.

That game was Wexford's equivalent of Clare's humbling by Kilkenny in the league final the previous season. Galway hammered Wexford 2–15 to 1–10, the Wexford goal arriving late from John O'Connor. There were excuses. Galway had spent the winter in Division One, whereas Wexford had been hurling away in the second tier losing to Limerick but racking up comfortable wins in their other games. The gym work and punishment on the beaches were geared for championship rather than league hurling but anyone who saw Wexford that day wouldn't have short-listed them for the All-Ireland title. Griffin, like Loughnane at the same juncture in 1995, refused to panic: 'We were beaten fair and square by a team that played better. We over carried when we had opportunities. We weren't taking long-range scores. We have work to do but in spots it was close to what we wanted.' Griffin knew that the hard slog had got what was essentially an ageing team into the physical condition of their lives. In the six weeks before the championship opener with Kilkenny, the imperative was to speed up their hurling and rid their minds of doubt.

The league final trilogy with Cork and drawn Leinster final against Kilkenny in 1993 had proven that Wexford had plenty of classy sticksmen – Martin Storey, Damien Fitzhenry, Larry O'Gorman, Larry Murphy, Adrian Fenlon, Liam Dunne, Sean Flood, Tom Dempsey and Rory McCarthy were good enough for any team in the country. In full flight, the Wexford style of hurling was a stirring sight; a combination of physicality and instinctive striking that was a throwback to the county's glory days of the 1950s and 1960s. The iconography of Wexford hurling was packed with names – the Rackards, Ned Wheeler, Nick O'Donnell, Martin Quigley, Tony Doran – that resonated of hurlers with a swashbuckling approach to winning matches. Too often, though, the bravery had faded and been replaced with a sort of wayward desperation when confronted in a tight corner by Kilkenny or, in latter years, Offaly. Wexford needed to ally some science to their better instincts and, in 1996, that essentially meant eliminating mindless clearances, Hail Mary shooting and the injection of some more ground hurling into the game plan. These are qualities that can be honed by good hurlers in five or six weeks quality training and while Rory Kinsella and Seamus Barron speeded up stickwork in drills and training matches,

Wexford veteran Billy Byrne celebrates his goal against Kilkenny in the 1996
Leinster hurling semi-final.

Griffin decided it was time to go to work on their minds and
brought sports psychologist Niamh Fitzpatrick into the camp.

Yet, all the nights in the gyms and sand dunes, the drills and
the psychology might have counted for nothing if it hadn't been
for the intervention of the veterans George O'Connor and Billy
Byrne in the second half against Kilkenny on 2 June. Kilkenny
started without D.J. Carey and John Power and included five
newcomers on the team and they looked to be in trouble when
they were five points down at half-time. The introduction of
Power after the break shook the game up and Kilkenny launched
a fightback closing the gap to one point by the 45th minute.
Their momentum had to be stopped and Wexford made some
changes bringing Martin Storey out to midfield and introducing
37-year-old O'Connor and 36-year-old Byrne to calm the situation. An old-style poacher, Byrne struck for the killer goal in the

63rd minute when Wexford were still just a point in front and it was enough to see his team hang on for a 1–14 to 0–14 victory. The euphoria of that victory was purged by an indifferent performance against Dublin in the semi-final two weeks later when Wexford scraped through to the final on a 2–12 to 1–9 scoreline, only managing four points in the second half.

As Wexford stuttered past Dublin, Clare faced a Limerick team buzzing after a 3–18 to 1–8 massacre of Jimmy Barry Murphy's Cork in Páirc Uí Chaoimh, Cork's first championship defeat on home soil since 1923 and biggest championship defeat since 1936. The Limerick–Clare Munster semi-final was played in the Gaelic Grounds before a capacity crowd in the sort of dead heat that had the occupants of the press box sweating before the sliotar was even thrown in. 'That game was one of the great days,' said Loughnane in *Raising the Banner*. 'I went to Limerick that morning about eleven o'clock to have a look at the pitch, just as the hawkers were setting up their stands. It was a lovely sunny morning and, even though there were only about 100 people there, you could feel the atmosphere. You just felt this was going to be something special. When we came in later, there was just a river of people in white shirts and in the Clare and Limerick colours, in a kind of shimmer of heat.'

Limerick led a hard but fair first half by 1–5 to 0–7 but, in the second half, the game appeared to be turning Clare's way. With all the usual suspects, McMahon, Daly, Doyle and, in particular, Brian Lohan in control at the back, they led by 0–15 to 1–9 with 12 minutes left. They missed a couple of chances to finish off the game, but still looked winners with five minutes left. Loughnane, though, had a presentiment that Clare's All-Ireland and Munster titles were slipping away, 'With about six or seven minutes to go, we seemed to lose all our energy. Near the end, when we were two points up, I met a Limerick selector Liam Lenihan, and he said, "Jesus, if we beat ye, it will be total robbery." I said, "Ye are going to beat us." I just felt that the tide had totally turned against us.' It did and in a manner that had shades of Offaly's onslaught in the last five minutes of the 1994 final.

Barry Foley narrowed the gap to two in the 66th minute. Gary Kirby closed it to one in the 69th and Foley, who had come on as late sub, levelled the match in the 70th. Clare, fatally, failed to win their own puck-out and the ball broke to Ciarán Carey just inside his own half. His man, Fergal Hegarty, slipped as Carey cut loose and soloed straight through the spine of the Clare defence, past McMahon and Lohan, to glide the ball over the bar from about 40 yards. Game Limerick: 1–13 to 0–15.

Given the heat and stakes, Carey's point was a super-human effort. Loughnane and Clare were strikingly sanguine and generous in defeat. Maybe it was the nature of Carey's score or an innate sense that there was a long road ahead, but there were no complaints or sour grapes afterwards. Loughnane was in expansive form when he addressed reporters outside the dressing room, 'In all my time in hurling, I was never part of anything like that today,' he said. 'This was a game that matched any epic games of hurling ever played, the kind of games we hear about from our fathers and grandfathers.' It wasn't even the end of June, and the All-Ireland champions and two of the 'Big Three', Cork and Kilkenny, had exited the championship.

July 1996 was a wicked month. The country basked in weeks of unbroken sunshine and the reflected glory from the Atlanta

Frankie Carroll (Limerick) celebrates in the 1996 Munster hurling final.

Olympics where Michelle Smith powered through the pool for three improbable gold medals that were later tarnished by a drugs scandal. Far away from Atlanta, hurling was experiencing another golden summer as the provincial finals in Munster and Leinster concluded. First up was the meeting of Limerick and Tipperary in Páirc Uí Chaoimh on 7 July. Playing some of their best hurling since the early 1990s, Tipp led by 10 points at the interval, 1–11 to 0–4. But, with Carey and Kirby again driving them forward, Limerick dug their heels in and closed down the avenues of space they had given Tipp in the first half. In an astounding 20 minutes, they scored 10 points without reply to level the game with less than 10 minutes left. Tipp pulled themselves off the ropes and led by two points in the final minute but Kirby, in the 70th, and Frankie Carroll, in the 72nd, landed the equalising scores: Tipperary 1–16 Limerick 0–19.

It was, agreed most commentators, the genuine article, a

Munster final classic. Griffin was so impressed that, looking ahead to the Leinster final, he coined his famous phrase about hurling being 'the *Riverdance* of sport'. The expression has since become almost as hackneyed as the 'Celtic Tiger' but was apt at a time when thousands of people, stimulated by the in-your-face Guinness advertising campaigns and RTÉ's live coverage of the big matches, rediscovered the game.

As the final seconds counted down in the Leinster final on 14 July, Wexford supporters had massed seven or eight deep all around Croke Park waiting for referee Aodan MacSuibhne to signal the end of Wexford's 19 ill-fated years in search of the provincial title. They were eight points ahead but, Martin Storey later recalled, there was alarm at the sight of the assembled supporters, 'One of the biggest memories I would have from that game was the ref trying to keep the crowd off the field. Tom Dempsey was signalling to the crowd to stay off the field. It was running through my mind that, God, if the crowd don't keep off the field, the game will be called off. Imagine that running through your head. I suppose it shows how much bad luck we had over the years. Even when we were eight points up, there was still a fear somewhere in my mind that the game could be taken off us. In all the years that I had been hurling for Wexford, the man above wasn't on our side. He wasn't even giving us a chance, he didn't even give us 50–50. We had lost titles when were four points up. We had given games away easily because we had lost our concentration or didn't stick to the game plan or allowed D.J. in with a heap of steps for soft goals.'

This time there was no D.J., no heartbreak, no doubts. The journey from Wexford to Croke Park that morning has since become part of hurling folklore. Griffin stopped the team bus at Scarnagh Cross on the Wexford–Wicklow border, told the players to get off and addressed them on the side of the road. 'Griffin stood almost in the ditch and gave a speech – Christ it still sends shivers down my spine,' recalled Liam Dunne. 'He gave a rendition of who we were and where we came from. He brought us back down the centuries to Vinegar Hill. The passionate way he spoke about Wexford brought tears to our eyes. It got worse when he spoke about our families and neighbours and ancestors and all the battles they'd had to fight over the years. And the fact they had risen, almost alone, in 1798 to give their blood in the cause of freedom. He asked for a complete focus and brought his oration to an end. "Lads," he roared, "we are walking out of our own county but we are coming back as Leinster champions this evening!"'

Griffin was true to his word as Wexford finally delivered in a game that ranks as one of the best of the era. 'Offaly were at their peak and the game had everything; goals, free flowing hurling, hard hitting,' said Storey. 'It was a savage game of hurling. I reckon that day against Offaly we produced our best hurling ever.' A penalty goal from goalkeeper Damien Fitzhenry helped Wexford to a one-point half-time lead, 1–10 to 1–9, three of the Wexford points coming from the baby of the team, Rory McCarthy. After the break, Wexford shot four without replay. Three points came from Man of the Match Larry Murphy and a Tom Dempsey goal in the 56th minute moved them 2–16 to 1–13 in front. Michael Duignan scored a goal for Offaly straight from the puck-out, but Wexford outscored the champions by seven points to two over the closing 12 minutes as their fitness and will to win kicked in. Final score: Wexford 2–23 Offaly 2–15.

The homecoming scenes on Sunday night and Monday were as rowdy and emotional as those witnessed in Clare the previous summer. On Monday night in Wexford town, Griffin rallied the crowd with another hair-raising call to arms: 'I have had a lot of questions asked of me about Wexford these last few years and I don't mind saying that I'm proud to have Wexford blood in my veins. I want you to be proud to be Wexford people,' he said. 'Hurling is a special game and our people can play it. I am not going to knock soccer, but Eric Cantona is from France and Paul Gascoigne from England. These people [the Wexford players] are your flesh and blood, they are your people. I want our game at the top and why shouldn't I? I have no intention of lying down.'

With all the emotion in the air, not to mention the inevitable marathon session, Wexford – again like Clare the year before – could have partied like it was 1956 and forgotten about the All-Ireland. But four nights later, Griffin and his players were back training for an All-Ireland semi-final against Galway. Limerick had beaten Tipperary by 4–7 to 0–16 in the Munster replay and, as August approached, the race for Clare's crown was wide open.

GALWAY'S FORM, AS USUAL, remained a mystery to themselves and everyone else. After beating Tipperary in the league final, they trained away, played challenge matches and had a comfortable workout against Roscommon in the revived Connacht final. Borrowing a leaf, perhaps, from Griffin's textbook, their manager Mattie Murphy was unusually forthcoming in an interview the day before the All-Ireland semi-final. 'The team to beat us isn't there at the moment,' he said. 'I honestly think that we have a better panel than any of those left in the championship. There is a pool of talent between 18 and 22 in Galway that isn't in any county in Ireland. That's one of the reasons why we don't fear anyone at the moment. There is a lot of belief in the squad. I would think that the Galway public are beginning to see that there is a team there for four or five years. They are a cut above the ordinary.'

They may have been a cut above the ordinary, but the absence of a reliable marksman was a costly handicap in a game of attrition with Wexford on 4 August. Galway were also slow to make changes. Joe Rabbitte broke a bone in his ankle in a throw-in with George O'Connor early in the first half but was only substituted late in the match. Wexford were more economical with their chances in the first half and led 1–9 to 2–5 at the break and continued to outscore a terribly wasteful Galway after half-time. In all, Galway hit 16 wides including six from very scoreable frees and, by the end of the match, had tried four different sharpshooters. The game could still have swung in their favour midway through the second half but Joe Cooney's shot from a penalty was saved on the line by Liam Dunne. Twelve minutes later, Billy Byrne found the net once more and three points from Martin Storey helped Wexford survive some fierce Galway pressure and advance to their first All-Ireland final in 19 years on an unconvincing 2–13 to 3–7 scoreline. In the other semi-final, Limerick defeated Antrim by 1–17 to 0–13 in another poor game.

Griffin wasn't too bothered about the quality of the hurling in the semi-final. It was arriving, not the manner of the passage to the final, that counted and, in the week before the final, he went into overdrive. Having learned that the Limerick team was spending a weekend in Dublin to attune the rhythms of an All-Ireland weekend, Griffin decided to go one better and brought his troops down to Ballytrent beach where they were billeted in an army tent for a weekend's training and bonding. Griffin had them out training at 5.15 in the morning and by way of consolation advised them that 'while we are down here getting ready for Limerick, they are asleep in Dublin. They are up there in a cosy hotel trying to get used to the pre-match routine but look at us and what we are doing. We are ready for them.'

Wexford's back-room team had covered every conceivable angle, right down to how the players should behave in the pre-match parade on 1 September. Limerick looked jittery and anxious for action as they marched behind the band, and broke early from the parade, but Wexford marched the whole way around the field with a military bearing and looked more composed and unfazed by the 65,849 crowd, the biggest in 24 years.

In the opening stages, the hurling was hard and reckless and Limerick expended a lot of their pent-up nervous energy in opening a 0–5 to 0–1 lead after 14 minutes, Barry Foley scoring two. Adrian Fenlon, probably the best hurler in the 1996 championship began to win quality ball for Wexford at midfield and, in the 20th minute, Wexford went ahead by a point when the veteran Tom Dempsey scored the game's only goal. It was never going to be a high-scoring, open game – Limerick had been waiting 23 years for an All-Ireland, Wexford 28 – but, from the start, players on both sides were guilty of some wild play and referee Pat Horan decided he had had enough when he sent off Wexford corner-forward Eamonn Scallon for a second dangerous pull on Stephen McDonagh.

Scallon had been booked a few minutes earlier in a bust-up involving more than a dozen players. In another incident, Limerick centre-forward Gary Kirby picked up a bad finger injury when he contested an aerial ball with Liam Dunne. Kirby's leadership of the Limerick attack and his accuracy from close and long-range frees meant that his well being was critical to his side's chances but, after the injury, he was a considerably reduced force. Dunne, later named as Man of the Match, denied that there was any malicious intent and insisted that he pulled legitimately. Suggestions that Wexford set out to physically intimidate Limerick are countered by the match statistics which show that their backs only conceded one free over the 70 minutes. Limerick had other grievances, notably having a Brian Tobin goal disallowed in the first half when referee Horan brought back play for a free.

On the scoreboard, it read 1–8 to 0–10 at half-time and, in theory, the force should have been with Limerick but instead it was Wexford, playing with a two-man full-forward line, who dominated the 15 minutes after the break. The younger Wexford players such as Fenlon, Rory McCarthy and full-forward Gary Laffan again showed well and two Laffan points along with scores from Dempsey and O'Gorman left Wexford four ahead – 1–13 to 0–12 – with quarter of an hour to go. There was no score for 12 minutes until Dave Clarke pointed for Limerick in the 67th minute. Carey added another, two minutes later but the late rally wasn't enough. Wexford stood their ground and, when Horan sounded the whistle, they were champions for the first time since 1968. Final score: Wexford 1–13 Limerick 0–14.

'Guts won it for us, pure guts,' said Griffin, who looked lost for words, as all around him Wexford supporters purged 28 years of anguish and yearning. In ways, Wexford's progress in 1996 was as compelling a hurling morality tale as Clare's in 1995. The bulk of the Wexford team had been hurling at senior level since the late 1980s. Players such as Ger Cushe, John O'Connor, Liam Dunne, George O'Connor, Martin Storey, Larry O'Gorman, Eamonn Scallon and Tom Dempsey had travelled to some dark places together before Griffin showed them that their careers in the county jersey didn't have to be about disappointment and humiliation. Wexford's 1996 All-Ireland was a triumph for perseverance and faith over calamity and doubt. Two weeks later, Mayo, their footballing soul brothers, came within a single bounce of achieving a similar feat.

Wexford All-Ireland Champions 1996

Damien Fitzhenry

Colm Kehoe   Ger Cushe   John O'Connor

Rod Guiney   Liam Dunne   Larry O'Gorman

Adrian Fenlon   George O'Connor

Rory McCarthy   Martin Storey   Larry Murphy

Eamonn Scallon   Gary Laffan   Tom Dempsey

Subs: Billy Byrne for Murphy, Paul Finn for Guiney,
Paul Codd for Laffan

1996

The Sorrowful
Mysteries of Mayo

*'In the 10 years that I have been playing, Mayo men never
went out to start mêlées or start fights.'*

Liam McHale, Mayo midfielder, September 1996

THE THURSDAY BEFORE the 1996 All-Ireland football final
between Mayo and Meath, two women from Ballinrobe decided
they would go the extra mile in devotion to their team and plant
a green and red flag at the summit of Croagh Patrick. When they
climbed to the top of the holy mountain, they discovered that
someone had beaten them to it. Undeterred, they scaled St
Patrick's Oratory and secured their flag there. It was an extreme
example of the fervour that seized Mayo as the county's footballers set out for Dublin in another attempt to win the Sam
Maguire for the first time since 1951. Wexford's success in that
year's hurling final should have been a good omen. Like Wexford's
followers, Mayo supporters are recidivist optimists and dreamers
who have been on a not so merry-go-round of defeat, near success
and worse defeat for decades. If Samuel Beckett had been a Gaelic

Mayo football manager, John Maughan.

football supporter rather than a cricket and golfing enthusiast, he might have followed Mayo. He would have appreciated their humorous resilience and stoical capacity to 'Try. Fail. Try again. Fail better.'

By the 1990s, the loyalty of hardened Mayo supporters was close to cracking. In 1989, they had come within three points of Cork in the All-Ireland final but stagnated afterwards – they didn't win Connacht again until 1992 when they lost one of the most dismal of All-Ireland semi-finals to Donegal by two points. That defeat was followed by a player mutiny against manager Brian McDonald and, when Jack O'Shea took charge for 1993, expectations revived again. Instead, after winning Connacht, Mayo were annihilated 5–15 to 0–10 by Cork in the All-Ireland semi-final. They mustered a tame-enough challenge against Leitrim in the 1994 Connacht final and, the following year, were well beaten by Galway. In September 1995, having had no luck with the outsiders, the Mayo County Board turned to one of their own, John Maughan, who had earned his management stripes with Clare. A popular choice, Maughan re-energised the camp, much as he had done with Clare. The older players respected him from his own playing days in the 1980s when he could potentially have been a Mayo great until a knee injury ended his career at 24. The younger Turks responded well to the discipline and camaraderie he brought to proceedings. The team enjoyed a good league run and victories over London and Roscommon brought them to Castlebar for the Connacht final against Galway in July.

The rivalry between the two counties is one of the enduring in football. It pre-dates Dublin and Meath, and the current northern enmities by decades, but doesn't have any of their atavism or record of indiscipline. If there's any genuinely Corinthian rivalry left in football, it's Mayo and Galway. There's a legacy of mutual respect between the counties going back to the 1920s and, in general, when they meet there's more value placed on pure football than aggressive posturing. In Connacht, everyone's spleen is reserved for Roscommon, for some not fully understood reason (unless you take their 'sheepstealers' nickname as having a serious historical basis).

The 1996 renewal between Mayo and Galway rated moderate to good. Galway travelled to Castlebar as defending Connacht champions, having come close to reaching the 1995 All-Ireland final, and the sides were level 2–7 to 1–10 until the 67th minute when Ray Dempsey scored the goal that saw Mayo regain the title on a 3–9 to 1–11 scoreline. The loss of Ja Fallon to injury after 55 minutes was a body blow for Galway, but Mayo still looked the better team. Kerry, under the management of Páidí Ó Sé, provided the opposition in the All-Ireland semi-final.

It's hard to believe it now but, in 1995, Kerry football was in meltdown. Losing three Munster finals to Cork was considered more than a crisis. Factor in the 1992 Munster final loss to Clare and the situation was considered catastrophic by Kerry supporters. It was the county's worst championship run since the years between 1914 and 1924 when Kerry was caught up in the throes of the War of Independence and the Civil War. There were genuine concerns that Kerry football, like Tipperary hurling in the 1970s and much of the 1980s, was slipping into permanent decline. Some commentators blamed the success of the Irish soccer team and the grip the 'Garrison Game' was gaining on the Kingdom's youngsters. Others pinpointed the loss of possession football values and the abandonment of the traditional Kerry catch-and-kick game. The inevitable populist response was to call for the head of manager Ogie Moran, while County Board chairman Seán Kelly also took a lot of flak for Sam Maguire's prolonged absence from home. However, a saviour was waiting in the wings.

Páidí Ó Sé had been bristling for the job since his retirement as a player in 1989. Mickey Ned O'Sullivan was given the nod ahead of Páidí that year and, three years later, P. Ó Sé finished last to Ogie Moran in a four-way contest for the toughest job in Gaelic football. By the winter of 1995, though, Páidí had an unbeatable hand to play after training the under-21s to an All-Ireland title.

'I don't think my appointment was ever really in doubt, certainly not with the chairman,' mused Páidí in his autobiography *Páidí*, 'I mean the county was desperate. We were facing a decade without an All-Ireland and we'd one Munster title in that period. There was panic among football folk in the Kingdom. My much-publicised passion for the Green and Gold was now seen as vital if we were to rehabilitate the fortunes of the county. The pressure was also mounting on Seán Kelly. He'd have to deliver to survive. It would have to be Páidí.'

And so it was. In October 1995, Páidí Ó Sé was named as team trainer and Seamus MacGearailt, Bernie O'Callaghan and Jack O'Connor from his under-21s back-room team also came on board.

In 1996, after a reasonable league campaign that ended with an extra-time defeat to Cork in the quarter-final, Kerry faced Tipperary in the first round of the championship and turned in a ropey enough performance until pulling away in the last 20 minutes to win by 11 points to set up the big tester against Cork. A fine performance from Maurice Fitzgerald was the difference between the teams in a tense game at Páirc Uí Chaoimh. Kerry won 0–14 to 0–11 and avoided the unthinkable vista of four successive championship defeats to the Rebels.

In their heart of hearts, Kerry underestimated the Mayo challenge in the All-Ireland semi-final. Páidí and the Kerry management didn't fully appreciate that Galway had upped the bar within Connacht in 1995 and that Mayo had responded in kind. Maughan's approach was so professional that he had held a 'debriefing session' for the Mayo team after the Connacht final. They were ideally primed for Kerry in the All-Ireland semi-final on 11 August. Only another superlative display from Maurice Fitzgerald saved Páidí and Kerry from a hiding. Mayo kicked some bad wides but led 1–8 to 1–4 at half-time, the goal a great strike from James Nallen, who finished off a move he had started in his own half. James Horan scored a spectacular second-half goal when he chipped the Kerry keeper, Declan O'Keeffe, from 40 yards and John Casey, with four points from play, played puck with Kerry in the second half. It finished Mayo 2–13 Kerry 1–10, Maurice Fitzgerald kicking 1–8 of Kerry's total.

'One Munster final does not a Kerry manager make,' admitted Ó Sé. 'What transpired over the next few weeks, culminating with our disastrous All-Ireland semi-final experience against

Mayo, would teach me more about management and preparation than any victory could have done. I learned enough to do me a fucking lifetime. When I think of it now, it makes me shudder. Raw. Unprofessional! Losing to Mayo in Croke Park changed the way I approached the job completely. You see a number of mistakes were made and I take full responsibility for them. Full responsibility. I couldn't get Cork out of my mind, my focus was way too narrow. When we beat them, I let rip. Celebrated with gusto. Even worse, I celebrated with the players. We had only three weeks to prepare and I didn't keep a tight rein on discipline, especially my own discipline. Huge mistake. I didn't keep a tight rein on the media. Huge mistake.'

PÁIDÍ COULD HAVE LEARNED some management tricks from Seán Boylan. Meath hadn't won a Leinster title since 1991 and, while they were hammered by Dublin in the 1995 Leinster final, there was no heave against Boylan. Meath people had immense respect for his achievements since 1982 and were prepared to give him time to build a new side. The All-Ireland winning side of 1987 and 1988 gradually dissolved after losing to Down in 1991 and, by 1996, just Colm Coyle and Martin O'Connell remained. Colm O'Rourke, on the cusp of 40, hung his boots up in the spring of 1996, but Boylan believed he had assembled the nucleus of another great team. Four players – Graham Geraghty, Enda McManus, Jimmy McGuinness and Trevor Giles – made the jump from the 1990 and 1993 All-Ireland minor and under-21 winning sides. Tommy Dowd, the novice in 1991, had matured into the team captain, John McDermott was a stern, physical presence in midfield and Coyle and O'Connell provided the leadership at the back. Still, the media felt that

Boylan was living on borrowed time if Meath failed again in the Leinster final against Dublin. 'Boylan can't go forever, can he?' queried one pundit the day before the game.

It was a first Leinster final for a third of the Meath team, but there were no wobbles during a cagey first half that ended with Dublin 0–4 to 0–3 in front. Meath gradually moved ahead after half-time, thanks to the accuracy of Giles, Brendan Reilly and the appetite and leadership of Tommy Dowd and won by 0–10 to 0–8. After the game, Dublin manager Mickey Whelan came under fire for some of his tactical and selection decisions. 'Our mental toughness wasn't there before the game as it was in the last couple of years. Why?' asked goalkeeper John O'Leary. 'I think it was just preparation. Fellows didn't seem enthusiastic

Brian Dooher (Tyrone) feels the pressure against Meath in the 1996 All-Ireland semi-final.

enough and didn't tune in to the game. Individually our attitude has to be questioned. We are the team and we can't blame anybody else at the end of the day.'

Meath had mental toughness and enthusiasm to spare when they faced Tyrone in the second All-Ireland semi-final on 18 August 1996. Having become the first Ulster champions in 20 years to retain their title after beating Down by a goal, Tyrone travelled south with plenty of confidence but were hit early and hard by a Meath side showing the benefits of their winter conditioning at Gormanstown College and the spring evenings spent running up and down the Hill of Tara. Graham Geraghty, Brendan Reilly and Barry Gallaghan cut loose for the first time that day and, while Tyrone were level at half-time – 1–6 to 0–9 – they faded badly in the second half and lost by 2–15 to 0–12. They had been out-muscled and out-manoeuvred by Meath and the sight of Ciarán McBride and Brian Dooher finishing the game with their heads swathed in bandages was grist to the theory that Meath had gone beyond the bounds of legitimate aggression in their game plan.

Boylan alluded to the criticisms of Meath's supposed roughhouse tactics in an interview the week before the All-Ireland final clash with Mayo on 15 September. 'Never, ever did I send a player out to do someone. I haven't and I never would. But we will fight tooth and nail for the ball and when you do that, accidents will happen.' In the same interview, Boylan admitted that the 10-point defeat to Dublin in 1995 had shocked him. 'I would go so far as to say that to see what was happening that day was frightening. Frightening because you felt so vulnerable. Everybody has this image of you as the person helping to create the environment for fellas to play football at the top level and they don't think you have done your job. It's easy to understand their annoyance. On a personal level, it's such a hollow feeling.'

While Boylan used the memory of the 1995 humiliation to Dublin to stoke up his players, Mayo manager John Maughan's main problem was preventing the hype from getting to his players as the entire county, to use a colloquialism, went pure cracked with excitement. There was only so much Maughan could do to insulate the team from the giddiness of football-mad people ravenous for some long-overdue glory, and he looked to his older players for a calming influence on the day of the game.

Players like McHale, Dermot Flanagan, Pat Holmes, Ray Dempsey and Anthony Finnerty had been there before in 1989 against Cork and McHale ran the show in the first half of the All-Ireland final as Mayo took a deserved 0-7 to 0-4 half-time lead, James Horan kicking three points from play. With 20 minutes on the clock, it looked as if the Ballinrobe women's dedication in climbing The Reek was to be rewarded. A goal in the 45th minute from Ray Dempsey pushed Mayo six points clear and one or two other points would surely have hauled them over the finish line. Instead, the rest of the match was a horror show for Mayo supporters. John McDermott and McGuinness took control at midfield and drove their side forward as Mayo retreated into a fragile defensive shell. Three points from Trevor Giles, two from Brendan Reilly and one from McDermott brought Meath within a point by the 66th minute, Mayo's only score in this period was a 59th-minute point from P.J. Loftus. The fates seemed to have turned against Mayo. A shot from Liam McHale struck the post and, while James Horan won the rebound, his effort hit the other post before being cleared to safety.

For all their problems, Mayo were still a point ahead entering the 70th minute when Colm Coyle drove a shot goalwards from midfield. Mayo goalkeeper John Madden advanced but misjudged the hop, and Coyle's shot had enough force to bounce over the bar. It was spookily reminiscent of P.J. Gillic's shot-to-nothing that earned Meath a draw in the first game against Dublin in 1991. Referee Pat McEnaney should have played three minutes of injury-time, but blew the whistle a few seconds after normal time. It was probably just as well for Mayo because Meath looked the side more likely to finish off the game. Final score: Meath 0–12 Mayo 1–9.

It was a poor enough final but had been played in a good spirit – unlike the replay two weeks later, which was one of the most notorious and controversial of All-Ireland deciders. Neither side had scored when all hell broke loose in the sixth minute. An initial skirmish led to a rolling brawl involving 27 players with digs, kicks and haymakers coming in from every angle. Nothing like it had ever been seen in an All-Ireland final and, when the tornado subsided, referee McEnaney sent off just one player from each team – McHale for Mayo and Coyle for Meath. Coyle, one of the survivors from 1987 and 1988, was an important player for Meath but McHale, given his form all year, was an inestimable loss for Mayo. Apart from his ball-winning

The infamous first-half brawl in the 1996 All-Ireland football final replay.

skills, McHale was adept at finding men in scoring positions and was good for a point or two in most games. He was also Maughan's lieutenant on the pitch, and Mayo's chances of an All-Ireland victory nosedived with his dismissal.

Even without McHale, Mayo looked the better side after the brawl. With Sheridan and Horan, again in good form, they were four points ahead before Giles got Meath's first score in the 18th minute. By the 30th minute, Mayo were 1–5 to 0–2 in front, thanks to a P.J. Loftus goal but, four minutes later, Meath were awarded a penalty, slotted away by Giles. It was a big score and Meath built on it after half-time when their captain Dowd, having a much better game this time, and Giles began to find gaps in the Mayo defence. The decisive score arrived in the 60th minute when Dowd got a toe to a quick free from Geraghty and poked the ball home for Meath's second goal. It was the first time the Royals had led in 130 minutes of football and, while James Horan kicked a 64th-minute equaliser for Mayo, Brendan Reilly had the final say in the 70th minute when he coolly slotted over the winner off his left. Final score: Meath 2–9 Mayo 1–11.

Meath celebrated, but the punch-up and sendings off sullied the final for most neutrals. The whole affair was an embarrassment to the GAA. Punch-ups and mêlées have always been part of Gaelic football but, in the 1990s, they began to occur with increasing frequency at every level and age-group and the oft-repeated video footage of Meath and Mayo going at it hammer and tongs was a public relations disaster for an organisation trying to persuade youngsters to play Gaelic rather than soccer or rugby.

There was another faux pas the day after the final, when Croke Park security staff refused to allow Boylan, team captain Tommy Dowd and several other Meath players into a reception being held in their honour because they didn't have the appropriate tickets. It required 45 minutes of negotiations before they were

◄ Anthony Molloy of Donegal lifts the Sam Maguire in 1992.

▼ Tipp legend Nicky English celebrates at the end of the 1991 All-Ireland hurling final.

John Troy and Johnny Pilkington celebrate at the final whistle after Offaly's spectacular five-minute final in 1994.

◄ Declan Darcy of Leitrim lifts the cup with Tom Gannon after the 1994 Connaught final.

©INPHO/Tom Honan

▼ The start of Jayo-mania – Jason Sherlock had a sensational championship in 1995.

©INPHO/Billy Stickland

©INPHO

Fans cheer on their teams in the 1996 Leinster Hurling final.

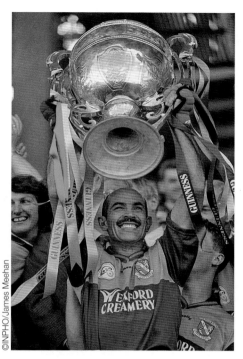

©INPHO/James Meehan

◀ Victory at last for George O'Connor and Wexford in the 1996 Leinster final.

▼ Ray Dempsey of Mayo celebrates his goal in the 1996 All-Ireland Football final against Meath.

©INPHO/Tom Honan

Páidí Ó Sé, managed Kerry to the 1997 All-Ireland football title.

Jamesie O'Connor gets his pass in for Clare during the 1998 Munster semi-final, watched by Brian Corcoran.

▲ All hell breaks loose in
the 1998 Munster hurling
final replay between
Clare and Waterford.

◄ Offaly veteran Joe
Dooley in action during
the 1998 championship.

The Sam Maguire crosses the Shannon after Galway's 1998 All-Ireland win.

allowed to join the party. It was an incident that added more fuel to the resentment felt by the top players at the slipshod manner in which they were treated by some sections of GAA officialdom.

The debate about the brawl and the dismissal of Coyle and McHale raged on for weeks. Referee McEnaney was hounded for his decision to single out McHale, in particular, and Mayo supporters claimed it had probably cost them the title. In an interview the following Sunday, a distraught McHale claimed the referee had taken 'an awful lot' away from him. 'Everything was going so well, there's no way I was as guilty as everybody else. I got three or four haymakers so I just started to take care of myself. It was scary in there. It was as rough as I have ever seen it. In the 10 years that I have been playing, Mayo men never went out to start mêlées or to start fights.' Wronged or not, McHale and Mayo had two choices: wallow in the wickedness of it all or, like Sisyphus, start to push the boulder up the hill again.

Meath All-Ireland Champions 1996

Conor Martin

Mark O'Reilly   Darren Fay   Martin O'Connell

Colm Coyle   Enda McManus   Paddy Reynolds

Jimmy McGuinness   John McDermott

Trevor Giles   Tommy Dowd   Graham Geraghty

Colm Brady   Brendan Reilly   Barry Callaghan

SUBS: Jody Devine for Callaghan, Ollie Murphy for Reilly

1997

THE FALLOUT FROM THE 1996 ALL-IRELAND FINAL lasted well into the 1997 season. In an interview early in the year, Mayo player Kevin O'Neill described the treatment meted out to top club and inter-county forwards: 'I have felt like packing it in so many times over the last couple of years. I have been stood on more times, spat on, abused verbally, kicked, punched…' There were plenty of more horror stories about worsening discipline in Gaelic football and, such was the clamour for action, the 1997 GAA Annual Congress approved the establishment of a National Development Committee for Gaelic Football whose remit was to examine all aspects of the game.

Meath, with some justification, felt they were demonised after the 1996 final. In the 1997 Leinster championship, they again proved they could play quality football as well as mix it when they faced Kildare in another replay saga that has been largely forgotten outside of the counties involved. Boylan's team had come close to losing their All-Ireland title against Dublin in June, winning by 1–13 to 1–10 after Paul Bealin missed an injury-time penalty. With Mick O'Dwyer back in charge, Kildare were inching their way towards a first Leinster title in 41 years until Trevor Giles stole a draw for Meath with a late equaliser. The replay, two weeks later on 20 July, was one of the games of the decade. Colm O'Rourke described it as the 'one of most incredible games of football I have ever watched and one of the greatest sporting occasions I have ever been fortunate to attend'. Kildare led by 1–7 to 0–7 at half-time and were still a goal in front with five minutes left when Trevor Giles converted a penalty and added a point for what appeared to be another archetypal Meath larceny. The referee, though, played five minutes of injury-time and substitute Paul McCormack got a fist to a Martin Lynch centre to punch over the Kildare equaliser. Final score: Kildare 2–14 Meath 2–14.

Kildare raced ahead in extra-time, and a goal from Willie McCreery left them 3–16 to 2–13 in front after the first period of play. Surely, Meath were finished now. No chance. They kicked six points without reply, four from Jody Devine, to again square the game. Final score AET: Kildare 3–16 Meath 2–19. Unfortunately, the third game represented a return to naked hostilities and Meath won 1–12 to 1–10 in a match that saw four players, two from each side, sent off and 51 frees awarded. Ollie Murphy, one of Boylan's new kids, was the match winner with 1–4, but the dismissal of Mark O'Reilly and Darren Fay was a blow as Meath prepared to play a resurgent Offaly in the Leinster final.

Graham Geraghty was already missing due to the suspension and Offaly fancied their prospects against a Meath team drained by the three games with Kildare. New manager Tommy Lyons had guided the Faithful from Division Four to the League title and had his team playing open, high-scoring football. They tore Meath to shreds in the Leinster final with the stylish Roy Malone striking for two goals to leave Offaly 2–6 to 0–7 in front at the break. Vinny Claffey, the crafty veteran, scored 1–5 and there were also big performances from Colm Quinn at wing-forward, and 18-year-old corner-back Barry Malone as Offaly savoured a 3–17 to 1–15 victory, their first Leinster title since 1982.

Afterwards, the analysts rushed to shower praise on Lyons and Offaly. 'The day Gaelic football was reborn,' was the verdict from the distinguished *Irish Times'* commentator Paddy Downey whilst, elsewhere, there was much talk of the game being rescued from cynicism and aggression.

There was also a temporary feel-good factor in Connacht where Galway and Mayo played out a blinder on 25 May. Thanks to live coverage, the game was the first time a nation-wide audience got to see new western stars, such as Michael Donnellan, Declan Meehan, David Nestor and Ciarán McDonald in action. Mayo hadn't beaten Galway in Tuam since 1951 but got off to a flying start and led by 1–4 to no score after 10 minutes, P.J. Loftus scored the goal. With James Nallen, Colm McManamon, Pat Fallon and Liam McHale ruling the middle third of the field, Galway had hardly a taste of the ball until player/manager Val Daly made a number of switches. He had started himself at centre-forward but switched 19-year-old Michael Donnellan out from the corner to curb Nallen and the move reaped quick results.

Donnellan terrorised the Mayo defence and the improved supply of ball saw Galway score nine points to Mayo's two during the remainder of the half, which ended level 0–9 to 1–6. Galway then went two points ahead with points from Niall Finnegan and John Donnellan but Mayo unleashed McDonald, their answer to Donnellan, and his two points, along with Maurice Sheridan's accuracy from frees and the experience of McHale and Holmes, was enough to see Mayo end the Tuam jinx. Final score: Mayo 1–16 Galway 0–15.

Mayo had seven points to spare over Leitrim in the semi-final in Castlebar but lost Colm McManamon for the rest of the summer after he was sent off, along with Leitrim's Gerry Flanagan, following a nasty punch-up that also saw John Maughan take a jab to the jaw. The Connacht final between Mayo and Sligo on 3 August at wet and gloomy Hyde Park was a throwback to the really bad days of Connacht football in the 1980s. Mayo played in a torpor, but Sligo were unable to punish them until the final five minutes when they scored 1–2. Final score: Mayo 0–11 Sligo 1–7.

Kerry, who had beaten a game Cavan team in the first semi-final, awaited the winners of the Mayo–Offaly clash on 31 August. Offaly were slight favourites on the basis of their 'total football' display against Meath, but they came out second best this time. Mayo kicked 17 wides but kept it tight at the back and at mid-field where Pat Fallon gave a Man of the Match performance. Mayo were six ahead before Offaly raised their first flag in the 24th minute and Mayo never let the lead slip. Offaly supporters were dismayed to see the full-forward line of Claffey, Malone and Brady, who had scored 3–8 against Meath, held to just a point. Maurice Sheridan, David Nestor and Ciarán McDonald did the bulk of the scoring for Mayo who qualified for their second successive All-Ireland final with six points to spare: 0–13 to 0–7.

Páidí and his young Kerry team recovered well from the trauma of losing to Mayo in the 1996 semi-final. With the manager setting the example, a Spartan approach was adopted and the first dividend arrived in April 1997 when they beat Cork in the League final. It was Kerry's first national title in 11 years, but any notions they had about themselves were rattled in the first round of the championship when they were given a serious fright by Tipperary in Tralee. Only one point separated the teams after 60 minutes but a Denis O'Dwyer goal saw Kerry squeeze through 2–12 to 1–10. On the other side of the draw, Clare caused the shock of the year by beating Cork when Martin Daly crashed home an injury-time goal in Ennis. The Clare men gave Kerry plenty to think about in the Munster final. Daly and wing-forward Ger Keane kicked some great points, but Kerry had the edge after a cracking individual goal from Pa Laide in the 39th minute. Final score: Kerry 1–13 Clare 0–11.

A few days before the 1997 All-Ireland football final, Maurice Fitzgerald rowed the short distance from Renard Point to Beiginish Island to meet to the Casey brothers, the last two inhabitants of the island. No doubt the Caseys, both in their nineties, talked to him about the Iveragh Peninsula's tradition of footballers. From the St Mary's Club in Cahirciveen on the tip of the peninsula, Fitzgerald was the inheritor of a flame of excellence that had been passed down from one generation of Iveragh players to the next. In the 1960s, Mick O'Connell – a man who, for a time, rowed in from Valentia Island for matches – had established himself as the greatest midfielder in the game and he passed the torch on to Jack O'Shea whose omission at midfield on the GAA's Team of the Millennium caused consternation in Kerry and beyond. O'Shea, also from Cahirciveen, was still playing when Fitzgerald made his debut for Kerry, but it was Fitzgerald's misfortune that Kerry were in decline as he was hitting his peak. He waited years for the opportunity to showcase his talents in an All-Ireland final and, when the chance arrived, he conjured up a display rated by Micheál Ó Muircheartaigh as the best performance by a Kerry player in an All-Ireland final since Sean Murphy in 1959 against Galway.

Fitzgerald's contribution aside, it was a forlorn sort of game between two teams who appeared more worried about avoiding defeat than actually going out to win the match. Mayo corner-back Dermot Flanagan pulled up with a hamstring injury after four minutes. The reshuffle of personnel that followed threw Maughan's team into disarray for most of the first half. The decision to start Liam McHale at full-forward struck most observers as an odd tactic and he was isolated inside until switched to midfield towards the end of the half. Mayo didn't score until the

23rd minute. And to heap woe upon woe, Maurice Sheridan, their most reliable scorer and freetaker, had to retire injured at half-time while Colm McManamon, back from suspension, wasn't his normal imposing self.

Kerry were struggling too. They had lost Billy O'Shea after 16 minutes when he broke a leg after he collided with Fitzgerald, but they had more focus and command of the basics. Liam O'Flaherty was an inspiring figure at

Maurice Fitzgerald on the attack for Kerry in the 1997 All-Ireland football final.

centre-back. Darragh Ó Sé and William Kirby were winning midfield and Pa Laide and Liam Hassett looked dangerous in attack. They led by 0–8 to 0–3 at half-time and more scores from Fitzgerald had them seven up until Mayo were given a lifeline in the form of a penalty. McDonald kept his head to beat O'Keeffe and two points from James Horan in as many minutes reduced the deficit to one. But the Mayo comeback faded as quickly as it began and they failed to score for the remainder of the match.

Fitzgerald scored a further two points to settle Kerry. In all, he scored nine of Kerry's 13 points including a few lovely scores from play. He was in a different class to most of the players on show. A few minutes from the final whistle, he emphasised just how different when he launched a 58-yard free from the Cusack Stand sideline over the bar to clinch Kerry's first title in 11 years. Final score: Kerry 0–13 Mayo 1–7.

Kerry celebrated as though it was their first rather than 31st All-Ireland. Mayo sloped away for another night on desolation row, although there was one Mayo man already preparing to put an end to Connacht teams' misery in Croke Park. John O'Mahony was officially named as Galway's new manager the week after the final. He and his team would breath new life back into not just Connacht football but the troubled old game itself.

Kerry All-Ireland Champions 1997

Declan O'Keeffe

Killian Burns   Barry O'Shea   Stephen Stack

Seamus Moynihan   Liam O'Faherty   Eamonn Breen

Darragh Ó Sé   William Kirby

Pa Laide   Liam Hassett   Denis O'Dwyer

Billy O'Shea   Dara Ó Cinnéide   Maurice Fitzgerald

Subs: John Crowley for Billy O'Shea, Donal Daly for Kirby, Michael Frank Russell for O'Cinnéide

Glory at Last for Cavan

It was a summer of surprises in Ulster where long-suffering Cavan ended a 28-year wait for an Ulster title by defeating Derry in a refreshingly open decider in Clones.

Cavan people have a serious passion for *peil* and the decades without at least an Ulster title to show for their efforts were an agony. Especially so for the generations reared on the exploits of the gallant John Joe Reilly, P.J. Dukes, Mick Higgins, John Wilson, Tony Tighe and the other players who had won five Ulsters and three All-Ireland titles between in the late 1940s and early 1950s, including the celebrated 1947 Polo Grounds Final in New York against Kerry.

The 50th anniversary of that final was always going to have a profound symbolism for Cavan football and, in 1994, the County Board looked beyond the county boundaries for help to revive their prospects ahead of 1997. They found an ideal candidate in Donegal's Martin McHugh who had been rejected for the vacant management position in his own county the same year.

McHugh knew there was plenty of raw talent in Cavan to match the tradition. Along with imposing the discipline essential for success, he also tweaked their style of play. Out went the predominantly catch-and-kick philosophy and in came an element of the more calculating, short-passing game Donegal had employed to such good effect in 1992. After beating Fermanagh in a replay, Cavan were drawn against Donegal in the 1997 Ulster semi-final. Several of McHugh's old team-mates ▶

Stephen King celebrates at the end of Cavan's win in the 1997 Ulster football final.

were still playing for Donegal but he cast those loyalties aside for 70 minutes in a high-scoring match where Ronan Carolan scored 1–7 as Cavan turned in a superb second half to win by 2–16 to 2–10.

The engine room of the team was the midfield pairing of 21-year old Dermot McCabe and 35-year-old Stephen King who was playing in his 17th championship for Cavan. The old warrior pulled a hamstring after 15 minutes of the Ulster final against Derry on 20 July, but soldiered on at full-forward until well into the second half. In his absence, McCabe and Damien O'Reilly produced a tour de force against Anthony Tohill and Dermot Heaney. It was a pacey, fluent game of football played in perfect conditions, a world away from some of rainy day, bone-crunchers of the early 1990s. The scores were level eight times in the first half, a ninth-minute goal from 21-year-old Jason Reilly the critical score for Cavan. Centre-forward Ronan Carolan was again a match winner, scoring three points in each half, and the Breffni County had other heroes in 19-year-old corner-forward Larry Reilly, the long-serving Fintan Cahill, corner-back Gerry Sheridan who curtailed Derry's dangerman Joe Brolly, and goalkeeper Paul O'Dowd. Final score: Cavan 1–14 Derry 0–16.

It was open season for sentimentalists. Fifty years after the Polo Grounds final, Cavan and Kerry again did battle, this time in the All-Ireland semi-final. Kerry were sluggish enough against Clare in the Munster final but started well in this game and were 0–3 to 0–1 ahead within five minutes before Cavan settled down and kicked three points without reply. Declan O'Keeffe foiled a Peter Reilly shot on goal but a cracker from Fintan Cahill gave Cavan a 1–7 to 0–9 half-time lead. The teams were still level until the 50th minute but Kerry took control and unveiled a new talent in Mike Frank Russell. He fired home a memorable goal on his debut and Kerry coasted through to another All-Ireland final. Final score: Kerry 1–17 to Cavan 1–11.

1997

The Golden Age of Hurling

'The thing is gone crazy, the pace of the game, the quality of the game… You can talk about the old days as much as you want but this is the greatest era of hurling, the greatest era ever.'

Ger Loughnane, June 1997

'The atmosphere of the game has been poisoned. The way things are now, hurling is hurtling towards a dark tunnel and unless something is done to check the momentum, the consequences could be horrific.'

Liam Horan, *Irish Independent*, August 1998

CLARE'S MUTATION FROM HURLING folk heroes in September 1995 to pariahs by the summer of 1998 is one of the strangest and most melodramatic stories in the GAA's history. It's hurling's equivalent of a Greek tragedy, leavened with plenty of farce and black comedy and peopled by a fantastical cast of characters. No one had expected Loughnane and his team to, in the words of captain Anthony Daly, 'feck off back to Doolin and drink pints' for the rest of their lives but few could have forecast the tornado they would unleash on their return to action in 1997. Although they had taken their defeat to Limerick in the first round of the 1996 Munster Championship like gentlemen and lain low afterwards, it was matter of when and how, rather than if, Clare would return. Winning the Munster and All-Ireland titles in 1995 had briefly sated Loughnane's ambitions but, given the youth and potential of his team, he was never going to rest easy until he had wiped the eye of Cork, Tipperary and Kilkenny in Munster and All-Ireland finals.

Hurling was in a state of robust good health at the start of the 1997 championship. The happy coincidence of Clare and Wexford's re-emergence, live television coverage of the big games and Guinness' sponsorship had seen attendances at the big fixtures soar during 1996 and hurling acquired a new respect, and even an element of glamour. The GAA's decision to introduce a 'back-door' system, allowing beaten provincial finalists back into the championship at a new quarter-final stage, for the 1997 championship upped the ante further, as did the experiment of starting the national league in March instead of October or November. Crowds in excess of 20,000 turned out for league matches that, a few years earlier, would have struggled to attract a few thousand supporters. It was all a far cry from the bleak mid-1980s when just over 8,000 supporters attended an All-Ireland semi-final between Galway and Cork. If you take 1995–99 as a golden age for hurling, 1997 was the apogee – although by the end of the year, the first tremors of implosion had begun to register loud and clear.

The first serious action of the year was the All-Ireland club final in Croke Park on St Patrick's Day between Athenry and Wolfe Tones from Shannon, the Galway club claiming their first title with three points to spare, 0–14 to 1–8. The dynamic Pascal Healy was Athenry's Man of the Match while their teenage full-forward Eugene Cloonan gave Brian Lohan something of a roasting, a score the Clare man would settle a few years later. It was minor blip for Lohan who was back to near his best on 8 June when Clare faced Cork in the Munster semi-final at Gaelic Grounds.

With an All-Ireland quarter-final place at stake, it was a winner-takes-all game and Jimmy Barry Murphy's new-look Cork side hurled out of their skins in the first half. Cork had been pitiful against Limerick the previous summer, but all the old dander was back for this game which saw the Rebels unveil several championship newcomers, including the diminutive Joe Deane and Seanie McGrath. The small men caused repeated problems for the Clare defence, particularly McGrath who scored five points from play. Along with Brian Corcoran, he was the catalyst for Cork's comeback after a blistering Clare opening. Clare led 0–9 to 0–8 at half-time and the second half was equally tight. Switching Ger O'Loughlin to full-forward proved a shrewd stroke for Clare with 'the Sparrow' scoring three quick points to re-establish their lead but Cork plugged away and the game was still there for the taking until Stephen McNamara grabbed the winning goal in the 70th minute. Cork protested that O'Loughlin had dropped his hurl before setting up McNamara for the goal but it was an academic argument and Clare survived to win by 1–19 to 0–18.

An encouraging aspect of the game for Clare was the distribution of scores. Apart from Jamesie O'Connor's six points, eight Clare players found the target, including the majestic McMahon with three points, and two apiece from newcomers David Forde and Colin Lynch who brought an additional cutting edge to Clare's midfield and attack.

On the other side of the draw, Tipperary had it far easier

against a Limerick side weary after their two losing assaults on the All-Ireland title. Tipp won by 1–20 to 0–13 and looked a potent force. Declan Ryan and John Leahy, two of six survivors from the 1991 All-Ireland winning team, had rediscovered their best form. Michael Cleary, another of the 1991 veterans, was as consistent as ever. The backbone of the defence was Noel Sheehy and Conal Bonnar and Tipp's manager Len Gaynor had successfully blooded players, such as Paul Shelley, Raymie Ryan, Conor Gleeson, Tommy Dunne and Liam Cahill. Next up for Gaynor were Clare, the team he had managed in 1993 and 1994.

Páirc Uí Chaoimh on 6 June 1997 was what Loughnane had dreamed about all his hurling life: Clare versus Tipperary in a Munster final on a glorious summer's day in front of a capacity 43,000 crowd. Defeat would see all the shibboleths about Clare's supposed inferiority to the traditional counties bubble up again; victory would elevate the Banner to a new position of strength. The memory of the Munster final wipeout against Tipp in 1993 and Nicky English's grin at the end of that game was still raw and alive in the minds of the Clare supporters and players, and Loughnane had his team psyched up as never before. They played spellbinding hurling in the opening 20 minutes and led 0–10 to 0–2 after 27 minutes.

The fundamental defensive values and spirit of 1995 had been augmented with slicker forward play and vastly improved striking of points from out the field. On this form, Clare looked unbeatable, but Tipperary called on all their innate hurling ability to drag themselves back from oblivion. Ten minutes before half-time, Gaynor moved Tommy Dunne to midfield in a switch with John Leahy, and both players immediately upped their game while Declan Ryan also found his form at centre-forward. Leahy struck two great points to spark the Tipp revival and, by half-time, they trailed by just five points, 0–13 to 0–8.

Colin Lynch celebrates Clare's 1997 Munster final victory over Tipperary.

Five Tipperary points in seven minutes after the break levelled the game until Sean McMahon broke the spell with a
morale-lifting, long-range free. Loughnane brought on David
Forde in the 48th minute and, four minutes later, Forde sliced
through the Tipp defence to strike a wonderful individual goal
that lifted Clare's confidence again. Jamesie O'Connor continued
to have one of the games of his life at midfield, but Clare had to
weather one final scare before regaining their Munster title. With
time almost up, the ball was still in the Clare danger area and it
broke towards Leahy. Standing 25 yards from the Clare goal and
willed on by the Tipperary supporters on the terrace behind

Davy Fitzgerald, he had his finger on the trigger awaiting the bounce when the sliotar appeared to hit a divot and he scuffed the shot. Final score: Clare 1–18 Tipperary 0–18. It was like 1995 all over again, as Clare supporters swarmed the field and Anthony Daly declared that the Banner were no longer willing to be 'the whipping boys' of Munster hurling. Those few words would lead to an escalation in hostilities later in the summer but, for now, Loughnane had reached Nirvana.

'The 1997 Munster final is the treasure of all treasures,' he wrote in *Raising the Banner*. 'We won two All-Irelands and they were brilliant, but this was unique. People outside Clare would find it very difficult to understand just how much it mattered. This was the dream for every Clare person for decades – to beat Tipperary in a Munster final. Forget about All-Irelands. Had we won six All-Irelands [but] hadn't beaten Tipp in a Munster final, it wouldn't have been as good but to win that day and go into the dressing room was sheer bliss. I made sure the dressing room was locked. The atmosphere inside was one of total and absolute contentment. We are not supposed to feel it in this lifetime. There was no need for a word to be said. The downside was that you knew there would never be a day like it again, but it is a feeling that will last forever.'

WHEN CLARE DEFEATED KILKENNY in the All-Ireland semi-final, Loughnane and his team had achieved the grand design of beating 'The Big Three' – Cork, Tipperary and Kilkenny – in one season. The only catch was that, because of the back-door system, they had to quell Tipperary again to reclaim the All-Ireland title. Tipperary had picked up the pieces after the Munster final by beating Down in the All-Ireland quarter-final in Clones. They had seven points to spare in the All-Ireland semi-final against Wexford, who had retained their Leinster title thanks to another late salvo from Billy Byrne. Wexford looked a tired team against Tipp, though, and suffered a serious setback when Rory McCarthy was forced off with an injury at half-time. They could never get any closer than four points to Tipperary who had made four changes in personnel and several positional switches from the team beaten by Clare.

The build-up to the second Clare–Tipperary encounter in the All-Ireland final saw the antagonism between the teams and their supporters ratcheted up a few more levels. Loughnane officially declared war after reading some comments made by the Tipperary PRO Liz Howard in the match programme for the Munster under-21 semi-final. She took exception to Anthony Daly's speech after the Munster final, in particular his declaration, justified given their history, that Clare were no longer willing to be 'the whipping boys' of Munster. Daly's comments were interpreted by Howard as evidence of an unhealthy arrogance creeping into Clare's mentality and were, she claimed, 'conduct unbecoming to hurling'. Loughnane responded by publishing an open letter to Liz Howard in *The Clare Champion* two weeks before the All-Ireland final.

The letter opened graciously with Loughnane recalling happier days of yore when Liz's father Garrett was the Garda Sergeant in Feakle:

'Dear Liz,

Congratulations to you and your county on reaching the All-Ireland final. Believe it or not, up to a couple of years ago I had thought that, since you were reared in Feakle, just like myself, you were a Clare woman. I remember your brother was in Seamus Durack's class in Feakle NS and I even remember you cycling to school in Tulla. Most of all, I remember well, with great fondness, your late father Garret. I used to go hunting with him with the beagles practically every Sunday morning during the winter months. I was enthralled by his vitality and I well remember as if it were yesterday, standing on Mike Henchy's hill watching the beagles chasing the hare and your father saying, "There, they go, hell for leather."'

The niceties out of the way, the Clare manager cut to the chase.

'I was outraged that a player I admired so much could be maligned for making a speech that I wish I could have made myself. Anthony Daly represented the people of Clare with the greatest of dignity. He has presented a modern, articulate image of the great game of hurling, something that was sorely lacking in the past and we are immensely proud of him. Because of people like Anthony Daly, Martin Storey and Rod Guiney, hurling is now drawing support from strands of our society who previously considered it a game for backward, ignorant people.'

Loughnane then went on to dissect the conversation he had with the Tipperary PRO at that year's All-Ireland quarter-final between Kilkenny and Galway in Thurles – before he was aware of her notes in the under-21 programme – when she said: 'Please don't say we are arrogant in Tipp.'

'When you returned and started your "we're not arrogant in Tipp" refrain, I wanted to tear strips off you. Instead, I just looked straight ahead at the open turf of this magnificent stadium and thought of the great days I was there as a player, mentor and spectator. I was there when Pat Fox scored that wonder goal with one hand in the replay against Cork. I remember well the roar that went up from the crowd and my young son said, "What was that?" "That,", I said, "was the Munster Championship."

'I wanted to tell you about a comment passed by one of your greatest players in recent times when he said that they knew they had reached an all-time low in 1986 when Clare beat them in Ennis. I wanted to tell you that a former Tipperary manager had said that if they didn't beat Clare by 10 points, they had no business taking on Cork... I wanted to remind you of the outrage we felt over the behaviour of certain Tipperary players in the Munster final of 1993. But, most of all, I wanted to tell you to shut up. And then I looked across and I actually felt sorry for you as I believe you are a genuine person. But do not ever again attack a Clare hurler and expect to get away with it.'

Loughnane concluded by asking Liz to 'please convey to Len [Gaynor] that we do not believe the "I wonder what the Clare lads think now" comment attributed to him after the semi-final as we are most grateful for the great work he did here and believe he is a man of the highest integrity as are the vast majority of people in the great hurling county of Tipperary. Up Feakle.'

It was an astonishing missive and vintage Loughnane: part sentiment, part mischief, but also aggressive and clever with a deadly sting in the tail. Loughnane believed Clare's best interests were served by reinforcing the siege mentality within the camp. And, for a time, his players seemed to thrive on all the mind games and brouhaha. In 1997, they combined what Loughnane later called a 'demonic ferocity' with enough discipline and focus

Tipperary manager, Len Gaynor.

to play some awesome hurling. It's a reflection of how good Tipperary were in this period that they brought the greatest team of the decade to the wire twice in one season.

From his time as Clare manager, Len Gaynor knew Loughnane's tricks well and he avoided any public verbal engagement with the Clare manager in the run-up to the final. As Loughnane stated in his letter to Liz Howard, Gaynor was a much-respected character of the 'highest integrity', but he was also under serious pressure within Tipperary to halt Clare's surge to the All-Ireland. A selector in 1984 when Tipperary came within a couple of minutes of victory in the centenary year Munster final against Cork, he stuck to the tried and tested Tipperary methods of preparing hurling teams. There were no psychologists, no motivation tapes, no emotive public cries from the heart. Gaynor was vindicated in his approach when Tipperary outhurled and outran Wexford in the semi-final. If the players were fit enough and had the right hurling instincts, that was good enough for Gaynor, although he was quick to make changes and switches where necessary.

The Tipperary team that lined out in the All-Ireland final against Clare on 14 September 1997 was unrecognisable from that which had taken the field in the Munster final. Liam Sheedy and Conal Bonnar replaced Raymie Ryan and Conor Gleeson in the half-back line. Gleeson was switched to midfield in place of Aidan Butler while Liam McGrath, Eugene O'Neill and Brian O'Meara started in the forwards in place of Liam Cahill, Kevin Tucker and Philip O'Dwyer. Tommy Dunne moved to midfield and John Leahy started at left half-forward. In contrast, Clare made just two changes: Conor Clancy and Niall Gilligan replacing Barry Murphy and Stephen McNamara in the forwards.

All the nonsense associated with the build-up was forgotten once the sliotar was thrown in. Captivating from start to finish, it was one of the games of the decade. This time, it was Tipp who enjoyed the flying start and they led by 0–9 to 0–3 after 27 minutes. Clare's forwards were unable to make worthwhile inroads against the regrouped Tipp defence and, with the wind at their backs, the Tipp forwards were flying; Leahy and Dunne the chief scorers and Declan Ryan disrupting McMahon's influence at centre-back. Loughnane then switched Gilligan out to the wing and brought Fergal Hegarty out to the other wing. The scores began to flow and 20-year-old Gilligan fired over two points to help reduce Tipp's half-time lead to a manageable 0–10 to 0–6.

As the Tipp players emerged for the second half, some choice comments were directed at Loughnane and he claims, in *Raising the Banner*, that he 'knew at that moment that Clare were going to win'.

'The Tipp lads were in too much of a frenzy. The bigger the rage they were in the better I liked it. I always believed that the best thing to do is to whip up the opposition into a complete frenzy. Before that All-Ireland, that's what I did. Deep down, I really feared that Tipp would pull one over on us. I knew the way Len operated. He's an emotional man and he'd go absolutely ballistic over some things. I put out the story that Tipperary thought nothing of us and that Len Gaynor told us that when he was with us. Before the final, Des Cahill came down to interview me. He asked me something. I paid no attention to the question but I brought up the question of how Nicky English had insulted Clare in 1993 and how that was really motivating me to manage Clare and to really sock it to Tipperary. The whole thing blew up again and it was driving Tipperary mad!'

Tipp did seem to lose their composure after the break. A Liam Doyle point after 10 seconds got Clare on a roll and with Jamesie O'Connor hurling up another storm on the wing, Baker grabbing a hold of the game at midfield and Forde again proving his worth as an impact sub, Clare led by 0–17 to 0–12 with 14 minutes left. As in the Munster final, their point scoring from distance and the distribution of scores among the team – nine players scored – emphasised how much the team had developed since 1995. Tipp were on the precipice, but a point from Leahy and a kicked goal from Liam Cahill in the space of two minutes reignited the game. After an exchange of points that kept Clare two ahead, Tipp briefly went into the lead in the 67th minute when Eugene O'Neill doubled the ball to the net after Tommy Dunne's 65 came off the crossbar. The unflappable Baker fired over the equaliser from the puck-out. Colin Lynch set up Jamesie for the lead point, the ball landing in Loughnane's hand when it dropped over the bar as the Clare manager shouted instructions to his forwards.

Tipp still had two more chances to salvage at least a draw. Leahy fielded a long ball from O'Meara in the final minute and was momentarily free within striking distance of goal. It was the Munster final all over again except, this time, he had the ball in the hand. Instead of taking the point, Leahy went for broke and aimed for the left-hand corner, but Fitzgerald got a stick to it at the last second. When Conor Gleeson's long-range effort for a point drifted wide, the game was up for Tipp. Clare were All-Ireland champions for the second time in two years. Final score: Clare 0–20 Tipperary 2–13.

Any doubts the traditionalist pedants had about Clare's worth had been erased. Cork, Tipperary, Kilkenny and Tipperary again had fallen beneath the Banner juggernaut and with most of the team still in their early to mid-20s, Clare looked a good bet to win a couple of more All-Irelands. They were still the people's champions, but the strain of the great leap forward was beginning to tell on Loughnane. It should have been a night for him to savour a few gin and tonics – his drink of choice – with the players, family and friends but instead he allowed himself to be hauled into yet another verbal ruckus, this time with *The Sunday Game's* match analyst Eamonn Cregan.

The Limerick man, who had coached Clare for a couple of seasons in the early 1980s, didn't agree with the consensus that it had been a classic All-Ireland. Loughnane saw red and, when *The Sunday Game* went live to the team's banquet, he opened fire on Cregan and his '10-minute whinge'. It might have been a crowd pleaser and settled some old scores for the Clare manager, but it was a discordant note to end the year on and set the tone for what became hurling's *annus horriblis*.

Clare All-Ireland Hurling Champions 1997

David Fitzgerald

Michael O'Halloran   Brian Lohan   Frank Lohan

Liam Doyle   Sean McMahon   Anthony Daly

Ollie Baker   Colin Lynch

Jamesie O'Connor   Conor Clancy   P.J. O'Connell

Niall Gilligan   Ger O'Loughlin   Fergus Tuohy

SUBS: Fergal Hegarty for Tuohy, David Forde for O'Connell,
Barry Murphy for Hegarty

1998

'We are like sheep running around in a heap...'

Michael 'Babs' Keating, Offaly manager, 5 July 1998

'It was as if the whole team had just one mind that they were going to battle today like never before. That was the attitude and I suppose it was the cause of the row at the start.'

Ger Loughnane, 19 July, 1998

1998 WAS THE YEAR OF THE OFFALY PLAYERS' REVOLT and the Colin Lynch affair. The year of a premature end to an All-Ireland semi-final, a Croke Park sit-down, sideline bans, mysterious priests in the Hogan Stand, cloak-and-dagger disciplinary hearings, Loughnane's broadcast on Clare FM. The year of Michael Bond, Brian Whelahan and, ultimately, the year Offaly won the war after losing one battle and almost losing another.

The Friday night after the 1998 Leinster final, the Offaly hurlers arrived in dribs and drabs for training in Tullamore and found a middle-aged stranger togging out in their dressing room. His name was Bond, Michael Bond. A native of Ardrahan, an area of south Galway steeped in hurling, Bond had managed a fine Galway under-21 team to an All-Ireland in 1983, but had then disappeared off the inter-county radar screen until resurfacing in July 1998. The principal of St Brigid's Vocational School in Loughrea, a feeder academy for Galway minor teams, Bond had been drafted in by the Offaly County Board as an emergency replacement for Michael 'Babs' Keating who had resigned as Offaly manager the Wednesday after the team's disappointing Leinster final exit. Kilkenny won a low-key and undistinguished final by 3–10 to 1–11, but the result was soon overtaken by Keating's post-match comments.

Keating is renowned for shooting from the hip, and his appraisal of Offaly's performance enraged a panel of players already on the brink of mutiny. 'That couldn't be described as Leinster senior championship hurling and I have no problem in saying that my job is to teach and show them what to do but it appears to be falling on deaf ears,' was his opening shot to the reporters gathered outside the Offaly dressing room. 'The players just aren't listening to me. We are like sheep running around in a heap. Lots of attitudes need to be changed in the next three weeks. I hate saying that in the middle of July. These are doubts and phrases I used last July when I came to Offaly,' continued the Tipperary man. 'I feel awful disappointed with the application of the stick and quality of play. You'd like to think you have something to contribute, but equally you'd like to think that you'd be listened to. There's a vein running through this Offaly team of individualism, of not thinking of their colleagues, not playing for their colleagues. The players just sail along. There's not a lot of disappointment in that dressing room. They just take every day as it comes.'

It was an unprecedented attack by a hurling manager on his players. This, after all, was the same group of Offaly players who had won the All-Ireland in 1994, lost the 1995 final by two points and who had almost beaten Wexford in 1997.

Relations had been poor between the Offaly players and Keating from the beginning. They felt he was trying to impose a style of Munster hurling alien to them, and Babs did himself

The Offaly rebels.

no favours with some comments he gave when Offaly failed to fulfil a challenge game against his native Tipperary in May. A real
traditional hurling county, i.e. Tipp, Cork or Kilkenny, would
never let themselves down like that, he suggested.

In spite of the dissension, Offaly denied injury-stricken
Wexford a Leinster three-in-a-row when they beat them by a
point in the provincial semi-final, a 70th-minute goal from Johnny
Dooley deciding the game. Laois came within a few minutes of
shocking Kilkenny in the other semi-final but lost by 3–11 to
2–11. Substitute Ken O'Shea scored 1–1 to steal it for the Cats
but, on the evidence of both semi-finals, it was a far from vintage
year in the east. The final was another poor game but Offaly
competed to a certain extent and probably would have won if it
hadn't been for D.J. Carey's two goals from 21-yard frees and
Charlie Carter's haul of 1–5. Offaly's body language, though,
spoke of a team in the throes of some turmoil and the sight of
Brian Whelahan engaging in a verbal battle with Keating midway
through the second half said it all. Babs' tirade after the game

gave the senior players in the Offaly dressing room the chance they had been waiting for.

Johnny Pilkington led the rebellion. Long before the Keating affair, Pilkington was an urban legend in hurling for his frank wit and refusal to adhere to the puritan lifestyle choices that were becoming the norm for inter-county players. He made no bones about his fondness for a pint, a smoke and living the *vida loca* and, along with several of his Offaly team-mates, he carried the torch for an alternative interpretation of the inter-county dream. His comment after Cork had beaten Offaly by a point in the 1999 semi-final – 'that's the last time I'll give up smoking for nine days' – was quintessential Pilkington.

But for all his supposedly dissolute ways, Pilkington had the knack of getting himself in shape for the summer months, not to mention Birr's winter campaigns in the Leinster and All-Ireland club championships. If anything, the older he got, the better a hurler he became and the longevity of his career was testament to his natural ability and hurling intelligence. The smokes and droll midland one-liners camouflaged the steel and self-belief he shared with a lot of the other Offaly players who were winners from their minor days. Babs was right in one sense, there was a streak of 'individualism' running through the Offaly team, but that was one of the qualities that made them such an intriguing and talented team in the first place. 'Individualism' aside, Babs had also underestimated the bonds that existed between the players. They had played together so long, particularly the Birr contingent, that they were never going to be bullied into changing their fundamental hurling principles. Babs had picked the wrong group of players to ridicule.

'It's stupid and unfair. Babs is washing his hands of all responsibility,' Pilkington told the *Irish Independent* the Tuesday after the Leinster final. 'The players are not taking criticism lying down. The comments are unbelievable. I don't think any manager anywhere has made comments of this nature after losing. Certain players, including myself, will have to take more responsibility but we don't need this kind of stuff from Babs. It's very unprofessional of him.'

Babs resigned as Offaly manager on Wednesday and, with Bond in place, Pilkington and his team-mates set about rescuing their season.

❖

THE KEATING AFFAIR was a localised spat compared to the chaos that was about to erupt in Munster. Clare were favourites to retain their title in the south and, in the final 10 minutes of their semi-final against Cork in Semple Stadium, they opened their shoulders and played the sort of hurling that had taken them to the summit in 1997. Once again, their point scoring, pace and all-round power marked them out as being in a different class to any other team in the province. Jimmy Barry Murphy's side stuck with Clare for 60 minutes but wilted in the final 10, as O'Connor, Gilligan, Markham and Taafe struck a sequence of unanswered points to secure a 0–21 to 0–13 victory for Clare.

Waterford were supposed to be the coming team in Munster for several seasons and they finally delivered and matched Clare's tally when they beat Tipperary by 0–21 to 2–12 in their semi-final clash on 7 July. Paul Flynn scored 10 points, Ken McGrath four, and Dan Shanahan, Tony Browne, and Billy O'Sullivan two apiece as Waterford blitzed an unsettled Tipperary side. They had one of the largest travelling armies of supporters in the country and they celebrated the success in Páirc Uí Chaoimh as though it were a Munster or All-Ireland victory. Two weeks later, they came within a puck of the ball of winning a first Munster title since

1963. With time almost up, Paul Flynn stood over a free 100 yards from the Clare goal to win the game for Waterford. He had the distance but his shot veered wide and the sides were deadlocked: Clare 1–16 Waterford 3–10. It would have been an audacious triumph for Waterford because they had only levelled the game in the 69th minute when Flynn found the net.

Tony Browne of Waterford.

Waterford revived memories of the teams of 1959 and 1963 with their performance in the second half when they refused to buckle after going in eight behind at half-time. Tony Browne was on fire at midfield and Anthony Kirwan plundered 2–1 off Brian Lohan. It was hectic and hard throughout and Clare's P.J. O'Connell was sent off in the second half for a high challenge on Browne. Waterford manager Gerard McCarthy was an animated figure throughout, repeatedly running onto the pitch to berate the officials and, a few days after the game, Clare selector Tony Considine claimed that McCarthy had unduly influenced referee Willie Barrett in P.J. O'Connell's sending off: 'We saw enough of those antics in the World Cup and we don't want to see the same thing creeping into our games,' said Considine, referring to the cynical diving prevalent in that year's World Cup finals in France. Considine's comments were the first shots of one of the bitterest conflicts in modern hurling.

Even though they had led by eight points at one stage, Clare looked flat and taken aback by Waterford's hunger and fervour in the second half of the drawn game. Loughnane attributed it to the effort they had invested in beating Cork but he also felt that, unlikely as it sounds, Clare had allowed themselves to be intimidated by Waterford. He was already formulating his own plans for the replay but the Clare players didn't need any promptings from their manager. A Waterford player called one of the Clare players a 'wife beater', a comment that enraged the rest of the Clare team.

Few teams have ever taken to a field as psyched up and wired as Clare were for the replay in Thurles on 19 July. Loughnane cried havoc and let loose his dogs of war. 'Before we went out on the pitch, I stared right into each player's eyes. They'd have taken on the German army. It was the only time I ever understood how soldiers could go into battle and not be afraid of dying,' he wrote in his autobiography. 'This was personal. Waterford were not going to be allowed to humiliate some of our players they way they had done the previous Sunday. We wanted to put them down. I admit completely, it was war without bullets.' Waterford were equally ready for a battle and the atmosphere in Semple Stadium before the game was heavy with acrimony.

Willie Barrett, one of the fairest and most accomplished of referees, was in charge of the match but he hadn't even thrown the ball in when the trouble started. Anthony Daly and Dan Shanahan were pulling wild on one wing. Jamesie O'Connor, a sportsman through and through, emerged with a broken hurl from an affray with Brian Greene on the other. Colin Lynch was pulling ferociously as Barrett attempted to steady the four midfielders for the throw-in and Browne, Quelly and even his own midfield partner Baker felt the heat of Lynch's ash. Four minutes after the sliotar got moving, tempers exploded. Brian Lohan and Waterford's Michael White became entangled and a mêlée began with Davy Fitzgerald racing from his goal to get involved. Barrett reached

Backs to the wall: Clare hurlers 1998.

for two reds. While he was dealing with this situation, more trouble started down the field with a linesman identifying Lynch as the culprit. A posse, including Loughnane and Daly, surrounded Barrett after he sent off Lohan and White. By now, Tony Browne was lying on the ground and, when Barrett somehow managed to restore order, he booked Lynch. The game restarted and Clare led 0–7 to 0–5 at half-time. Clare were better equipped than Waterford to revert from a war footing to normal hurling and they destroyed the pretenders to their crown by 2–9 to 0–4 in the last half hour. Final score: Clare 2–16 Waterford 0–10.

'There was a totally different attitude coming down here today,' Loughnane told reporters afterwards. 'Completely different all through the week, but especially last night. I have never been as tense in myself even when I was playing, even going to All-Irelands. There was a single-mindedness. It was if the whole team had just one mind that we were going to battle today like never before. That was the attitude, and I suppose it was the cause of the row at the start. Everybody was so keyed up. I know a big deal will be made of it when it's shown on telly. All kinds of nutters will be ringing the radio stations about it but everyone got it out of their systems and it became a sporting contest with hard knocks given and taken. There's no doubt we felt Waterford had put it up to us physically the last day. We weren't going to be pushed around. We were determined to hurl from the soles of our feet to the tops of our heads.'

Anthony Daly echoed his manager's sentiments when he accepted the Munster Cup: 'We refuse to yield,' he roared to the Clare supporters.

Loughnane was right about the calls to the radio stations, particularly RTÉ's *Sportscall* programme on Monday evening. The switchboards were jammed with callers straining to outdo each other in their criticism of Loughnane and his players. Clare had become the demons of hurling and they were accused of everything from 'orchestrated violence' to using 'steroids'. One caller suggested Loughnane was 'unfit' for his job as a teacher.

Waterford were sad, stiff and sore. Paddy Joe Ryan, their County Board secretary, was incensed by what he claimed was a deliberate attempt by Clare to 'take out' their best player Tony Browne. 'Tony was battered and bruised but he is super fit and can take a lot. He was hit two or three times. The feeling here in Waterford is that the physical exchanges took too much out of our players.' Waterford played Galway the following Sunday, 26 July, in the All-Ireland quarter-final in Croke Park and won by 10 points, 1–20 to 1–10, in front of a disappointing crowd of 26,000. Tony Browne was Man of the Match but his altercation with Colin Lynch in the Munster final replay resurfaced when Lynch was charged with 'repeated striking with the hurley on opponents' and requested to attend a Munster Council disciplinary hearing on 7 August.

Waterford's goalkeeper Brendan Landers after the 1998 Munster final replay.

The situation spiralled out of control. Clare officials claimed Lynch had no case to answer as he hadn't been cited in the referee's report. Loughnane circled the wagons and claimed that a conspiracy was being waged against Clare by a motley coalition comprising everyone from 'spivs in journalism' to 'jealous people' in the traditional counties. Clare County Chairman Robert Frost reported back on a conversation he overheard between three priests sitting in the VIP section of Hogan Stand at the Waterford–Galway game. 'Their main discussion was on the Clare team. It went along the lines that the Clare team were tinkers, Loughnane was a tramp and the Clare team must be on drugs,' reported Frost, who also claimed to have heard one of the priests state the Munster Council was going to suspend Colin Lynch for three months.

That last piece of information fed Loughnane's conviction that the Munster Council was engaged in a witchhunt on Lynch and, by extension, the Clare team and himself. The controversy had become an all-consuming distraction from the primary duty of preparing the team for their All-Ireland semi-final against Offaly on 9 August. Offaly had beaten Antrim by 2–18 to 2–9 in their quarter-final. It was an unconvincing display, but Offaly were motoring along nicely under the encouragement of Bond who focused entirely on drills to sharpen the team's first touch and ground hurling.

Antrim had more to worry about than their first touch. They had been unable to train collectively in the weeks before the quarter-final because of the dangers of travelling throughout north Antrim during what was a particularly violent and volatile loyalist marching season.

The Munster Council was due to meet on Friday night, 7 August, to deliberate on the charges against Colin Lynch, but Loughnane again put the cat among the pigeons the day before the hearing when he addressed the people of Clare in a 90-minute broadcast on Clare FM's mid-morning radio show hosted by Colm O'Connor. 'Sunday is a day when we have to make a stand. If we have to fight on our backs on Sunday, we just have to stick it down the throats of all those people who have been castigating us,' he told the faithful. From the safe distance of eight years, it's priceless material for the neutral listener. Loughnane ranged far and wide and there was more comedy when he quoted one old stalwart who claimed that he had often 'seen more pushing and shoving coming out of Crusheen mass on a Sunday' than he had seen in the Munster final replay!

The Munster Council didn't see it that way, and suspended Lynch for three months after the player's attempted High Court injunction against the legality of the hearing on 7 August was dismissed. The hurling finally resumed on 9 August when Clare, minus Lynch and Brian Lohan, faced Offaly in the All-Ireland semi-final in Croke Park. Offaly were a far different proposition from the listless outfit beaten in the Leinster final. They controlled the first half, taking full advantage of Lohan's absence, and led by three points in the 43rd minute when Fitzgerald made a brilliant save from a Johnny Dooley piledriver. The save lifted Clare and Loughnane, watching from the stands because of his touchline ban, sent Fergus Tuohy into the fray. Tuohy scored 1-1 and Clare led by 1-12 to 0-11 entering the final 10 minutes – but a Pilkington goal and two points from Dooley and Pilkington again appeared to have snatched it for Offaly until Jamesie O'Connor scored an equalising free. Final score: Clare 1-13 Offaly 1-13.

The replay two weeks later saw the hurling summer fork off on another bizarre tangent. Having survived one game without Brian Lohan and Lynch and recovered their focus, Clare were again hurling with the assurance of 1997. Loughnane started two championship newcomers, Christy Chaplin at midfield, along-side Baker, and Alan Markham on the wing. And it was a goal from Markham in the 23rd minute that put Clare 1–5 to 0–2 ahead and emphasised their superiority in virtually every position on the field. With McMahon landing three 65s in the first half, Clare led by 1–9 to 0–4 at half-time and there didn't appear to be any way back for Offaly. Points from Markham and Baker after the break stretched Clare's lead to 10. They had one foot in the final until the Dooleys intervened. Points from Joe and Johnny and a goal from Billy narrowed the deficit to five. It was game on and, while points from O'Connor steadied Clare, Joe Errity found the net in the 57th minute to close the gap to three. The next 10 minutes produced some intense hurling from both sides. Clare reopened a 5-point advantage but Brian Whelahan, playing in the forwards, and Billy Dooley brought it back to one score – but with less than three minutes left – Offaly desperately needed a third goal.

Possession was with Clare when Jimmy Cooney blew for full-time but it immediately became apparent that he had ended the game two and half minutes early. The logical solution would have been to restart the game but, once the whistle went, Cooney was surrounded by agitated officials from both teams as opposing players shook hands and swapped jerseys. Cooney was whisked off the field by Croke Park minders before he could remedy his error of consulting the wrong stopwatch. While all this was happening, the under-21 hurlers from Kerry and Kildare raced onto the field for their All-Ireland B semi-final. They never got to play it. Once word of the lost time was confirmed, the Offaly supporters poured onto the pitch and staged a sit-down protest demanding a replay. The hardcore refused to budge, until an official announcement that the game 'had not fulfilled its full duration'. The following day, the GAA Games

Offaly supporters stage a sitdown protest after the premature end of the 1998
All-Ireland semi-final replay.

Administration Committee (GAC) announced that the refixture would take place in Thurles the following Saturday with all the match receipts going to the fund for victims of the Real IRA's bombing atrocity that claimed 29 lives in Omagh on 15 August.

It was a heaven-sent reprieve for Offaly. Clare were clearly the better team in the second game but physically, mentally, every way, the advantage was now with Offaly and they won the third and best game of the series by 0–16 to 0–13 in front a near-capacity crowd in Semple Stadium. Brian Lohan was back for Clare, but the match turned on some great saves from Offaly goalkeeper Stephen Byrne and a Man of the Match display at the other end of the field from veteran corner-forward Joe Dooley. At 35, he was the only survivor from the 1984 Offaly team who had lost the Centenary All-Ireland to Cork in Thurles, and his five points from play broke Clare's hearts. Offaly were six to the good with five minutes left but Clare, weary and all as they were, battled on and closed the gap to three as full-time approached. Substitute Fergal Hegarty had one last chance to force the tie into injury time, but Byrne denied him with another nerveless save. Final score: Offaly 0–16 Clare 0–13.

Kilkenny had beaten Waterford by a point in the other semi-final and the pairing of the two Leinster sides in the All-Ireland final on 13 September was described by one commentator as the 'second-best team in Leinster facing the third-best team in the country'. Clare's absence devalued the final for some people and there was an unusually subdued build-up with tickets readily available on the morning of the game. When news of Brian Whelahan's debilitating flu leaked out, the feeling was that there was another 'handy All-Ireland' there for Kilkenny who had been rocked earlier in the year when D.J. Carey announced his retirement. After a week or two or drama, D.J. returned to action but, for most of the season, Kilkenny still resembled a team in transition rather than All-Ireland contenders until the mayhem in Munster galvanised them into action.

Whelahan rose from his sickbed to start in his customary right half-back position but was clearly a weakened presence and conceded two points to Brian McEvoy in the first 15 minutes and also allowed his man set up a third. In the meantime, Charlie Carter had scored a 12th-minute goal. The Offaly mentors took quick action and moved Whelahan to wing-forward in a swap with Michael Duignan in the hope of getting their most influential player into the match.

The switch worked wonders. Duignan, Hubert Rigney, the outstanding Kevin Martin, Johnny Pilkington and Johnny Dooley took control of the midfield battle and Offaly fought back to trail by just two points at half-time. Whelahan moved into full-forward in the second half and produced a master class as Offaly hit their finest form in years and attacked Kilkenny with all the venom of old. They drew level in the 47th minute and went ahead a few minutes later when Joe Errity finished a solo run with a goal. He added a point for good measure and Offaly were 1–13 to 1–9 ahead when Kilkenny were awarded a 57th-minute penalty. D.J. went for goal but his shot powered over the bar. Brian Whelahan had taken his place on the line to face the blast and, 10 minutes later, secured the title for Offaly when he scored the second goal after Errity had again done the spadework. Final score: Offaly 2–16 Kilkenny 1–13.

Whelahan scored 1–6 in total, 1–3 from play, and it was probably the performance that clinched his place on the GAA's Millennium Team of the Century. One of his second-half points should be preserved for posterity.

John Troy addressed a sideline cut underneath the Hogan Stand. Whelahan indicated he wanted possession and darted out from goal. Troy obliged by delicately chipping the cut at the right angle for Whelahan to catch it at chest height and he swivelled and pointed without breaking stride. The move took about five seconds and was an exquisite example of what Offaly were capable of when they were in the mood. Whelahan's sickbed conversion from defender to highest scorer epitomised Offaly's spirit on a day when Errity, Troy, Duignan, Martin, Rigney, the Dooleys, and the full-back line of Martin Hanamy, Kevin Kinahan and Simon Whelahan were superb.

There will always be question marks because of Clare's absence, but Offaly played with the verve and class of champions and would probably have beaten any opposition as they peaked to perfection for September. Their performance the following year when the lost their title to Cork was heroic and confirmed their worth as champions.

The Offaly supporters acclaimed Bond for restoring their team's dormant style and swagger. 'Personally, I feel great that I have been able to help them in any way because no matter who you look after, you must treat them right,' said Bond afterwards. 'If you treat them right, they will respond and if you have talent and motivate them then it will fall in place. I have done very little because all of these players have extraordinary talents. They had it in 1994 and they had it in 1995 and they simply don't lose it overnight.'

It was a remarkable Offaly team's final fling. They were caught at the death by Cork's youth in 1999 and, although they subdued the Rebels in the 2000 All-Ireland semi-final, they were mauled by Kilkenny in the final.

Clare never fully recovered from the trauma of the summer of 1998. Loughnane's team remained a constant threat but

Munster and All-Ireland titles eluded them in years when they should have put at least two and possibly three All-Irelands back-to-back. The revolution was over. The 'Big Three' regained control in 1999 and haven't relinquished it since. But, for all the controversy and paranoia of 1998, history will judge Loughnane and his Clare team kindly. They were liberators who brought hurling to a new level of intensity and excitement and forced the traditional counties to completely re-evaluate their approach to the game. It could be decades before we see their likes again.

Offaly All-Ireland Hurling Champions 1998

Stephen Byrne

Simon Whelahan   Kevin Kinahan   Martin Hanamy

Brian Whelahan   Hubert Rigney   Kevin Martin

Johnny Pilkington   Johnny Dooley

Michael Duignan   John Troy   Gary Hanniffy

Billy Dooley   Joe Errity   Joe Dooley

SUBS: Paudie Mulhare for Hanniffy, Darren Hanniffy for Billy Dooley, John Ryan for Johnny Dooley

1998

Revenge of the Fancy Dans

'That's the end of 32 dirty, rotten, miserable oul years.'

Galway supporter leaving the Canal End, 27 September 1998

'The GAA should get down on their knees and give thanks for John O'Mahony and his gallant Galway players. Yesterday in Croke Park they reinvented the great old game of Gaelic football.'

Eugene McGee, Irish Independent, 28 September 1998

WHILE THIS BOOK WAS BEING WRITTEN, Seán Purcell, one of the true icons of Gaelic football died at the age of 76 in Blackrock Clinic. Many of those who were fortunate enough to see him play would rate the Tuam Stars and Galway virtuoso as the greatest Gaelic footballer of his own or any other generation. An

176

undisputed selection at centre-forward on the GAA's Football Team of the Millennium, Purcell's genius lay in his mobility, vision, bravery and apparently effortless command of the game's most subtle tricks and skills. He played most of his football at midfield but was famously versatile – one of his seminal displays was at full-back for Galway in the 1954 Connacht semi-final against Mayo in Tuam. His bravura performance in that match launched a young team on its way to an All-Ireland title two years later. That final against Cork is remembered most for Frank Stockwell's tally of 2–5 from play, Purcell orchestrating the show from centre-forward. Purcell and his Tuam Stars team-mate Stockwell became immortalised in football as 'the Terrible Twins', a sobriquet passed on in 2005 to Galway under-21s Michael Meehan and Sean Armstrong after their six-goal haul in the All-Ireland under-21 final against Down.

Purcell had retired by the time Galway embarked on their three-in-a-row of All-Ireland titles in the 1960s, but he remained an ever-present at Galway, Tuam Stars and St Jarlath's matches over the years. Galway's long, slow decline after losing three All-Ireland finals in 1971, 1972 and 1974 must have saddened a purist like Purcell, particularly the nadir of the county's capitulation to Dublin in the notorious 1983 final. Disillusion was rife among Galway football people in the early 1990s and a new rock bottom was reached in 1995 when the football County Board sold just 53 tickets ahead of the Connacht championship first-round game against Sligo at Markievicz Park. Galway won that match and the 1995 Connacht title. And the revival looked more convincing when they went close to defeating a Peter Canavan-inspired Tyrone in the All-Ireland semi-final. Their manager Bosco McDermott, a corner-back on the 1960s three-in-a-row team, was non-committal about his own future after the game but predicted great things for his young team: 'I don't know yet if I will be with them but they are a fine bunch of lads, full of intellect and character and I know there is an All-Ireland in them.' The forecast came good three years later when seven of Bosco's team helped bring the Sam Maguire west for the first time since 1966.

The weekend of Seán Purcell's death, Jimmy Magee dedicated a lengthy chunk of the *Sunday Sport* programme on RTÉ Radio 1 to 'The Master'. It was a wonderful piece of radio and featured tributes from Roscommon great Gerry O'Malley, the RTÉ broadcaster and *Tuam Herald* journalist Jim Carney, Dublin's Tony Hanahoe and Sean Bán Breathnach of RnaG and TG4. They spoke as much about Purcell's essential decency and substance as a person as they did about his prowess on the field although the conversation inevitably wound its way back to football. Sean Bán concluded his contribution with an anecdote about meeting Purcell in the Sacre Coeur Hotel in Salthill the week after Galway won the 1998 All-Ireland final. Purcell was riveted to a rerun of the final and, after watching one particular Galway surge in the second half, he turned to Sean Bán and said, 'Now that's football!' It was succinct and high praise. Purcell, like countless football people throughout the country, had been thrilled by the dash and openness of Galway's unexpected victory over Kildare. Eugene McGee captured the reaction well when he wrote: 'The game of Gaelic football was the big winner yesterday because Galway revived three great skills – catching, kicking and scoring long-range points. It is not an overstatement to say that yesterday's game may mark a turning point for Gaelic football as we approach the 21st century.'

Put simply, by 1998 Gaelic football had regressed and, at times, degenerated as a spectacle in the vacuum left following the break-up of the Kerry side that won eight All-Ireland titles between 1975 and 1986. Their dominance wasn't healthy for the game and, in Kerry's wake, success was often the preserve of teams who adhered more to a negative, spoiling and macho ethos than to the skills and principles that can make Gaelic football such an engaging code when played well. The warning bells were sounded when Kerry were still harvesting All-Ireland titles. In *Over the Bar*, his caustic and frank autobiographical reflection on the GAA first published in 1984, Brendán Ó hEithir wrote: 'I find it most appropriate that a medical doctor [Dr Mick Loftus] has been elected President at a time when football, if it were human and his patient, would probably be in an intensive care unit. Much as I favour the advancement of hurling, it must be admitted that the resolution of the problems of football is the GAA's single most pressing problem at the moment. Tinkering with the rules has failed to eradicate the major blemishes of what is essentially an evolving game… It would make for a healthy start if the GAA, like the alcoholic, were to admit publicly and sincerely that the problem exists and that Gaelic football may not survive without immediate help. Once it has got the rules in order, it can then tackle the equally important problem of standards of refereeing and interpretation of the rules.'

Like the neverending fretting about the precarious health of hurling, the rules of Gaelic football and their interpretation are a perennial headache for the GAA but the game was in serious trouble by the mid-1990s. The 1995, 1996 and 1997 deciders don't feature too often in reruns of classic All-Irelands and the 1997 GAA Congress acknowledged that there were fundamental problems with the game when it established a National Development Committee for Gaelic football.

Ó h'Eithir, a native of the Aran Islands with family roots in Clare would have relished the style of Galway's achievement in 1998 and the fact that it was a Connacht team who halted Gaelic football's latest descent into mediocrity. The middle-aged Galway-man leaving the Canal End after the All-Ireland Final was right

– for Connacht, the years since Galway last took the title west in 1966 had been dirty, rotten and miserable. Years of neverending *mi-adh* and defeat: Galway's three losing finals in 1971, 1973 and 1974 to Offaly, Cork and Dublin; Roscommon's failure to finish off Kerry when they had them on the ropes in 1980; the shame of 14-man Galway's surrender to the 12 Dubs in 1983; Mayo's hard-luck story in the 1989 final against Cork, and the same county's woes in 1996 and 1997. Clann na Gael of Roscommon lost four All-Ireland club finals in Croke Park in the 1980s and then there were Mayo's calamitous semi-final defeat to Cork in 1993. Prior to 1998, the last Connacht football team to win a final in Croke Park were Galway minors in 1986.

It was fitting that John O'Mahony, the keenest football brain in the province, masterminded the end of the misery. He had worked the oracle with Leitrim in 1994 and the Galway County Board's decision to appoint him as senior manager in September 1997 was auspicious. McDermott's team from 1995 had faltered twice against Mayo but were maturing well and players such as Kevin Walsh and Tomas Mannion – minors in 1986 – Jarlath Fallon, Niall Finnegan, Seán Óg de Paor, Ray Silke and Gary Fahey were augmented by an influx of fresh talent drawn primarily from the St Jarlath's team that had won a Hogan Cup title in 1994.

It was the sort of colleges team that only appears once in a lifetime and six of them – Michael Donnellan, Pádhraic Joyce, John Divilly, Tomás Meehan, Derek Savage and Tommy Joyce – went on to win All-Ireland senior medals with Galway. St Jarlath's, who won their first Hogan Cup in 1947 when Purcell played midfield, had a reputation for turning out 'pure' footballers but, even by Jarlath's standards, the 1994 crop was exceptional. In the final against St Pat's of Maghera, John Concannon totally outplayed Sean Marty Lockhart who went on to become an All-Star and International Rules defender. Derek Reilly scored the winning goal and, four years later, he was the leading scorer when his club, Corofin, broke the Connacht hoodoo in Croke Park by beating Erin's Isle of Dublin in the All-Ireland club final. Concannon and Reilly never graduated to the Galway senior team and, instead, it was Pádhraic Joyce and Michael Donnellan who provided the spark of youthful inspiration for the 1998 All-Ireland winners. There was a lot more to the Galway team than Joyce and Donnellan but no one would dispute that it was their brashness and class that gave O'Mahoney's team the extra edge in a four-year period when they won two All-Ireland titles, by very different routes, and came within inches of winning a third.

The O'Mahony era began in earnest on 24 May 1998 when 34,000 supporters crammed into McHale Park in Castlebar for the Connacht semi-final between Galway and Mayo. It was biggest crowd seen in the province for years and, even though Galway were clearly the better side, there was enough flux and dramatics to keep the crowd entertained until the final whistle. The sides were level 2–5 to 1–8 at half-time, the Galway goal coming from Derek Savage, another prodigy who prospered under O'Mahony's tutelage. After the break, the experienced hands of Kevin Walsh at midfield and Jarlath Fallon steadied Galway but they struggled for scores and Mayo were still just a point behind entering the last 10 minutes. Galway goalkeeper Martin McNamara more than made up for a first-half gaffe when he saved a point-blank shot from Ciarán McDonald in the 57th minute, and three minutes later McDonald saw another shot come off the crossbar. That was the signal for Galway to move through the gears and they kicked three points in the last five minutes, two from the underrated Niall Finnegan, for a 1–13 to 2–6 victory.

Finnegan had been a regular since the early 1990s and Galway's season could have ended prematurely only for his *sang froid* at the death in the Connacht final a few weeks later. Roscommon, as unpredictable and bullish as ever, had staged a remarkable recovery in their semi-final against Sligo, scoring 2–1 in the final minutes to steal a draw. They won the replay by a point and were on the verge of the Connacht title when a controversial decision by Leitrim referee Seamus Prior swayed the game in Galway's favour. Time was almost up when Gary Fahey appeared to lift the ball off the ground 25 yards from his own goal

Galway's attacking wing-back Seán Óg de Paor.

but Prior waved play on and Fahey was fouled as he attempted to clear his lines. Donnellan won possession from the free and, in turn, was fouled 35 yards from the Roscommon goal. With the rain pouring down, Finnegan guided the pressure kick over the bar to level the game 0–11 apiece. Roscommon moaned about the provenance of Galway's equaliser but there had also been doubts about the free leading to their lead point, and a draw was a fair result in a game memorable for Roscommon wing-forward Eddie Lohan's eight points, four of them from play. Roscommon had a man sent off in the first half and Galway should have cruised to the title, but they kicked 17 wides and were a relieved team to get a second crack at 'the Rossies' in Hyde Park on 1 August.

The replay in front of a full house in Hyde Park on a fine Saturday evening was a terrific game of football and the high fetching, points from distance and general abandon of the exchanges was a welcome antidote to the dour, short-passing game then in vogue in so many counties. Veteran observers rated it as the best Connacht final since Galway and Mayo in 1948. Lohan was on fire again for Roscommon and landed another eight points. His efforts and some spectacular points from Nigel Dineen, Tommy Grehan and Fergal O'Donnell left Roscommon 0–10 to 0–8 ahead after 57 minutes but Finnegan squared the match with two points and Seán Óg de Paor, Galway's Man of the Match, pushed them ahead with a point after one of his distinctive raids from defence. Roscommon weren't finished though and Lohan sent the game into extra-time with a late equaliser from a free. The game turned on a mistake by Roscommon keeper Derek Thompson 30 seconds into the second period of extra-time. After fielding a harmless enough ball, Thompson mulled too long over his clearance, was dispossessed by Galway substitute Shay Walsh and Michael Donnellan blasted the loose ball into the net. The goal and Ja Fallon's three points in the first period gave Galway a five-point cushion and they survived another Roscommon rally to win 1–17 to 0–17.

Between McDonald's shot off the crossbar in Castlebar and the disputed free in the drawn game with Roscommon, Galway definitely rode their luck in Connacht. Once they reached Croke Park, though, they played like a liberated team and made quick work of an ageing Derry in the All-Ireland semi-final. Donnellan, de Paor, Fallon and Joyce were the architects of a 0–16 to 1–8 victory. Galway played with the breeze in the first half and their tactic of running at the Derry defence yielded plenty of scoreable frees for Joyce, giving them a 0–10 to 0–4 lead at half-time. Derry improved on the restart and it took two great saves from Martin McNamara to help steer Galway through a difficult third quarter. A couple of sweet points from Fallon and Joyce finished off the Ulster team whose goal came from a last-minute penalty.

While Galway were blazing a trail out of the west, Kildare were also crawling their way to redemption in Leinster. Their hunger and need for some sort of success was so stark they wouldn't have felt out of place in Connacht. They hadn't won a Leinster title since 1956 and you had to go back to 1928 for their last All-Ireland. Yet, for all the poverty of their achievements, the Kildare supporters seemed to have curiously high expectations of success. They had a sense of entitlement born of growing up listening to stories about an ever-receding era of glory. The Lilywhites three-game series with Kerry for the 1903 champ-ionship was credited with giving birth to Gaelic football as we know it and, while Kildare lost, the saga earned them huge respect nationally. They won their first All-Ireland in 1905 and added a second in 1919 with a team captained by the famed Larry Stanley who, apart from being a consummate footballer, was also an international class high-jumper. The Lilywhite heritage was enriched further in the 1920s and 1930s when they won six Leinster titles and two All-Irelands between 1926 and 1931. But the lights went out after the six-in-a-row and the 1956 Leinster title was a lone beacon of hope until 1990, when Mick O'Dwyer arrived from Kerry amid much hype to take over as manager.

Even with Micko on board, the burden of history dogged Kildare and they seemed doomed to always collapse when their usual tormentors Meath and Dublin were almost out of sight. 1997 was especially cruel when Kildare blew a six-point, extra-time lead in the epic 3–20 (Kildare) to 2–17 (Meath) Leinster semi-final replay. Meath finished the job in a nasty second replay but Kildare regrouped for another assault on the championship in 1998.

The one-point victory over Dublin in the Leinster quarter-final was the turning point for O'Dwyer's team. As was their wont, they kicked some shocking wides but had the character to keep shooting from distance and that proved the winning of a tense and mediocre game. Niall Buckley and Padraig Gravin kicked some powerful points and Kildare led 0–12 to 0–8 until they conceded a last-minute goal but there was no time for any more torture and the Lilywhite supporters were delirious after a first championship victory over Dublin since 1972. They were far more confident in the semi-final, racking up 2–13 against a raw Laois team.

The acid test was the Leinster final against Meath on 2 August. It was another day of trench warfare in Croke Park but, this time, Kildare didn't surrender. They battled and scrapped and, although Meath scored three points without reply to level the game in the final minute, Kildare finally found the wherewithal to respond and score 1–2 for a 1–12 to 0–10 triumph that ended the decades of torment. Martin Lynch set up Cork import Brian Murphy for the goal that spelled deliverance and the grace-note points were supplied by Eddie McCormack and Willie McCreery. 'Yesterday was the day when Kildare finally took their place in the game of Gaelic football and finally laid to rest the ghosts of Larry Stanley and all the other greats of a bygone era,' observed Eugene McGee. 'Kildare's achievement in snatching victory at the very end in a game of such importance was the most significant aspect of yesterday's game. So often have they failed in similar situations, but yesterday was the final indication that we must now scrap all the old clichés for Kildare football. Out go words like "gutless", "leaderless" and "a crowd of wasters" and in come terms like mature, brave, and streetwise.'

They needed all those qualities in abundance when facing All-Ireland champions Kerry in the All-Ireland semi-final. Much of the build-up to the game focused on the conflict between O'Dwyer and his native county. Páidí Ó Sé, one of of O'Dwyer's most trusted players in Kerry's years of dominance, was naturally a little unnerved by the prospect of pitting his management wits against O'Dwyer and he attempted some mind games before the game began. 'I would have to try every trick in the book to stop this man,' he admitted in his autobiography *Páidí*. 'Turn the tables on him. Step back into the past, see what I could find. I knew O'Dwyer well, really well. Knew if he pissed crooked. But I feared him. When it came to match day, high on my priority was securing the dugout closest to the Canal End. Why? *Piseoga*. I knew Dwyer wanted it. Even if his team was dispatched to the Hill 16 end of Croker for the pre-match warm-up, he'd insist on the Canal End. He achieved far too much success at that end for him to overlook it.'

Páidí succeeded in securing the Canal End dugout, but the *piseoga* turned against Kerry as Kildare galloped to a 0–13 to 1–9 victory. Kildare were the better team for most of the game and the win was all the more commendable given the absence of scoring ace Niall Buckley because of injury. The intensity of their running and tackling had Kerry on the back foot from the start. McCreery and Dermot Earley controlled midfield and the scores were well distributed among Cravin, McCormack, Karl O'Dwyer and Martin Lynch. For once, Kildare were a model of economy in attack. Kerry, by contrast, missed some good chances in the first 15 minutes. Maurice Fitzgerald, recovering from injury, had an off-day from frees and was hounded in general play by Brian Lacey, a Tipperary recruit to the Lilywhite cause. Kildare led by 0–9 to 0–4 until John Crowley stemmed the tide with a Kerry goal. Drawing on the experience of the Dublin and Meath games, Kildare weathered the crisis and restored a 0–13 to 1–7 advantage although Kerry's Denis O'Dwyer had what looked like a legitimate goal in the 65th minute disallowed for a square ball. Kerry chipped away at the lead in the closing minutes but Kildare survived to reach a first All-Ireland final in 64 years.

By the end of the 70 minutes on 27 September, however, the Lilywhites were bewildered and deflated. Their supporters hadn't countenanced defeat in the weeks leading up to the final and the highrollers lumped on a Kildare victory, narrowing the team's odds to less than evens by the day of the final. The consensus in Kildare and elsewhere was that, having beaten the two previous All-Ireland champions en route to the final, they would have no difficulty with Galway who, the theory went, wouldn't have the power or experience to cope with Mick O'Dwyer's outfit. The fact that none of Kildare's victories against Dublin, Meath and Kerry produced football to match that served by Galway, Mayo and Roscommon in the Connacht Championship was ignored, as were the injury problems within the Kildare camp. Niall Buckley was short of match fitness, Glen Ryan required a cortisone injection to line out and full-back Ronan Quinn was sidelined by injury.

Galway had a fully fit panel of players and the suffocating focus on Kildare was heaven-sent for O'Mahony, a manager with an almost pathological distaste for hype and people talking up his teams. The scene was set for a western ambush and Galway led by three points after 13 minutes. Michael Donnellan roamed far and wide in those early stages and electrified the crowd with his solo runs into the heart of the Kildare defence. The opening burst laid down some ground rules for the

Michael Donnellan celebrates Galway's 1998 All-Ireland victory.

encounter, but Kildare gradually settled and more or less dominated the rest of the half, a goal from Dermot Earley giving
them a 1–5 to 0–5 half-time lead.

Galway had lost their way in the second quarter. Ja Fallon, in
particular, seemed at odds with himself but he and the rest of
the side, caught fire in another explosive 10-minute burst after
the break that effectively decided the game. Reverting to the
basics of catch and kick, they ripped Kildare apart. Fallon landed a wunderpoint and, when the goal arrived, it was thrilling in
its simplicity and execution. Divilly drove a long ball down the

field to Donnellan who kicked a precision pass into Joyce. He sidestepped around Kildare goalkeeper Christy Byrne and finished to the empty net. Fallon and Finnegan added three more points as Galway scored 1–4 without reply to take a 1–9 to 1–5 lead. Galway mixed catch-and-kick and short-passing tactics and, with the injuries taking a toll, the Lilywhites began to spring leaks all over the field. Walsh and O'Domhnaill, who landed a killer point from distance, destroyed them at midfield in the second half and their forwards were well shackled by the canny Galway backs, especially the warrior Tomás Mannion in the corner. He produced an exhibition of the finer defensive arts and was a contender for Man of the Match with Donnellan and Fallon.

The honour, though, had to go to Donnellan for the tearaway exuberance and intelligence of his play that simply tore up the rulebook and bamboozled Kildare's defensive strategy. Galway may have been the underdogs, but Donnellan had to cope with the most personal and intense form of pre-match pressure. His father John (1964) and grandfather Mick (1925) had won All-Ireland senior medals and Michael's presence on the Galway team was treated as good portent by the more superstitious Galway supporters – and he played as though it was his destiny to lead his tribe to victory in Croke Park.

While Donnellan, Fallon and Joyce stole the headlines, another story was the presence of players such as O'Domhnaill, de Paor and Walsh from clubs west of the Corrib and the Gaeltacht areas that had been under-represented on Galway teams in previous decades. The honour of lifting the Sam Maguire went to Ray Silke who, earlier in the year, had also captained his club Corofin to their All-Ireland title. It was the first of several heady days in Croke Park for O'Mahony and Galway, but first they would have to absorb the shock of learning to lose all over again.

Galway All-Ireland Football Champions 1998

Martin McNamara

Tomás Meehan   Gary Fahey   Tomás Mannion

Ray Silke   John Divilly   Séan Óg de Paor

Kevin Walsh   Sean O'Domhnaill

Shay Walsh   Jarlath Fallon   Michael Donnellan

Derek Savage   Pádhraic Joyce   Niall Finnegan

Subs: Paul Clancy for Shay Walsh

1999

1999 WAS A STRANGE AND UNDISTINGUISHED YEAR for football. The prospect of a new direction for the game held out by Galway's success in 1998 never really materialised.

It had taken Galway 32 years to regain the All-Ireland title and just 70 minutes to wave it goodbye, as Mayo ground out the most satisfying of victories in Tuam Stadium. The down-at-heel venue would have been hard pressed to accommodate the 31,000 attendance on a fine day, never mind a July Sunday that saw the rain pour down hard and steady from midday. It wasn't as bad as the Ulster final in Clones in 1993 but conditions were still dangerous for spectators and weren't much better for the players who managed to provide an engrossing enough contest for the muted and sodden throng. Mayo didn't begrudge Galway their All-Ireland, even if had magnified their own shortcomings in 1996 and 1997. Former Mayo player Martin Carney articulated the mood when he said, 'We ran the race, we set the pace, they breasted the tape. It was like doing a marathon, being ahead for 26 miles and in the last 300 yards all of a sudden they went past us.' Mayo manager John Maughan held a couple of aces in reserve for the showdown in shape of Pat Fallon and Ciarán McDonald and their introduction with 20 minutes remaining swung the game in Mayo's favour.

Galway led by 1–10 by 1–8 before Fallon's arrival but he soon began to win some clean ball for Mayo around midfield and McDonald caused panic in the Galway defence when he followed

Fallon into the fray. He scored a point and had a part in three more as Mayo pushed on for a 1–14 to 1–10 victory that purged some of the bad memories from 1996 and 1997. It was a maudlin anti-climax for Galway. Several of their star performers from 1998, especially Donnellan, Fallon and Finnegan, didn't do themselves any justice. The alarm bells had sounded a few weeks earlier when they needed an injury-time point for a draw in their semi-final against Sligo. The decisive winning margin in the replay only papered over a weariness that became apparent when their fiercest rivals asked the hardest questions in the most demanding of conditions. The All-Ireland semi-final beckoned for Mayo although, by now, some of their supporters would have preferred a barefooted, night-time ascent of Croagh Patrick to the prospect of another losing 70 minutes in Croke Park.

The honeymoon ended too for Páidí Ó Sé and Kerry who lost their Munster crown the same day Galway exited the championship. Conditions in Páirc Uí Chaoimh were as dismal as those in Tuam, but Cork turned the clock back to the early 1990s when they out-fought and out-witted Páidí's troops, who could only muster two points after half-time. Aodán MacGearailt scored two goals to give Kerry a 2–2 to 0–5 lead at the break but, after that, it was all Cork with Michael Lynch from Carberry Rangers, Podsie O'Mahoney and Philip Clifford leading the charge as Larry Tompkins' team regained the Munster title on a 2–10 to 2–4 scoreline. After a bad start, Seán Óg Ó hAilpín recovered and held on to his place as he chased an All-Ireland football and hurling medal double.

There was change, too, in Leinster where Kildare had crashed out in the first round and Meath reasserted their dominance over Dublin in a poor Leinster final winning by a comfortable 1–14 to 0–12. Dublin manager Tommy Carr and his selectors persisted with Peadar Andrews at corner-back on Ollie Murphy who

Cork celebrate their 1999 Munster championship success.

had scored 1–5 before the rookie St Brigid's player was finally called ashore with 10 minutes left. Andrews showed commendable spirit to recover from the ransacking and establish himself as a lynchpin of the Dublin side in the new millennium. He was the scapegoat for a woeful Dublin display that saw them score just two points from play. Meath manager Seán Boylan drafted in several new players to bolster his 1996 All-Ireland winning team and the two Nigels – Nestor and Crawford – and Hank Traynor proved their worth as the Royals advanced to meet new Ulster champions Armagh in the semi-final.

Armagh were one of the dark horses of the championship and their semi-final clash with Meath witnessed the embryonic stages of the massed defence or 'swarm' tactics that they would employ to such controversial but successful effect in the years ahead. Meath won the game by 0–15 to 2–5 and were helped no end by six Armagh wides on the trot after half-time when accomplished marksmen, such as Oisín McConville, Diarmaid

Graham Geraghty and Seán Boylan raise the Sam Maguire in 1999.

Marsden and Tony McEntee, all came down with a bad case of the Croke Park 'yips'. The Ulster champions scored one point in the second half and, even though they went through some long barren patches themselves, Meath ground out the result thanks to the promptings of Trevor Giles, Graham Geraghty and Raymond Magee.

It didn't offer much in the way of entertainment value for the 60,000-plus crowd and the game was a microcosm of everything that was bad about the 1999 season. 'Champagne football it wasn't,' wrote Liam Horan in the *Irish Independent*. 'More like a cheap, deadly poitín… When negativity infects the minds of football men, the results can be horrific and dread inevitably came to pass in the form of a grinding, attritional affair that lends grist to those mills churning out the view that Gaelic football is an unpretty and unloved game.' Cork defeated Mayo by 2–12 to 0–12 in the other semi-final.

The Meath–Cork All-Ireland final was a reprise of the 1990 decider when Cork survived an all-out battle to complete the All-Ireland football and hurling double. Seán Óg Ó hAilpín already had a hurling medal in his pocket when he lined out at full-back for Cork, but his double dream died as Meath proved too crafty and economical in what was a good game of football compared to most of the fare on offer that summer. Cork looked potential winners in the first half but squandered too many chances especially in the 10 minutes after the break when they failed to make the most of two good breaks.

Cork's goalkeeper Kevin O'Dwyer saved a Trevor Giles penalty and then Cork were lifted further by a spectacular goal from Joe Kavanagh (who had opened the 1993 final against Derry with a similar individual effort) that gave Cork a 1–6 to 1–5 lead. The force was with Tompkins' team but they didn't increase their lead during a critical 10-minute period when Meath were there to be beaten. Instead, Boylan made all the right calls as he realigned his forwards. Trevor Giles moved out to the wing from full-forward and started to mop up Cork's short kick-outs. Richie Kealy was brought in at centre-forward to liven up the Meath attack and his introduction brought the best out of Graham Geraghty who kicked three second-half points. In defence, Mark O'Reilly saw off Mark O'Sullivan and Fionán Murray to claim the Man of the Match award.

It was Boylan's fourth title in 17 years and another victory for the defining Meath qualities of toughness, patience and unshakeable self-belief. They were a young team and most Meath supporters expected them to win at least another one or two All-Ireland titles. But Gaelic football was already starting to evolve in a whole new direction and Meath would prove to be one of the high-profile casualties of the revolution fermenting in the North.

Meath All-Ireland Football Champions 1999

Cormac Sullivan

Mark O'Reilly   Darren Fay   Cormac Murphy

Paddy Reynolds   Enda McManus   Hank Traynor

Nigel Crawford   John McDermott

Evan Kelly   Trevor Giles   Nigel Nestor

Ollie Murphy   Graham Geraghty   Donal Curtis

Subs: Richie Kealy for Nestor, Barry Gallaghan for Traynor, Tommy Dowd for Kelly

Brian Murphy of Kildare celebrates after scoring the winning goal against Meath in the 1998 Leinster football final.

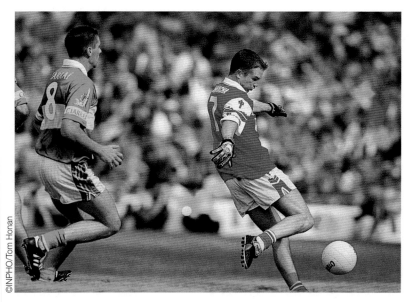

Andrew McCann scores the equalising goal for Armagh in the 2000 All-Ireland football semi-final.

©INPHO/Tom Honan

Clare goalkeeper David Fitzgerald strikes a last-minute equalising goal against Tipperary in the 1999 Munster semi-final.

©INPHO/Billy Stickland

Jimmy Barry Murphy, Cork manager for the All-Ireland winning 1999 season.

The Cork team before the 1999 Munster hurling final.

Kilkenny's Henry Shefflin celebrates a goal in the 2000 All-Ireland hurling final.

The Limerick defence fail to prevent Damien Fitzhenry scoring the winning goal for Wexford in the 2001 All-Ireland hurling quarter-final.

©INPHO/Lorraine O'Sullivan

©INPHO/Andrew Paton

▲ Armagh's Oisín McConville celebrates at the final whistle of the 2002 All-Ireland football final.

◄ Mickey Harte managed Tyrone to a first All-Ireland senior football title in 2003.

Space-age Croker.

The teams arrive for the Opening Ceremony of the 2003 Special Olympics.

Wexford's Michael Jacob celebrates scoring a last-minute, match-winning goal in the 2004 Leinster hurling championship.

Captain Dara Ó Cinnéide raises the Sam Maguire in 2004 after Kerry's 33rd All-Ireland title victory.

2000

THE KERRY–GALWAY ALL-IRELAND FOOTBALL FINAL that the purists and the not-so-pure longed for finally came to pass in millennium year. After the slump of 1999, it was a year of recovery for football as three of the main protagonists from 1998 returned to prominence and a vastly improved Armagh side laid the groundwork for their first All-Ireland title in 2002.

Galway were determined to quash doubts that 1998 had been a 'soft' All-Ireland title. They enjoyed a quixotic passage through Connacht. After beating New York, they travelled to Markievicz Park to face Sligo in a sell-out game. Sligo registered a rare win over world-weary Mayo in the first round and were genuinely confident that they could turn Galway over but, by half-time, the game had become a horror show for the home team when Galway led by a shocking 0–14 to 0–0.

Galway gave a sublime display of total football and, even allowing for the fragility of the opposition, it was arguably their finest performance of the O'Mahony era. They were rapacious and disciplined in defence and there was a hypnotic quality about their passing, movement off the ball and point scoring. Nineteen of the final tally of 22 points came from play with Joyce, Donnellan, Savage, Finnegan and Joe Bergin, the 19-year-old newcomer at midfield, finding the target at will. Sligo didn't score until the 40th minute and finished the match with four points.

Galway were more subdued in a comfortable Connacht final

victory over a spirited Leitrim side whose year's mission had been accomplished when they sucker-punched Roscommon in Hyde Park.

Winning a Connacht title without beating either Roscommon or Mayo wasn't the best preparation for an All-Ireland semi-final and Galway also had to prepare without the services of the 1998 Footballer of the Year, Jarlath Fallon. The Tuam Stars man suffered a cruciate ligament injury the week after the New York beano and was ruled out of action for the entire season. The wear and tear of more than a decade of football began to catch up on Kevin Walsh and injuries also limited him to sporadic contributions during the summer.

Galway were still too strong for Kildare in their semi-final clash at a wet and windy Croke Park on 27 August. It was a tighter and more physical game than the 1998 decider and there were just seven scores in the first half, Kildare leading 1-2 to 0-4 at half-time thanks to a Tadhg Fennin goal. Galway resumed normal service after the break with points from Paul Clancy, Donnellan and Joyce but were rattled again when Kildare scored 1-3 to lead by 2-5 to 0-8 after 45 minutes. Kevin Walsh, who had come as a substitute, calmed the game down for a Galway who systematically reeled Kildare in. As in 1998, they bombarded the Lilywhites' defence with long, probing balls and Donnellan and Joyce applied the finishing touches – Donnellan was back to his brilliant best and John Finn was sent off in the 63rd minute for persistent fouling on the Dunmore McHales man whose point from a 55-yard free sealed the Galway win, 0-15 to 2-6. It was a devastating setback for Kildare, who had come from six points behind at half-time to beat Dublin by five in the Leinster final two weeks earlier.

❖

THE REALLY SERIOUS DRAMA of the summer came in the other semi-final between Kerry and Armagh. Páidí Ó Sé had taken the expected flak after the 1999 Munster final collapse and ran into more criticism when he dropped Maurice Fitzgerald for the 2000 opener against Cork. Páidí claimed that Maurice hadn't recovered enough fitness from two bad ankle injuries for 70 minutes of championship football. The player's body language and impact when introduced as a sub in all of Kerry's championship games suggested otherwise, and the rift between the manager and his talisman would dog Páidí for the next two years. Two converted penalties from Dara Ó Cinnéide gave Kerry a 2–9 to 0–5 half-time platform against Cork, but they had to weather a fierce Rebel onslaught that reduced the deficit to two by the 62nd minute before winning by 2–15 to 1–13. Clare were put to the sword by 16 points in the Munster final.

Fitzgerald bailed out Kerry and Páidí with a point in the fourth minute of injury-time against Armagh in a gripping All-Ireland semi-final on 20 August. Armagh could have stolen the game when they scored a goal and a point in the closing minutes to lead Kerry for the first time but that would have been rough justice on a Kerry side who looked the likely winners throughout the game. Kerry led 1–3 to no score after six minutes, Dara Ó Cinnéide planting another penalty, but Kerry sat back on the lead and Armagh had levelled the match by 14th minute. That exchange set the pattern for the match: Kerry opening up commanding leads and then lapsing into complacency and allowing Armagh back into the game. The Ulster side had finessed their tactics considerably since 1999. They played Oisín McConville and Steven McDonnell as a two-man full-forward line and the direct ball into this duo worked well until they decided to revert to the laboured slow build-up which was meat and drink for Kerry full-back Seamus Moynihan. Armagh trailed by 1–7 to 1–5

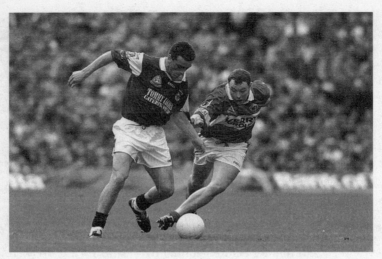

Pádhraic Joyce (Galway) and Seamus Moynihan (Kerry) tussle in the 2000 All-Ireland football final.

at half-time and, as in the Meath game in 1999, kicked some atrocious wides after the break. When Maurice Fitzgerald waltzed through for one of the goals of the year in the 57th minute, Armagh looked finished but dogged persistence was rewarded in the 69th minute when Andrew McCann stunned Kerry with the equalising goal. Two minutes later Kieran McGeeney gave Armagh a brief lead before Denis O'Dwyer won the free for the Fitzgerald equaliser. Final score: Kerry 2–11 Armagh 2–11.

Fitzgerald was a sub again for the replay six days later. This was another close encounter except that, this time, Armagh set the early pace. An Oisín McConville goal gave them a four-point half-time lead and they went six in front before fatally circling the wagons and regressing into a what-we-have-we-hold defensive mode. Kerry kicked four points, and a goal from Mike Frank Russell put them in front before McConville rescued Armagh with a late free. Kerry were the classier and more assured side in extra-time and a second goal from Mike Frank Russell sealed their 2–15 to 1–15 passage into the All-Ireland final.

The final on 24 September was too patchy and nervous to fully satisfy its pre-match billing as the dream decider between 'the two best footballing sides in the country'. Galway had three clear-cut chances to win it in the closing minutes when the sides were level, but Derek Savage dropped a shot short when Pádhraic Joyce was pleading for possession in the type of position from which he doesn't miss. Donnellan and de Paor also went close to clinching it for Galway but the 0–14 apiece draw was a satisfactory outcome in a game that veered from the ordinary to the masterful. Galway would have been grateful for the second chance when they languished 0–7 to 0–1 behind after 25 minutes. Much had been made beforehand of the confrontation between Moynihan and Joyce who were close friends and former teammates on a Tralee IT Sigerson Cup winning team but direct opponents in the final. Moynihan won that battle in the first half but, when Galway switched Joyce out to centre-forward and brought on Kevin Walsh for their teenage midfielder Bergin, the game forked off on another tangent. Walsh and O'Domhnaill started to get the better of Donal Daly and Darragh Ó Sé at midfield and the Galway forwards cranked into action with Donnellan drawing the frees for Joyce and Finnegan to point.

Kerry led by two points at half-time, 0–10 to 0–8, and two quick scores after the break from Ó Cinnéide and Darragh Ó Sé were probably the saving of the game for them. They only scored twice in the remaining half hour and not even the introduction of Fitzgerald in the 48th minute could stem the Galway fight back. Joyce levelled the game in the 66th minute and, while Galway probably should have pushed on from there, Kerry had the final opportunity but Denis O'Dwyer's shot to nothing drifted left and wide.

There was no disputing the better team in the replay. Galway had gambled on Kevin Walsh's fitness for the second game, but he was forced off with a fresh injury in the 17th minute and, while he returned to the action in the second half, Galway needed a full 70 minutes from the Killanin giant to better Kerry. Jarlath Fallon was sorely missed as well and Kerry exploited the fissures in Galway's gameplan by bringing on Maurice Fitzgerald before half-time. Overall, Kerry were a more disciplined side than in the drawn game. Moynihan was again colossal at full-back and, along with his corner men Mike Hassett and Michael McCarthy, only allowed Joyce, Savage and Finnegan one point from play between them.

Kerry led 0–8 to 1–3 at half-time and Galway supporters' only crumb of consolation afterwards was reliving Declan Meehan's third-minute goal, one of the best ever scored in Croke Park. The move began with Walsh winning possession under his own cross-bar and transferring the ball out the field where it eventually found Paul Clancy. While the ball was being worked out of defence, Meehan – a national championship class sprinter – tore up the field and Clancy landed a spectacular cross-field pass into the Caltra player's hands. Meehan kept moving and planted the ball past Declan O'Keeffe.

Kerry momentarily admired Galway's handiwork and then set about winning the All-Ireland. Galway grafted hard enough after half-time to land four unanswered points for a one point lead by the 48th minute but Kerry quickly regained control. Fitzgerald called the shots in the middle of the park in the final 20 minutes and, with Ó Cinnéide, Russell and Liam Hassett kicking the points, Kerry were well worth their four-point winning margin. Final score: Kerry 0–17 Galway 1–10.

It was an autumn of bliss and reprieve for Páidí and his Kerry players, but one of the county's worst days in Croke Park loomed as the GAA prepared itself for the year of the back-door.

Kerry players celebrate their 32nd All-Ireland title

Kerry All-Ireland Champions 2000

Declan O'Keeffe

Mike Hassett   Seamus Moynihan   Michael McCarthy

Tomás Ó Sé   Tom O'Sullivan   Eamonn Fitzmaurice

Darragh Ó Sé   Donal Daly

Aodán MacGearailt   Liam Hassett   Noel Kennelly

Mike Frank Russell Dara Ó Cinnéide   John Crowley

SUBS: Maurice Fitzgerald for Kennelly,
Tommy Griffin for O'Sullivan

1999

The Rebels Return

'There were times when I didn't think we would see this day. That maybe they wouldn't want me, that they'd have to bring in someone else and if that happened I'd have no problem with that either. I'd have just walked away from the job content that I'd given Cork the best years I could.'

Cork Manager, Jimmy Barry Murphy, July 1999

ONE OF THE ENDURING IMAGES from the 1999 hurling championship is that of Cork manager Jimmy Barry Murphy racing across the pitch at Semple Stadium to greet his players after they had defeated Waterford in the Munster hurling semi-final. Being Jimmy Barry, it wasn't a whooping and hollering sort of display. It was more graceful than that, but his uninhibited delight spoke volumes about the changes that had occurred in hurling since he sported and played with such distinction for Cork.

Jimmy Barry won five All-Ireland and 10 Munster medals as a player but, by 1999, he was in his fourth year as manager and the parameters of ambition had narrowed to reaching a Munster final. All the old Cork certainties had been blasted away by Loughnane's storm troopers with Limerick landing another knockout blow for good measure. Jimmy Barry's management and Cork's position among the elite of hurling had come down to 70 minutes against Waterford in Thurles on 13 June 1999. Win and they were at least guaranteed an All-Ireland quarter-final place; lose and it was goodbye Jimmy Barry and God knows what for Cork hurling.

Nine years without an All-Ireland title, Cork hadn't reached a Munster final since 1992. They hadn't won a championship game of any consequence since 1996 when Jimmy Barry endured a nightmare managerial debut in Páirc Uí Chaoimh. Limerick won that match by 3–8 to 1–8 in what was Cork's first champ-ionship defeat on home soil since 1923. 'Maybe it was a bit naïve going into that game thinking we could win it but it raised a huge level of self-doubt about myself and my ability to handle senior players at this level,' reflected Jimmy Barry two years later. 'Leaving the park that evening was just total devastation. That width of defeat was frightening.' The following year, Cork's honour was salvaged when they pushed Clare to the wire in Limerick but, in 1998, they were ransacked in the final 10 minutes by the Banner who won 0–21 to 0–13.

Cork hurling hadn't been this close to the precipice of self-doubt since the unspeakable years between 1954 and 1966 when they won a solitary Munster title (1956) and endured 12 years without an All-Ireland. Then, in 1966, the legendary trainer and character Jim 'Tough' Barry, who had trained his first Cork All-Ireland winning team back in 1926, stepped into the breach. An old IRA man who had been an accomplished boxer, swimmer and singer in his time, Barry welded a team of under-21s and committed journeymen and veterans together for one of the county's most celebrated All-Irelands. There were plenty of parallels between the situation in 1966 and the late 1990s. For Tipp in the 1960s substitute Clare in the 1990s. Justin McCarthy's description of the Tipperary team that annihilated Cork in the

1965 Munster decider was equally apt for Loughnane's Clare in their prime: 'If it wasn't one fella killing you it was another,' recalled McCarthy in his autobiography *Hooked*. 'They had options all over the field. And yet they were better than the sum of their parts. They could move the ball in any direction because they could all read each other's play. They were strong mentally, physically and collectively. They were like… Godzilla. We needed to play a different brand of hurling to beat them. Being told to go out there and play "Cork hurling" wasn't the way to go about it. We tried to play no-nonsense, direct, hip-to-hip hurling which was suicide against such a physical side. Getting "stuck in" against them was just what they wanted us to do, especially their "Hell's Kitchen" full-back line.'

Cork had avoided the 'Godzilla' Tipperary team in 1966 thanks to Eamonn Cregan who scored 3–5 against the 'Hell's Kitchen' full-back line when Limerick shocked the reigning All-Ireland champions in the first round of the Munster championship. But there was no avoiding the modern Godzilla of Clare in 1999 if Cork were to end the losing cycle in Munster. First up, though, were Waterford managed by Gerald McCarthy, one of the young players Jim Barry had drafted into the Cork team in 1966. Waterford were as ravenous for success as Cork and with their Clare-style approach to training and supposed physical edge were favourites to beat Cork. Jimmy Barry and his selectors had refused to go down the route of sand dunes and searching for hard men as a means of dealing with the new reality in hurling. Instead, they looked to a promising bunch of under-21s and named six championship debutantes and nine players under the age of 22 for the Waterford game.

One of the most controversial selection decisions was to start under-21 Mickey O'Connell, who hadn't even been in the panel in May, at midfield alongside Mark Landers. O'Connell's performance in scoring five points from play summed up Cork's day. They took the best Waterford had to throw at them in the first half and led by 0–10 to 0–7 at half-time. Paul Flynn's goal from a penalty in the 55th minute left it 0–18 to 1–14 and should have been the signal for Waterford to take control but, instead, it was Cork who took full advantage of some dubious refereeing decisions to regain the advantage with points from Landers and O'Connell. Final score: Cork 0–24 Waterford 1–15.

Like Jim Barry in 1966, Jimmy Barry's trust in youth to resurrect Cork fortunes was vindicated. Along with his selectors Tom Cashman and Tony O'Sullivan he had struck on an unusual but convincing team. O'Connell, Timmy McCarthy, Neil Ronan and Ben O'Connor had all delivered in their first championship game and the small men Joe Deane and Seanie McGrath continued to prosper. Alan Browne was a crafty and physical full-forward. At full-back, Diarmuid 'The Rock' O'Sullivan was a man who would have felt right at home in the environs of 'Hell's Kitchen'. New goalkeeper Donal Óg Cusack looked the natural successor to Ger Cunningham. Brian Corcoran, the 1992 Hurler of the Year, was the anchor at centre-back, and Seán Óg Ó hAilpín, Wayne Sherlock, John Browne and Fergal Ryan completed a compact and miserly Cork defence.

Cork's return as contenders further enlivened a hurling championship rich with possibilities. The Munster semi-final between Clare and Tipperary on 4 June was billed as the potential game of the year and it matched the hype. Tipperary had appointed Nicky English as manager and it looked as if the recently retired living legend had silenced Clare's wrath when his team led by 0–18 to 1–12 after 71 minutes, but the game was decided by two Davy Fitzgerald epiphanies. In the 67th minute, he produced a wonderful save to stop a goal-bound shot from Paul Shelley that would have wrapped up the game for Tipp.

Four minutes later, Clare won a penalty when substitute Conor Clancy was dragged to the ground by Feargal Heaney. Fitzgerald trotted up the field and drove a low shot inside his opposite number for the equalising goal: Tipperary 0–18 Clare 2–12.

Tipperary should have won what was a thunderous match played in front of a packed Páirc Uí Chaoimh. Their centre-back, David Kennedy, was commanding throughout and for once his opposite number Seanie McMahon was eclipsed. Tommy Dunne and Liam Cahill picked off the scores and Paul Shelley bothered both Lohans. Clare were in serious trouble until an otherwise subdued Jamesie O'Connor scored the 44th-minute goal. O'Connor, like his Doora-Barefield team-mates McMahon and Baker, looked drained from the exertion expended on the successful All-Ireland club campaign in the spring and it was the industry of Niall Gilligan and David Forde and substitute Clancy that kept Clare in a game that was level 10 times.

Six days later, Clare produced arguably the most complete hurling performance of the decade. They simply destroyed Tipperary. The weariness of the drawn game was replaced by a sustained purpose and venom. The Clare defence conceded just two points from play in the entire 70 minutes as Baker and Man of the Match Colin Lynch dictated proceedings from midfield. Anthony Daly's early long-range point was a taster of what was to come and for the rest of the game the points flowed freely for Alan Markham, Barry Murphy, Gilligan, Forde and Lynch. Markham's goal after seven minutes helped Clare to a commanding half-time lead and, while English reshuffled his pack as best he could, there was no respite in the second half. Only for Declan Ryan's goal from a 20-yard free and Dunne's 10 points from frees and play, it would have been one of the darkest days of all for Tipperary hurling. Final score: Clare 1–21 Tipperary 1–11.

It was the higher high of Loughnane's management career. 'We gave the most perfect performance the team ever gave,' he said in *Raising the Banner*. 'I always longed for the day that the team would give a display I'd be totally and utterly satisfied with. That was the display. It was so commanding; we overpowered them, outwitted them and were more skilful. Every aspect you could possibly judge a good performance on, that one had. Afterwards, there was a great feeling that this was the ultimate collective performance.' Loughnane never possessed the same need or force-of-nature quality on the sideline again. The titles had been won and Clare's worth already proven beyond the most unreasonable of doubts during four years of engagement against Tipperary, Cork and Kilkenny. The 1999 replay against Tipperary was Loughnane's *satori*, the 70 minutes when he finally attained hurling enlightenment. Having experienced perfection, in his heart of hearts he had no more battles to wage.

Who knows how far his players had reached within themselves physically, mentally and emotionally for the depth of that performance. It was astonishing achievement when set against all they had been through since 1995. They were bound to be vulnerable afterwards, and Cork took full advantage in the Munster final on Independence Day, 4 July, in Semple Stadium before close on 55,000 spectators. Jamesie O'Connor was ruled out because of a broken collar bone and his club-mate, Baker, hobbled off with an ankle injury in the 53rd minute. Baker's loss came at a time when Clare had recovered from a flat first half that left them 1–10 to 0–7 behind at the break. Joe Deane scored the goal in the 33rd minute after Seanie McGrath retrieved a ball Brian Lohan protested had gone wide. A couple of more Cork scores could have buried Clare but they recovered their champions' bearing and Baker powered the revival from midfield after half-time. He scored two points and won an amount of ball as

Clare outscored Cork by 0–6 to 0–1 to close the gap to one point, but Baker's forced withdrawal enabled Cork to get back into the game. Jimmy Barry also made a shrewd move by switching Alan Browne out to wing-forward to curb Liam Doyle's drives forward. Cork overcame their nerves and some bad shooting to pull away with the final three points after David Forde missed a free that would have levelled the game for Clare. Final score: Cork 1–15 Clare 0–14.

THE CHAMPIONSHIP was far more subdued in Leinster, where a familiar sequence of results was played out: a good hiding for Wexford from Offaly, and then a walloping in turn for Offaly from Kilkenny in the final. Kilkenny had nine points to spare in 1998. This time the margin was increased to 10 points and it was a turkey shoot for D.J. Carey, Charlie Carter, Brian McEvoy and the latest black and amber prodigy Henry Shefflin. As in 1998, though, Offaly's luck was in when they drew Ulster champions, Antrim, in the quarter-final. With the Ulster team struggling, Offaly had enough time to jump that hurdle and shape up in time for the All-Ireland semi-final against Cork on 8 August.

Offaly were the only county who opposed the introduction of the back-door system for the hurling championship in 1997 but they had quickly adjusted to rhythms of the new system. In the semi-final against Cork, they were unrecognisable to the listless crew that lay down in front of Kilkenny the previous month. It was a clash between experience and age, craft and speed that deserves a place on any shortlist of the decade's great games. Offaly started with 11 players who had tasted action in the 1994 All-Ireland final and some of their ground hurling and precision of their striking was a joy to watch on a wet and gloomy day in

Croke Park. They led 0–10 to 0–9 at half-time and could have been four or five ahead given the possession they enjoyed. There was a sense that if they had managed to break Cork's cover for even one goal that would have been it, but Donal Óg Cusack along with Diarmuid O'Sullivan, John Browne and Fergal Ryan in the Cork full-back line held firm. Two of Cork's trademark scoring bursts decided the game. They scored four points in six minutes after half-time, Seanie McGrath and Ben O'Connor making the most of Martin Hanamy's travails in the left corner. But with Brian Whelehan giving a master class on the wing, Johnny Dooley and Johnny Pilkington driving them forward from midfield and John Troy pilfering possession from Brian Corcoran, Offaly regained the lead and were a point ahead by the 66th minute when Joe Deane levelled the game with a point from a disputed free.

Youth won out in the final minutes. O'Sullivan, Corcoran and Ó hAilpín lifted Cork with their clearances and in the final seven minutes, their lightweight forwards finally found the legs on the Offaly rearguard with Deane, Seanie McGrath and Ben O'Connor striking three points. Offaly almost managed an equaliser when Johnny Pilkington burst through the cover to set up Paudie Mulhare with a half chance but his shot bobbled off the post and wide. Cork held on for a 0–19 to 0–16 victory.

Diarmuid O'Sullivan celebrates the All-Ireland hurling semi-final victory.

It was a sweet triumph for Jimmy Barry and his players who, as in the Waterford and Clare games, survived the physical exchanges against a stronger side and found enough in reserve to finish with a deadly flourish. Offaly were devastated and felt, with some conviction, that three of Cork's points had come from dubious decisions by referee Dickie Murphy. They also queried the four minutes of injury-time he played at the end of first half, a period when Cork scored two points. Brian Whelehan said the result could have signalled the break-up of the team. 'I thought maybe it might be a break-up after an All-Ireland final. I just hope it's not going to be 100 years before you see Offaly in the All-Ireland series again. We're all on the go a long time. You know you can't just keep going year after year.'

Offaly's complaints about Dickie Murphy's time-keeping was another example of a team left powerless in the face of a GAA referee's eccentric interpretation of what did and didn't constitute lost time. The 1998 semi-final farce should have been the final proof of the necessity for some independent system of time-keeping but, for reasons best known to themselves, the GAA preferred to leave this most fundamental of considerations 'at the discretion' of the referee. Referee Padhraic Horan's decision to blow the whistle after a mere 10 seconds of injury-time in the All-Ireland quarter-final between Galway and Clare on 25 July may have cost Galway a place in the All-Ireland semi-final. Horan should have played at least three minutes 'lost time' and supporters drew their own conclusions when he blew the whistle after Galway had won a free within scoring distance. It was an unsatisfactory conclusion to a marvellous game that's one of the lost classics from the era.

Games between Clare and Galway can be fiery and unpredictable affairs. It's one of the lesser rivalries in hurling but has a colourful history. Seven decades before the foundation of the

GAA, 10,000 people are said to have gathered at Lord Clonbrock's estate in Ahascragh near Ballinsloe in 1812 to watch the counties play a challenge under organised rules. Galway won that encounter and a contemporary report concluded with the immortal line that the day passed off splendidly with 'not a skull cracked or a heart broken'. Plenty of Galway hearts were broken after the 1932 All-Ireland semi-final in Limerick, the most famous clash between the teams. In a game of wildly fluctuating fortunes, Galway led by 4–9 to 2–0 after half-time but lost by 9–4 to 4–14, with Clare's Tull Considine scoring seven goals.

Galway never lost their propensity for blowing big leads. In 1999, they were nine points ahead after 20 minutes and squandered plenty more scoring opportunities as they threatened to swamp Clare in the first half of the quarter-final. Mattie Murphy was back for his second term as Galway manager and they were a different team to the one that had surrendered so meekly to Waterford at the same stage in 1998. Joe Cooney rolled back the years with a masterful display at midfield and Ollie Fahey, Kevin

Niall Gilligan (15) scores Clare's fist goal in the 1999 All-Ireland hurling quarter-final.

Broderick and Eugene Cloonan were Galway's chief scorers but Clare put together a vital sequence of three points before half-time and were back in the match at 1–9 to 0–8. Jamesie O'Connor was still sidelined through injury but that was evened up when Galway's full-back Brian Feeney was forced off with an injury after seven minutes. Feeney's Athenry team-mate Eugene Cloonan departed the action at half-time with a head injury. Ollie Fahey scored a second goal in the 50th minute to push Galway nine clear again but in such an open and furious game that wasn't an insurmountable gap for Clare. The introduction of Jamesie O'Connor, in spite of his heavily bandaged arm, lifted the team and goals from Gilligan and Markham along with points from McMahon drew Clare level before Baker gave them the lead for the first time with seven minutes left. Galway fought back and were a point ahead when Ollie Canning had the chance to finish Clare off but his shot rebounded off the cross-bar. Two McMahon points from a free and a 65 levelled the game before Padhraic Horan prematurely called time. McMahon's five points from frees and 65s had saved Clare and, eight days later, Galway, like Waterford and Tipperary before them, learned that this Clare team exacted full retribution in replays. Eugene Cloonan scored 2–10 from placed balls and play but still ended up on the losing team as Galway slumped to a 3–18 to 2–14 defeat on the August Bank Holiday Monday. Gilligan scored 2–3 for Clare and with O'Connor back in the starting line-up and Daly, McMahon and Doyle wiping out the Galway half-forward line, they advanced to the semi-final against Kilkenny.

Brian Cody had taken over as Kilkenny manager from Nicky Brennan and had spent the summer assembling and reassembling the ingredients of a potentially lethal side. Back into the team came John Power, centre-back Pat O'Neill and corner-back Philly Larkin. Canice Brennan was relocated to full-back and Denis Byrne, the team captain, to midfield. Peter Barry, who had been tried at midfield and wing-forward, was switched to wing-back. Barry was a contender for Man of the Match in the semi-final on a day his defensive colleagues O'Neill and Willie O'Connor weren't far behind him as Kilkenny carved out a convincing 2–14 to 1–13 passage to the final. The Kilkenny forwards matched their backs for effort and application and prevented the Clare half-back line from dictating the pattern of play in a hard and absorbing contest. Brian McEvoy scored four points off Daly and John Power was as combustible and driven as ever at centre-forward.

A goal from D.J. Carey in the 55th minute finished off a Clare team and Kilkenny hastened the end of the Loughnane era. 'When Kilkenny beat us in the All-Ireland semi-final in 1999, I said to myself in the dressing room, "We'll not climb this mountain again. We're not going to be here again." I had no desire to be there again. That was even worse,' he recalled in *Raising the Banner*. Loughnane had planned to retire in 1999 and, while he was persuaded to stay on for one more year, the fire inside had diminished. He remained on to smooth the way for his successor Cyril Lyons but later admitted, 'I just didn't have the same bite in me as before... In 2000, I had been involved for such a long time that the thing had gone a bit dreary – a bit dead. When we were beaten by Tipperary in the championship, instead of being disappointed, I was just relieved. The day you feel relieved to be beaten is the day to give up. It was time to take a break from it.'

Jimmy Barry remained on as Cork manager for another season after leading the team back to the promised land in the 1999 All-Ireland final. 'I'd have to say it's the greatest day of my sporting life to see Cork back on top again,' the Cork manager said afterwards. 'I feel vindicated in the policy we decided upon after that hammering by Limerick in 1996. This day is the culmination of a lot of hard work, the fruit of what we decided back then on one of the worst days of our life.'

For neutrals, that final was a dull and disappointing conclusion to an intriguing and exciting summer but, after seven years away from the summit, bliss it was to be a Rebel on that wet and overcast September Sunday. Cork's capacity to finish strongly was again their saving ace. An Andy Comerford point put Kilkenny 0–11 to 0–8 in front with 11 minutes left and Kilkenny's superior heft and experience as All-Ireland finalists in 1998 should have seen them close the game out in the rain and heavy conditions. Cork's switch of Man of the Match Timmy McCarthy to midfield for the final 20 minutes was vital and a reminder of Cork's traditional cuteness on the line. McCarthy broke Comerford and Denis Byrne's grip at midfield and Seanie McGrath responded by firing over the winning points in the final five minutes and Cork secured a 0–13 to 0–12 title victory.

McGrath's scores were jewels on a day both sides shot 17 wides. Cork's other heroes were at the back where Corcoran was

Cork's All-Ireland match winner Seanie McGrath.

back to his form of 1992. He subdued John Power and without Power's rampaging runs and passes, the rest of the Kilkenny forward suffered, none more than D.J. Carey. He had a poor final and was tried on four different markers to no avail. Charlie Carter and Brian McEvoy also drew a blank.

For Cork, the natural order had been restored and they

defended their title in style when beating Tipperary in a Millennium Munster final that won the approval of the purists. They appeared on course for another All-Ireland final until systematically ambushed by Offaly's last stand in the 2000 semifinal. Cork lost their way badly in the two years after that defeat and it would take one of the biggest upheavals in the GAA's history to steer them back to winning ways.

Cork All-Ireland Hurling Champions 1999

Donal Óg Cusack

Fergal Ryan   Diarmuid O'Sullivan   John Browne

Wayne Sherlock   Brian Corcoran   Seán Óg Ó hAilpín

Mark Landers   Mickey O'Connell

Timmy McCarthy Fergal McCormack   Seanie McGrath

Ben O'Connor   Niall Ronan   Joe Deane

Subs: Alan Browne, Kevin Murray

2000

Millennium Cats

'Throw it in to D.J. and he'll hang it.'

Kilkenny hurler John Power

'You should never have a fear about your own ability. If you have done it in the past, you've no reason to lack any confidence. I have been there, done that. Played well, played bad. I don't worry about the possibility of playing poorly because I always think I am going to play well.'

D.J. Carey, August 2002

A 20-FOOT HIGH SCULPTURE of D.J. Carey was the centre-piece of the hurling-themed closing parade at the Kilkenny Arts Week in August 1999. It was carried through the mediaeval streets like a pagan deity in tribute to D.J.'s status as the people's hurler. His was the most recognisable face and name in the game in the 1990s but a minority of the *cognoscenti* doubted D.J.'s worthiness of a place in the pantheon of true hurling giants. Their contention was that D.J.'s All-Ireland medals, All Stars, and so on, didn't automatically assure him a plinth alongside the immortals until he produced a *galactico* performance in an All-Ireland final. They quibbled that, in his five All-Ireland finals to the end of 1999, he had only scored one goal and didn't score from play in either the 1998 or 1999 finals. It was an absolutist argument. One that conveniently ignored the dozens of match-winning performances he had conjured up for St Kieran's, Young Irelands and Kilkenny down the years – and the obvious point that opposition teams expended so much defensive energy curbing his influence, his very presence on the field was a match winner for Kilkenny. And it wasn't as if he was anonymous when he won his All-Ireland medals in 1992 and 1993. He scored 1–4 against Cork in 1992 and landed two critical frees from distance in the last 10 minutes of the 1993 decider with Galway, a final Kilkenny wouldn't have reached if it hadn't been for his late spurt of scores to see off Offaly in the Leinster semi-final.

For more than a decade, he routinely tormented Offaly, Wexford, Laois and Dublin in Leinster and you won't find too many hurling people in Galway questioning D.J.'s greatness. Kilkenny faced meltdown in the 1997 All-Ireland quarter-final against the westerners in Thurles when they trailed by nine points at half-time. It had taken Kilkenny a few years to recover from a Galway hiding at the same venue in 1986 and the situation this time round looked possibly worse until John Power's raw pride and D.J.'s artistry rescued the game. D.J. scored 1–4 in 13 minutes after half-time and finished with 2–7 as Kilkenny won an overlooked thriller by 4–15 to 3–16.

The doubts about D.J. may have had as much to do with his demeanour on and off the field as his perceived failures in All-Ireland finals. He didn't possess Mick Mackey's devil-may-care charisma, Christy Ring's aura, Nicky Rackard's braveheart glamour or the warrior quality of latter-day defensive icons such as Brian Whelehan, Ciarán Carey, Brian Lohan and Seanie McMahon. His game was about rarefied pace and reflexes, uncanny opportunism and an almost incidental courage. Off-the-field, he wasn't a bar-room legend or party animal. He didn't drink or smoke and came across as a private individual who kept his emotions and thoughts under wraps. When he wasn't working long hours building up his cleaning products business (D.J. Carey Enterprises) or at home with the wife and kids, he was hurling or playing handball. The closest thing he had to a vice was his fondness for a round of golf – hardly material for scandal. But the reward for his clean living ways and industriousness was a torrent of bad-minded gossip that caused him to announce his retirement from the game at the age of 27 in February 1998.

The doubters he could handle but the rumours about his professional and personal life were too much. He was still young and sensitive enough to be undermined and threatened by the gossip. There were stories about his company being on the verge of bankruptcy, D.J.'s golf obsession, greedy demands for appearance fees, extra-marital affairs and his interference in team selections. His retirement was bombshell news but such was the groundswell of support, locally and nationally, that six weeks later he was back in the Kilkenny fold. The rumours died down but the doubts about his place in the grand scheme of hurling lingered on. He had a poor game in the 1998 All-Ireland final when Kilkenny lost to Offaly and had another bad one when they were beaten by Cork in the 1999 final. His lack of impact in those two finals probably cost him his place on the GAA's Hurling Team of the Millennium, and, when Kilkenny reached a third successive final in 2000, D.J. was under the microscope like never before.

At the beginning of 2000, hurling never had it so good. The day after the 1999 All-Ireland hurling final, the GAA and Guinness announced a £4 million extension of their sponsorship deal for the hurling championship – £2 million was a direct cash transfer to the GAA, while Guinness committed itself to spending an additional £2 million on marketing the game and other promotional activities. As a spectator sport, hurling had blossomed at a pace way beyond the wildest dreams of either the drinks company or the GAA since the first sponsorship deal was brokered in 1995. A good example was the rivalry between Clare and Tipperary. When the counties met in the first round of the Munster championship in 1994, the attendance was 18,215; by 1999, the corresponding fixture was a 50,000 plus sellout, and attracted a television audience in excess of 400,000 viewers.

Five years after Kilkenny's Nicky Brennan warned the GAA's Annual Congress that hurling was 'dying on its feet', there was even optimism that the Guinness-financed investment in coaching would eventually lift underachievers – such as Laois, Dublin, Westmeath and Roscommon – into the ranks of genuine contenders. 'We are talking about gradual progress and an improvement in relative terms,' said GAA President Joe McDonagh in an interview before the 1999 hurling final. 'This year's biggest result was Westmeath minors running Kilkenny to two points in the Leinster minor hurling final. They have been one of the counties who have really embraced our coaching schemes. I don't think it's unreasonable to think that some of the weaker counties can be competitive in 20 years time.' McDonagh's long-term prognosis may yet prove correct but, by 2000, the championship was already slipping back into a familiar groove as the big beasts of the hurling jungle reasserted their supremacy.

Kilkenny enjoyed an untroubled march to the coveted millennium year All-Ireland. Overall, it was a flat sort of championship compared to 1999 and the helter-skelter drama of 1997 and 1998. The standard remained high in Munster, where Tipperary edged out Clare in the first round by 1–15 to 0–14 in Ger Loughnane's last match in charge of the Banner. After beating

Cork forward ace, Joe Deane.

Waterford in the semi-final, Tipp advanced to meet Cork in the Munster final. Played in ideal conditions before a sellout crowd of 55,000, it was a game worthy of the occasion with Cork again pulling ahead in the final minutes to win 0–23 to 3–12.

Joe Deane with 10 points including three from play, Seanie McGrath, Ben O'Connor and Alan Browne at wing-forward were Cork's main scorers but Tipp's barnstorming approach to scoring goals meant that a draw was a possibility right to the end. Cork started the better but a Eugene O'Neill goal drew the sides level, 1–5 to 0–8, at half-time. Cork brought Pat Ryan on for Mickey O'Connell at midfield in the 40th minute and Ryan broke Tipp's dominance at midfield and his team led 0–16 to 1–10 before Tommy Dunne rifled Tipp's second goal in the 54th minute. The challengers were awarded a penalty in the 56th minute but John Leahy's shot was saved and Cork upped their efforts another notch and were five points clear with three minutes. Tommy Dunne scored a second goal and Paul Kelly added a point as Tipp closed the gap to a point in injury-time but Seanie McGrath had the last word to secure the Munster title for Cork. Both teams would have fancied their chances of progressing to a potential showdown with Kilkenny in September but, by mid-August, they had fallen to the outsiders from Offaly and Galway.

Tipperary were the first of the Munster duo to exit when they were beaten 1–14 to 0–15 by Galway in the All-Ireland quarter-final on 24 July. It was Galway's first championship win since the semi-final victory against the same opposition in 1993 and a deeply satisfying result for manager Mattie Murphy and his players. It was a no-quarters-asked-or-given-type of affair, with Galway upping their physical commitment at the sight of the blue and gold. The Athenry players Eugene Cloonan, Joe Rabbitte, and Brian Feeney, who had won an All-Ireland club title in March, along with Rory Gantley, Cathal Moore and Liam Hodgkins did most to send Tipp packing. Cloonan blasted a goal from a 25-yard free in the 14th minute and with Rabbitte winning the aerial battle, Galway opened an early six-point lead. Tipp closed the lead to two by half-time but the loss of wing-back Eamonn Corcoran after 24 minutes and John Leahy early in the second half combined with the continued absence of Declan Ryan was too much for them to overcome. They laid siege to Galway's goal in the final minutes but referee Dickie Murphy called time after a shot to nothing from 30 yards by goalkeeper Brendan Cummins was stopped on the line.

In the other quarter-final, Offaly took on Derry who earlier in the summer had won their first Ulster title in 92 years. It was no walkover for Offaly, who had to survive some serious scares before winning by 2–24 to 2–17. The quarter-final game against the Ulster champions had become an annual rehabilitation exercise for Offaly. Earlier in the summer they crushed Wexford 3–15 to 1–8 in the Leinster semi-final but, having done enough to secure the All-Ireland quarter-final place, offered only passive resistance to Kilkenny in the Leinster final. The suspicion that Offaly weren't all that bothered about the Leinster title was borne out a month later when the team of the 1990s summoned up one last show of defiance to dethrone the reigning All-Ireland champions Cork in the All-Ireland semi-final.

Cork's 3/10 price in the bookies tells its own story and, in the opening 20 minutes, it did look bleak for Offaly as Deane and McGrath weaved their familiar darting patterns. Deane gave Offaly full-back Kevin Kinahan a roasting and scored eight points, four from frees, as Cork took a 0–12 to 0–10 half-time lead, but Offaly turned the form-book on its head in the second 35 minutes. Kinahan opted to play Deane from the front and he probably couldn't believe his luck when Cork started to rain high ball down on the Offaly square. Simon Whelehan was flawless in the corner and further out field Kevin Martin, Johnny Pilkington, with four points from play, Johnny Dooley, seven points, Michael Duignan and 37-year-old Joe Dooley, who scored two points, won their personal battles hands down. Cork's problems were magnified when centre-forward Gary Hanniffy began to run Brian Corcoran ragged. It was one of the few occasions in his illustrious career that Corcoran was comprehensively outplayed as Hanniffy charged repeatedly through the centre of the Cork defence to score three points and create several more. Cork still led by three points after 40 minutes but they then went 18 minutes without a score and had substituted two of their half-forwards – Feargal McCormack and Tommy McCarthy – by the final quarter. As Offaly reeled them in with an economical and hard-hitting but measured approach, Cork panicked and shot some bad wides – 16 in total over the 70 minutes, compared to Offaly's five. By the final whistle, it was the ageing 'Biffos' who looked the more energetic and sprightly team. Final score: Offaly 0–19 Cork 0–15.

A week later, Kilkenny made it an all-Leinster All-Ireland final when they dismantled Galway in the second half of their semi-final clash. Galway started well and scored some spectacular points and conceded nothing in the physical stakes to lead 0–12 to 1–8 at half-time. Andy Comerford scored the first Kilkenny goal but it was the second from D.J. Carey in the 39th minute that hastened Galway's exit. Full-back Brian Feeney, who had curtailed the maestro well until then, was caught a few yards the wrong side of Carey as a high ball floated in and Carey blasted it past Michael Crimmins. Galway never recovered from that setback and Carey, Shefflin and Denis Byrne, who struck eight points including five from play, finished off the job for Kilkenny on a 2–19 to 0–17 scoreline.

Brian Cody's side were equally clinical and convincing in an All-Ireland final which was terribly deflating for Offaly and neutrals alike. Kilkenny had no shortage of motivation to sharpen their appetite. The most pressing being a determination to avoid becoming the first team in hurling history to lose three successive finals. They wanted revenge for the 1998 defeat to Offaly and also wanted to prove the Leinster final hammerings they routinely inflicted on Offaly were a true reflection of the balance of power in the province in spite of the midlanders' adventures through the backdoor. D.J. Carey had his own agenda and he silenced all but the most extreme of his doubters with a Man of the Match performance in Kilkenny's 5–15 to 1–14 victory. He scored his first goal after six minutes and claimed a second three minutes later when he appeared to get the final touch to a Shefflin shot. Offaly were in serious trouble but restored a semblance of stability when they cut Kilkenny's lead to five points in the 29th minute but Kilkenny simply upped the intensity again and led 3–8 to 0–7 at half-time.

It was a harrowing day for Offaly. Their backs were overwhelmed by Carey (2–4), Carter (1–3) and Shefflin (1–3) and even the switch of Brian Whelehan to the forwards made little difference against a Kilkenny defence well marshalled by centre-back Eamonn Kennedy. Kilkenny were four goals clear by the 55th minute and supporters had begun to leave Croke Park when

D.J. Carey wins his third All-Ireland medal.

Johnny Pilkington's score raised a green flag for the losers in the 59th minute. Offaly battled on and preserved some dignity on a final day of reckoning for some of their older players. Kilkenny supporters' thoughts turned to back-to-back titles or, depending on the volume of Smithicks consumed, even a three-in-a-row after a championship in which no team had gone any closer than eight points to D.J. & Co. But, like Cork before them, Kilkenny discovered that semi-finals can be treacherous places for favourites and any nascent hubris on the part of some players and their supporters was banished by the events of 20 August 2001.

Kilkenny All-Ireland Champions 2000

James McGarry

Michael Kavanagh   Noel Hickey   Willie O'Connor

Philly Larkin   Eamonn Kennedy   Peter Barry

Andy Comerford   Brian McEvoy

Denis Byrne   John Power   John Hoyne

Charlie Carter   D.J. Carey   Henry Shefflin

Subs: Canice Brennan for McEvoy,
Eddie Brennan for Brennan

2001

THE 1990S WERE A PAINFUL AND CONFUSING decade for Galway hurlers. They won a solitary championship game between 1993 and 2000 and their repeated failures in Croke Park had as much to do with poor administration and an exasperating absence of patience in the boardroom as it did with deficiencies on the pitch. Expectations were unrealistic since the back-to-back All-Irelands of 1987 and 1988 and club delegates didn't allow managers the time to develop a team over a period of three or four years. Dozens of players were tried and discarded and Galway's board-room shuffles became a near annual end-of-season blood sport for the media. When Noel Lane took over in the autumn of 2000 he was Galway's fifth manager in eight years (Jarlath Cloonan 1993–94; Mattie Murphy 1995–96; Cyril Farrell 1997–98; Mattie Murphy again 1999–2000). Galway supporters looked at the wave of quality underage teams produced in the lost decade and what was then the strongest club championship in the country and wondered where it all had gone wrong.

Along with Birr and the Clare sides, Doora-Barefield and Sixmiledbridge, Galway sides dominated the All-Ireland club championship for a decade. Kilkenny, Cork and Tipperary clubs didn't win a single club title between 1992 and 2003, another indication of the shifting sands in hurling in this era. The Galway clubs' golden years began with a Kiltormer victory after a second replay against Cashel King Cormac's in 1992 and continued with

Sarsfields in 1993–94. Joe Cooney, one of the great modern hurlers, led Sarsfields to back-to-back titles and was seen to his best effect at this level in the years when Galway were invariably knocked out of the All-Ireland championship after one game. Athenry won their first All-Ireland title in 1997, and were unlucky not to win another in 1999 when they were beaten a point by Doora-Barefield in controversial circumstances involving a disallowed point. They recaptured the All-Ireland in 2000 when they defeated the same opposition. In 2001, they matched Sarsfield's achievement by retaining the title with a thrilling 3–24 to 2–19 victory after extra-time in the final against Graigue-Ballycallan. The Kilkenny team led by a goal with seconds left before Eugene Cloonan scrambled an equaliser and Athenry pulled away in extra-time of a final switched from St Patrick's Day to Easter Monday because of the national foot-and-mouth disease scare. Cloonan was seen by many as the potential inheritor of Joe Cooney's legacy as the consummate Galway hurler and he strengthened his case

Galway prodigy, Eugene Cloonan.

when Galway played Kilkenny in the All-Ireland semi-final on 20 August.

The only change in Leinster that year was that Wexford, rather than Offaly, were the recipients of the annual hiding as Kilkenny secured a fourth provincial title in a row on a 2–19 to 0–12 score-line. Brian Cody tried to weed out complacency but there was a consensus in Kilkenny and beyond that all they had to do was show up against Galway to reach another All-Ireland final. A small number of shrewd punters looked at Galway's 4/1 price and decided it was time to gamble on the sort of semi-final ambush the Tribesmen specialised in since regaining a position among hurling's elite in the 1970s. They had ended Cork's bid for a four-in-a-row in the 1979 semi-final; humiliated Kilkenny in the 1986 semi-final in Thurles; and shocked Tipperary at the penultimate point in 1993. By the summer of 2001, Galway were ready for another sting.

Noel Lane's recruitment of Clare's physical trainer Mike McNamara was the factor that had swung the Galway manage-ment position Lane's way and McNamara set about toughening up the supposedly fragile Galway psyche. 'I suppose the perception outside Galway was that they needed a bit of maybe strengthen-ing up,' he reflected in an interview before the Kilkenny game. 'That they had beautiful hurlers but watching for years and playing against them on a couple of occasions on big days, as I did with Clare, we always had the feeling that if you stay at them, and at them, they'll buckle towards the end of a match.'

McNamara's role with Clare was sometimes overlooked because of the sheer force and colour of Ger Loughnane's per-sonality, but he again proved his worth with Galway where Lane had drafted in some fresh talent for the Clare man to work on. McNamara had carefully conceived ideas about the type of player he wanted: 'I suppose my ideal player is a strong, forceful player with an incredible, burning desire to succeed. A virtue epitomised I suppose by Brian Lohan maybe more than any other player in Ireland. He refused to buckle under any pressure or strain and can match physical strength with skill and can change his game to suit a particular man or type of player.' In the same interview, McNamara offered an interesting slant on the D.J. Carey debate: 'It [hurling] is a Celtic sport which means there's a ferocity in it and as a nation we tend to admire fellas who have little bit of the devil in them, that little bit of ferocity. And while, without doubt, D.J. Carey is the outstanding sportsman in hurling terms of this generation we often look to somebody else. Maybe Willie O'Connor we might admire more. We have that tendency to admire that type of player who lifts a team.'

Galway's new-found ferocity was in evidence before referee Pat O'Connor had even thrown the ball in for the start of the semi-final with Kilkenny. Nineteen-year-old Richie Murray squared up to Brian McEvoy and David Tierney stood his ground in the midfield rutting while John Power emerged with a broken hurl from his jostling with Liam Hodgins. These exchanges set the tone for a game in which Kilkenny were burned off the field by the unanticipated fervour and steel of Lane's and McNamara's side. The new Galway players like Murray, Mark Kerins and Derek Hardiman sparkled, particularly Kerins who got the best of Eamonn Kennedy. Murray and Tierney were so fired up, their direct opponents Andy Comerford and Brian McEvoy were both substituted in the second half. Ollie Canning fine-tuned his reinvention as the most stylish corner-back in the game by limiting Charlie Carter the unstoppable scoring machine to a single point while Joe Rabbitte and Kevin Broderick stretched the Kilkenny defence.

Most of all, the day belonged to Eugene Cloonan. He scored a flukey goal after four minutes from a 60-yard free to set Galway

John Power (Kilkenny) and Kevin Broderick (Galway) clash in the 2001 All-Ireland hurling semi-final.

on their way and he put six between the teams when he kicked the ball to the net in the 53rd minute. His 2–9 tally included six frees, two 65s and a marvellous point from play before half-time to leave Galway 1–6 to 0–6 ahead. They had corner-back Greg Kennedy sent off in the 28th minute but were going so well that his departure caused minimal disruption. Lane and McNamara replaced corner-forward Feargal Healy with Athenry's wing-back terrier Brian Higgins and he enhanced Galway's grip around the middle third with a series of uplifting clearances.

Galway led by seven points with 10 minutes left and, in the 68th minute, Kevin Broderick landed one of the great points when he soloed from deep in his own half and, having used up the permitted two catches, flicked the ball over Eamonn Kennedy's head, caught it on the hurl and scored on the run. It was another blow to Kilkenny's pride on their worst day in Croke Park since the 1995 Leinster final against Offaly. D.J.

Carey scored a goal from a 21-yard free in the 70th minute but failed to score from play. Shefflin scored nine frees but, like Carey, was held scoreless in the loose, and three points from play was a sorry total for what was supposed to be the most lethal strike force in the game. Overall, Kilkenny appeared ill-prepared to cope with McNamara's tornado and, while Cody was philosophical after the match, the defeat caused him to re-evaluate his management style to ensure that no team of his would ever be caught lounging in the comfort zone again.

It was a gratifying coup for Lane, McNamara and the Galway squad. They had faced down the All-Ireland champions and responded superbly to McNamara's pre-match exhortation to 'reach for the damn thing'. They went close in the All-Ireland final on 9 September but, ultimately, came up short against a Tipperary team that had been building patiently towards a title since Nicky English had taken over as manager in 1999.

English's team had survived a far more testing route to the final than Galway. They edged out Clare by a point, 0–15 to 0–14, in the Munster semi-final and two late points from Brian O'Meara and substitute John O'Brien broke Limerick hearts in the decider. Two first-half goals from Declan Ryan and Lar Corbett left the sides level, 2–8 to 1–11, at half-time. Tipp pulled three clear by the 46th minute but scored just one point for the next 20 minutes as Limerick, driven forward by Man of the Match Mark Foley at wing-back, scored four points to level the game again. They had winning chances in this period but Tipp held their nerve and the two late points from O'Meara and O'Brien secured the Premier county's first Munster title in eight years. Final score: Tipperary 2–16 Limerick 1–17.

Four weeks later, Limerick lost the quarter-final by a point in another thrilling game remembered most for the exploits of Wexford goalkeeper Damien Fizthenry. There was an old-fashioned flux about the game with the scores flowing freely from the second minute when Rory McCarthy scored Wexford's first goal. Fitzhenry gifted a goal to Limerick's Barry Foley in the 29th minute when he was hooked on an attempted clearance. He compensated two minutes later when he scored a penalty and a Paul Codd goal from a 21-yard free gave Wexford a 3–6 to 2–5 interval lead. Limerick outscored Wexford by 0–10 to 0–4 in the second half and appeared set for an All-Ireland semi-final rematch with Tipperary until Fitzhenry scored his second goal in the 71st minute after Clem Smith had dragged McCarthy to the ground for another 21-yard free. Final score: Wexford 4–10 Limerick 2–15.

Wexford had rebuilt their side since 1996 but it was one of the veterans, Larry O'Gorman, who saved the day in the All-Ireland semi-final against Tipperary who blitzed the Leinster side in the first half to open up an eight-point lead. O'Gorman, playing at midfield, barrelled his way through for two goals after half-time and Rory McCarthy scored a third to level the game. Paul Codd was wide from a late free that would have given Wexford a sensational passage to the All-Ireland final but the draw was perceived as a moral victory after the devastation of their Leinster final defeat to Kilkenny.

The second game was a testy affair played in miserable conditions the following Saturday. Tipp won by 3–12 to 0–10 in a match that made the headlines for the controversial sending off of Tipperary's Brian O'Meara and Wexford wing-back Liam Dunne early in the first half. Pat O'Connor produced the red cards after O'Meara and Dunne were spotted by linesman Par Ahearne butting each other in the ribs with the sharp end of their hurls. There were protests that referee Pat Horan had over-reacted. The 'it's a man's game' philosophers claimed that Dunne and O'Meara were merely engaged in 'handbag' stuff that is an unwritten part of the game. Dunne was left to brood on a second successive championship dismissal but the consequences were far more serious for O'Meara who received an automatic one-month suspension for his straight red. He appealed the sentence and was supported by a 'Men Not Wimps' campaign in *The Star* but no pardon was forthcoming from Croke Park and he missed the All-Ireland final against Galway.

In O'Meara's absence, Mark O'Leary's two goals were the critical scores in Tipperary's 2–18 to 2–15 victory in the best final since 1997. O'Leary's first goal in the 22nd minute gave Tipperary a six-point lead and while Eugene Cloonan replied in kind almost immediately, Galway were always chasing the game. They trailed 1–9 to 1–7 at half-time after shooting four unanswered points, but their momentum was broken in the 39th minute when O'Leary capitalised on the indecision in the Galway defence to dribble home his second goal. Some great points from Kevin Broderick, who finished with five from play, and a spectacular goal from Feargal Healy closed the gap to a single point by the 60th minute but Tipperary, steadied by Tommy Dunne's industry at midfield and Declan Ryan's cuteness, outscored Galway by 0–5 to 0–3 in the final 10 minutes for the county's first title since 1991. Apart from Dunne, O'Leary and Ryan, goalkeeper Brendan Cummins was another key figure for a team who deserved an All-Ireland for their gutsy persistence and progressive improvement during the three years of Nicky English's management. Galway supporters pondered the two Feargal Healy shots that came off the posts and Broderick's late disallowed goal, but the reality was that their team had been undone as much by the lack of a rigorous examination on the way to the final as bad luck. The challenge for them was to regroup and push on for the 2002 title but their neighbours in Clare resurfaced again like a bad dream to end Lane's reign and set Galway's grail quest back another few years.

Tipperary All-Ireland Champions 2001

Brendan Cummins

Tom Costello   Philip Maher   Paul Ormonde

Eamonn Corcoran   David Kennedy   Paul Kelly

Tommy Dunne   Eddie Enright

Mark O'Leary   John Carroll   Lar Corbett

Eoin Kelly   Declan Ryan   Eugene O'Neill

Subs: Dermot Fahey for Costello, Paul O'Brien for O'Neill, Michael Ryan for Paul Kelly, Conor Gleeson for Kennedy

2002

THREE SUCCESSIVE TITLES FOR CORK, Kilkenny and Tipperary suggested a long-term restoration of the old order but another long-suffering pretender stormed through Munster in the summer of 2002 to inject renewed excitement back into the championship. Waterford had repeatedly tantalised and traumatised their supporters during the 1990s and the series of defeats to Clare, Kilkenny, Cork and Limerick between 1998 and 2001 suggested that another generation of Deise hurlers had missed out on the opportunity to win the county's first Munster title since 1963. Gerald McCarthy retired as manager after the Limerick game in 2001 and was replaced by another McCarthy – Justin – who had brought Clare close to the summit in 1977 and 1978 and gone on to coach Cork to the centenary year All-Ireland title and Cashel King Cormacs to their first Tipperary and Munster club titles. McCarthy was optimistic that he could rejuvenate players such as Tony Browne, Paul Flynn, Feargal Hartley, Tom Feeney, Brian Greene, Ken McGrath and Peter Queally for another tilt at the Munster title. Fresh talent was there too, in the shape of Eoin McGrath, Eoin Kelly and John Mullane and in his auto-biography *Hooked* published at the end of 2001, McCarthy argued that 'there is only a puck of the ball between the nine top counties'. 'My job is to get Waterford on the right side of that puck or break of the ball. If I can get every Waterford player to improve a little bit, then the whole team improves considerably. Waterford have as good a chance of any team of winning the 2002 All-Ireland. People argue that this team is too old. I don't buy that argument. Wexford had a similar age profile when they won the 1996 All-Ireland. Experience is vital; look at what Wexford did under Griffin or Cashel did when I was there. There's a popular theory now that hurling is a young man's game. But why's that? Because there has been an overemphasis on physical fitness. We won't be making that mistake in Waterford. We're focusing on quality rather than quantity. Come the championship, we'll be hurling fit.'

It was a bold prediction given Waterford's penchant for self-destruction, but the players confirmed McCarthy's faith in them by beating Cork 1–16 to 1–15 in the 2002 Munster semi-final – Waterford's first championship win over Cork in 13 years. Ken McGrath scored the winning point but the much-maligned Paul Flynn was Waterford's saviour, scoring 12 points, nine of them from frees, including two from over 100 yards in the first half. Cork led by a point at half-time after playing against the stiff breeze in Semple Stadium but Tony Browne's 43rd-minute goal kickstarted the Waterford challenge in earnest and some great defending from Feeney, James Murray, Hartley and Brian Flannery kept Cork at bay as Waterford advanced to meet Tipperary in the Munster final. The reigning champions had already beaten Clare for the fourth year running, scraping past an ominously resilient Banner side by 1–18 to 2–13. Tipp had seven points to spare against Limerick in the semi-final and were strong favourites to retain their title when they faced Waterford on 30 June in Páirc Uí Chaoimh.

It was another tremendous battle in the south on day when McCarthy's pre-season prescience about Waterford emulating Wexford came good right down to his team's final tally. Like Wexford against Offaly in 1996, Waterford scored 2–23 and pulled away in the final quarter with a bravura burst of hurling that was hair-raising in its excellence and the emotion it generated on the terraces. Waterford supporters, probably the loyalist in the country considering the torments they had endured in modern times, finally got to taste the primal bliss of the breakthrough.

It had taken them a generation to recover from the terrible defeats to Cork in the 1982 and 1983 Munster finals and the 1998 Munster final struggle with Clare could have been another fatal setback. Instead, Waterford played the type of quality hurling the

Deliverance day for Brian Flannery and Waterford.

optimists, such as McCarthy, believed was there underneath all the self-doubt and frustration. Man of the Match Ken McGrath led the assault from centre-forward with seven points from play and Tipperary were eventually overwhelmed by his mastery and the pace of Mullane, Eoin Kelly and Eoin McGrath. Paul Flynn chipped in with 1–5 from frees. His 16th-minute goal from a 21-yard free was a vital score and saw Waterford trail by just 1–10 to 1–9 at half-time after playing against the breeze. Benny Dunne kept Tipp in contention with two goals but Tony Browne's 52nd-minute goal was the signal for Waterford's liberation. Four days before the match, McCarthy had brought in Tom Cheasty, Martin Óg Morrissey and Frankie Walsh from the 1963 Munster-winning side to talk to his players. He later maintained the veterans' encouragement helped rid the players of the neuroses that had plagued the team for years. The bad times, it seemed, were over at last.

In hindsight, the six-week break between the Munster final and the All-Ireland semi-final against Clare did not do the new Munster champions any favours. While Waterford recovered from their celebrations, Clare walloped Wexford 3–15 to 3–7 in the qualifiers to make it to the quarter-final clash with Galway. A 72nd-minute point from Colin Lynch saw them through that game by 1–15 to 0–17 and, with two restorative wins under their belts, they were ideally tuned up for the Waterford challenge in the first All-Ireland semi-final on 12 August. Early delight for the Waterford supporters turned to anxiety after half-time and eventually to despair by the time Pat O'Connor called time. They scored four points in the first four minutes, led by 1–7 to 0–5 after 22 minutes but gradually disintegrated and were a shambles at the end when Clare claimed a 1–16 to 1–13 victory. Loughnane's successor Cyril Lyons had managed to blend players such as Brian Quinn, David Hoey, John Reddan, Tony Griffin and Tony

Carmody into the side, but it was the old hands O'Connor, Gilligan and Markham who did most of the scoring while McMahon and Brian Lohan vied for the Man of the Match award. Waterford's woe was compounded by an off-the-ball incident in which Clare wing-back Gerry Quinn suffered a serious hand injury.

The second semi-final a week later between Kilkenny and Tipperary had commentators searching for adequate superlatives. Hurling had been on such a roll for a couple of years that there was a tendency in some places to bestow classic or epic status on what were often merely moderate to good games, but this encounter was the real deal. Tipp were the one county in the game who held the whip hand on Kilkenny, having lost only one championship game – the 1967 All-Ireland final – against the Black and Amber in 80 years. If Tipp had been competitive in the 1970s, they probably would have lost more to the great Kilkenny side of Eddie Keher, Pat Delaney, Kieran Purcell *et al* but ancient history counted for nothing in a game that marked the return of D.J. Carey to competitive action. Carey had gone into a second 'retirement' after the 2001 loss to Galway but, after Kilkenny struggled in a 0–19 to 0–17 victory over Wexford in the 2002 Leinster final, Brian Cody coaxed him back to training – and he was the difference between winning and losing a game that was in a completely different class to the previous Sunday's fare. Carey scored four points, two from play, but it was his general menace that unhinged Tipp and, 11 minutes from time, he sprinted through from the half-forward line, drew the cover and hand-passed the ball to sub Jimmy Coogan who drove home the match-winning goal. Final score: Kilkenny 1–20 Tipperary 1–16.

However, it was another anti-climactic All-Ireland final. The opening act saw D.J. drift in behind the Clare full-back line for a fourth-minute goal and they were five points ahead after six minutes. The Lohan and McMahon axis was disrupted by Shefflin and Martin Comerford's combative running and Clare were in such trouble in the midfield against Andy Comerford and Derek Lyng that they sent on Baker after just 20 minutes to try and shore things up.

The Clare forwards laboured for scores compared to the fluency of Carey and Shefflin and the Banner's starting six up front scored just three points between them as Hickey, Kavanagh and Larkin reigned supreme in the Kilkenny full-back line. Centre-back Seanie McMahon was Clare's top scorer with six points from placed balls and Jamesie O'Connor fired over four from frees and their accuracy prevented an unseemly humiliation. Kilkenny led 1–11 to 0–8 at half-time and, while Clare closed the gap to a goal by the 48th minute, Kilkenny eased ahead without any great fuss and shot six points without reply including Carey's 52nd-minute effort when he soloed past a flailing Baker and shot a point off the hurl from the Hogan Stand sideline. Shefflin's 64th-minute goal was the final incision and Brian Cody gave John Power a valedictory taste of competitive action in Croke Park when he belatedly brought on one of Kilkenny's greatest servants ever in the 71st minute. Power and D.J. collected their fourth All-Ireland medals and Power, a farmer, memorably shrugged off the honour as 'another bale in the trailer'. He may have been understandably upset at only getting a minute or so of action given the commitment and fearlessness he had brought to Kilkenny's various campaigns since 1991. In his own way, he was as important to the cause as D.J. and had made a huge effort to make the team in his final year before surrendering his place on the 40 to Shefflin. While hurling was a poorer and less colourful place for Power's passing, Shefflin was a worthy successor as Cody and Kilkenny pressed on for total redemption in 2003.

Kilkenny All-Ireland Champions 2002

James McGarry

Michael Kavanagh   Noel Hickey   Philly Larkin

Richie Mullaly   Peter Barry   J.J. Deleney

Andy Comerford   Derek Lyng

John Hoyne   Henry Shefflin   Jimmy Coogan

Eddie Brennan   Martin Comerford   D.J. Carey

SUBS: Charlie Carter for Coogan, Brian McEvoy for Hoyne, John Power for Brennan

2001

21st Century Croker

'Architect Des McMahon remembers overhearing well-to-do women in a south Dublin pub boasting of how many times they had been to Croke Park that year. The term 'Croke Park chic' was used to describe the phenomenon. Unbelievably, Croke Park had become trendy.'

Tim Carey, *Croke Park: A History*

BY THE SUMMER OF 2001, the GAA entered the final phase of constructing a stadium that combined 21st-century architectural values with a reverence for the organisation's heritage and an acknowledgement of the corporate realities of modern Ireland. The new Cusack and Canal End stands had been completed on time and within budget and, in October 1999, work began on the reconstruction of the Hogan Stand. A government decision in April 2001 to give the GAA a once-off grant of €78 million towards the completion of the stadium allayed growing anxieties within the GAA that the Hogan Stand redevelopment might have to be put on hold because of escalating construction costs.

The government grant came against a backdrop of intrigue and debate about the opening up of Croke Park to other sports, the GAA's participation in the proposed national stadium project – the 'Bertie Bowl' in Abbotstown – and even the possibility that Croke Park might become the state's national stadium. The politics surrounding the €78 million grant rumbled on for another three years but, in the meantime, the promise of the additional state funding gave the GAA the impetus to press ahead with the Hogan Stand redevelopment which would be ready in its entirety for the 2002 All-Ireland hurling final between Clare and Kilkenny.

The fully enclosed, all-seater, U-shaped arena was a breathtaking sight. The lingering presence of the painfully modest Nally Stand and the old Hill 16 only served to underline the vastness of the new stadium. A tour of the new Cusack Stand gave the visitor a snapshot of the shrewd balancing act the GAA had struck between tradition and modernity. The ground-level museum, opened in 1998, provided an atmospheric reminder of the strength of the GAA's roots and history while the packed corporate boxes on the upper tiers were evidence of the organisation's success in forging alliances with some of the most powerful business interests in the country. The new Croke Park was a powerful symbol of regeneration and the GAA's confidence in its future.

What had once been an often backward, insular organisation hostile to change was now a vibrant, modern movement, that revealed a canny ability to anticipate the national zeitgeist. While other sporting bodies and the State floundered on even making a decision about where or when to build a stadium, the GAA pragmatically pressed on and delivered one of the few enduring public monuments in an era of previously undreamt of national prosperity and wealth. It's a typical GAA paradox that the redevelopment of Croke Park was conceived and launched long before the boom when Ireland was considered the economic sick man of Europe, and the GAA was perceived by some 'progressive' thinkers as one of the forces for stagnation in the country.

The 1983 All-Ireland football final occupies a prominent place in the GAA's annals of infamy. It was the day that Dublin's 'Dirty Dozen' or 'Twelve Apostles' defeated a 14-man Galway team in one of the worst and most foul-humoured finals ever – but it was events on the terraces which were to have a pivotal impact on the GAA's future. In his encyclopaedic and quirky history of Croke Park, Tim Carey – a former curator of the GAA Museum – traces back the genesis of the modern Croke Park to the events of that murky and fateful day when it was considered a miracle that fatalities were avoided in the post-match rush from Hill 16. An official attendance of 71,988 – the third largest since 1966 – was packed into the stadium and, writes Carey, 'It was noticed on the day that the crowd were in poor form – narky, grumpy, cantankerous. Trouble was not inevitable but there was an unhealthy atmosphere around the ground.'

Trouble on the Hill had been a frequent problem since the 1970s and garda baton charges of rowdy supporters were a frequent sight that the GAA authorities preferred to ignore. The Hill was gripped by a particularly hostile mood during the 1983 decider, reflecting the nastiness of the exchanges on the field. Overcrowding on the terrace saw one group of supporters break through the barrier separating the Hill from the Cusack Stand, forcing ticket holders from their seats. On the other side of the Hill, pensioners and students in the Nally Stand were pelted with missiles.

'Finally, at the end of the match, the most serious incident occurred. Behind the Hill was a walkway with a single set of concrete steps going to ground level. On one side of the steps were steep, grassy banks. Normally, the crowd would wait to go down the stairs, or slowly make their way down the slope. On this occasion, people slid at speed down the wet banks, often before the people who had gone before them were able to move

Referee John Gough talks to another player during the 1983 All-Ireland football final.

away. It was reported that it was a near miracle that people hadn't been killed. Fatalities were only avoided by the slimmest of margins and the intervention of gardaí and stewards.' The events of 18 September 1983 made the redevelopment of the Hill and the rest of Croke Park an urgent priority for the organisation's Director General Liam Mulvihill and the then President Paddy Buggy of Kilkenny.

For all the pageantry and affection surrounding the big match days involving Dublin, Kerry, Galway, Cork, Offaly, Kilkenny and Limerick in the 1970s, 'headquarters' had been in dire need of modernisation for well over a decade. The stadium had remained unchanged since the opening of the new, 16,000-seater Hogan Stand in 1958 (at a cost of £250,000). It was considered the height of sophistication at the time and brought the total capacity of the ground to almost 90,000 for All-Ireland finals.

The ground's ability to accommodate such a horde was pushed to the limit in 1960 when an official attendance of 87,768 spectators watched Down beat Kerry to take the Sam Maguire north for the first time. Twelve months later, Down were back to defend their title against Offaly in front of a record crowd of 90,556. The gates had been closed almost two hours before the throw-in and an estimated 25,000 to 30,000 supporters were locked out. In the 1940s and 1950s, it wasn't unusual for the gates to be rushed when the full-house notices went up but, on this occasion, common sense, mercifully, prevailed. Carey quotes contemporary reports that found the atmosphere in the stadium 'curiously flat' in spite of the huge crowd: 'It is likely that they were muted by their own size. They were jammed into every corner of Croke Park like never before. What is looked on as one of the greatest days of the Association could just as easily have been its blackest day. A shuttle of ambulances ran between Croke Park and the Dublin hospitals carrying those who had fainted or were injured in the crush. Perhaps, it was the only the muted behaviour and self-restraint of the crowd, wary of its own power in such circumstances, which saved the situation from possible catastrophe.'

By the end of the 1960s, the days of 90,000 crowds belonged to another era. The GAA experienced one of its periodic slumps in popularity and, while the Dublin–Kerry rivalry of the 1970s brought the crowds back to Croke Park, the 1950s-built stadium had begun to age badly. Its creaking decline was lyrically summed up by one observer writing in the commemorative programme for the opening of the new Canal End Stand in 2000. 'In the 1970s, while Croke Park could be utterly magical, it was a gum-blackened, down on its luck tangle of metal, stone and moisture... gaunt, mildewed and basic. A place immune to market research... symptomatic of a national mindset. We lacked ambition and self-confidence.'

The GAA's Director General, Liam Mulvihill, couldn't be accused of lacking in ambition or confidence. More than any other individual, it was his drive and vision for the organisation that pushed the GAA in the direction of a €275 million stadium that would become the third largest in Europe. A native of Kenagh in County Longford, Mulvihill had been an accomplished colleges footballer with St Mel's and played corner-back on the team that won a Hogan Cup title in 1963. He later played under-21 and senior for his county, but it as an administrator that he made his name, and he was just 24 when he was appointed Chairman of the Longford County Board in 1969. Ten years later, he became the GAA's youngest Director General when he succeeded Sean O'Siochain. Mulvihill was no firebrand and in his early years in the position – effectively the GAA's equivalent of a private sector Chief Executive – he did little to challenge the status quo. But his handling of the Croke Park redevelopment, support for the restructuring of the championships and input into the debates on Rule 21 and Rule 42 have marked him out as a practical and reasonable voice for change during a period when the GAA could have been driven apart by internal politics.

The initial reaction to the chaos of the 1983 final was to rebuild Hill 16 but, by the late 1980s, events abroad pushed the GAA in the direction of a complete reconstruction of Croke Park. The 1988 Hillsborough disaster prompted a reassessment of safety at sporting venues all over Europe – and Croke Park fared badly when judged on modern health and safety criteria. While the problems on Hill 16 had been addressed, the Cusack Stand remained a potential deathtrap. Opened in 1938, by its golden anniversary, it was found to be 'in an advanced stage of dilapidation' and the access and exit area through a 15-feet wide passageway was no longer acceptable for capacity crowds of 14,000.

There were also fundamental structural problems in the Hogan Stand and Canal End and the GAA began to consider the construction of a new 90,000-capacity stadium. After rejecting an engineering-driven option that would have seen additional seating added to a modified Cusack Stand and seating installed in the Canal End, the GAA looked abroad for a new vision of Croke Park and shortlisted two design consultants – HOK and Lobb. They had different visions. One favoured the American 'super-bowl' model with a significant corporate element, the other the European model maximising seat capacity and facilities for the ordinary spectator. As a compromise, the GAA asked both companies to share their expertise and produce a joint master plan for a new Croke Park. The two international practices agreed and the master plan was presented in 1990. Another significant development was the GAA's decision to appoint the Dublin firm of Gilroy McMahon as executive architects. Des McMahon, a partner in the firm, was from Beragh in County Tyrone and had played football for the county. He had an instinctive grasp of where the GAA was coming from and where it wanted to go. 'Maybe I understood their requirements and unclarified aspirations and I was able to bridge that gap,' he recalled as the project neared completion.

The design team, including Liam Mulvihill, embarked on a research tour before drawing up the final model for Croke Park. Stadiums including the Nou Camp, Bernabeu, Twickenham, the Stadium of Light in Lisbon, the venues for Italia '90, and American arenas, such as the Giants Stadium in New Jersey and Joe Robby Stadium in Miami, were all visited and assessed as possible models. An indication of the commitment to the project was GAA President John Dowling climbing to the very last row of the upper deck of Joe Robby Stadium to see a sliotar on the pitch. 'The Offaly man suffered from a severe fear of heights and five people had to help him down,' Tim Carey recalled in his Croke Park history.

All the effort was worthwhile when the design team unveiled the model for Croke Park in February 1992. The papers hailed it as 'Space Age Croker' and the boldness and scale of the project suggested a whole new direction for the GAA. The project was costed at £115 million and the four distinct construction phases were expected to take 15 years to complete. When the planning process got underway, Mulvihill, McMahon and the new GAA President Peter Quinn set about selling the project to an unconvinced grassroots membership. There were genuine concerns that the redevelopment would prove a crippling financial burden for the association and that the corporate element was a betrayal of the GAA's amateur ethos. Quinn proved a persuasive advocate. Along with Dermot Power of Bank of Ireland, he devised an ingenious finance package for the new Cusack Stand that envisaged the entire cost of the project being offset by the sale of corporate boxes and premium-level seats. £8 million would come from the sale of corporate boxes and the additional £14 million of the total £22 million would come from the sale of premium-level seats. The clinching argument was that the premium-level

Reconstruction of the Canal End at Croke Park.

seats would only account for 3,000 seats of the new stand's 24,000 capacity. The GAA, argued Quinn, was effectively increasing the number of seats available to ordinary supporters while getting the corporate sector to bankroll the entire development. An added incentive was that the premium-level seats would become available for resale after 10 years.

Quinn won the day and a similar financing package was also successful in getting the Canal End phase of the development underway. Demolition work on the old Cusack Stand began the day after the 1993 All-Ireland football final between Derry and Cork and the lower section was completed in time for the 1995 Leinster hurling final between Kilkenny and Offaly. The premium level was ready for the 1996 All-Irelands and work on Phase Two, the Canal End Stand, began after the 1998 All-Ireland football final between Galway and Kildare.

A remarkable feature of the whole project was that the work was scheduled in such a way the GAA was able to maintain a full programme of fixtures between October 1993 and completion in 2004. The demolition work took place in the winter and, in the spring, the attention switched to the provision of additional seating for that summer's games. One poignant milestone was the demolition of the old Hogan Stand which began the day after the Mayo–Monaghan All-Ireland women's football final in October 1999. The first seats in the new Hogan came on stream in 2000 when the completed Canal End was also opened in time for the All-Ireland finals.

THE NEW CROKE PARK STADIUM came of age during the 2002 season. Tim Carey wrote: 'During [that] season 1.3 million people attended matches in Croke Park. As the months progressed, the crowds began to move along the upper deck of the Hogan as more seats became ready. The first occasion on which the entirety of the Cusack, Canal and Hogan were occupied was the hurling final of 2002. Croke Park had come so far that the Nally Stand now looked shabby and Hill 16 diminutive.'

The teams paraded before the throw-in against a wall of noise. Any fears about the new stadium lacking in atmosphere were emphatically dispelled. The new Croke Park had opened and the reviews were ecstatic. Tom Humphries in *The Irish Times* wrote: 'If you grew up in the GAA, the new Croke Park is a dream-world. For all the vainglorious talk down through the generations of the glory of hurling and football, the GAA never gave its jewels a showcase. The new Croke Park is perfect. Its inviolable pitch, its softly curved roofing, its teeming terraces and its handsome bars. It's a uniquely Irish place.' Vincent Hogan in the *Irish Independent* was equally bedazzled: 'It is as it should be then. The new Croke Park honouring the old. Modern, self-confident, yet freighted with proud history. It is a fusion of two worlds. Each

The scene before the 2002 All-Ireland hurling final.

one beautifully enhanced by this fusion of stone and steel and human intellect.'

The ecstatic reviews were public reward for the design team, main contractors and dozens of specialist subcontractors who had faced new challenges on an almost weekly basis. The challenge of reconstructing a stadium on a 15-acre site bounded at one end by a canal and railway line at the other presented all kinds of architectural and engineering headaches. Minimising disruption to residents in the densely populated streets around Croke Park was also a constant concern. Budget overruns in the late 1990s, caused by accelerating wages inflation in the construction industry and rising materials costs, could have set the completion date back years until the government's timely intervention in 2001. There were also planning headaches, such as the initial insistence by An Bord Pleanála in 1999 that Hill 16 be rebuilt as a seated area. The GAA successfully appealed this decision on the grounds that the Hill was an integral part of the Croke Park experience and that the redesigned terrace would offer faster exit than that available in the seated areas. The redesigned Hill 16 and the new Nally Terrace Stand between the Hill and the Hogan Stand opened in autumn 2004 and marked the completion of the entire €275 million project.

The aerial shots from the 2005 All-Ireland football final between Kerry and Tyrone captured the new stadium in all its glory for the first time, and Tyrone's victory was appropriate for the mood of change and progress the new Croke Park evokes. It was the GAA's good fortune that the reconstruction of Croke Park coincided with the 'golden age of hurling' and, in latter years, the phenomenon of renewed northern dominance in Gaelic football. But the stadium itself was also a catalyst in the regeneration of interest in the games and emergence of new challengers for major honours. On a purely practical level, the

GAA needed more big games to finance the redevelopment and this helped defeat traditional arguments against the introduction of the back-door and qualifier systems in the championships.

The qualifiers, in turn, have seen teams and supporters from counties such as Sligo, Westmeath and Fermanagh escape from the tyranny of the provincial system to enjoy their day in the sun at headquarters. Watching their teams play in Croke Park can only increase the enthusiasm of children in the 'weaker' counties for football and hurling. The feelgood factor, and cycle of progress and renewal created by the new stadium should continue for decades.

In 2003, Croke Park was unveiled to a global audience when the stadium hosted the Special Olympics' opening and closing ceremonies. Two years later, it received Bono's imprimatur when U2 played three sell-out shows 20 years after their first Croke Park performance.

In the past, the GAA's alignment with Church and state – twin pillars of conservatism – meant that, for a significant minority of Irish people, Croke Park was more a symbol of repression than an arena of happiness and belonging. In the years after Independence right up to the 1970s, it was regularly the venue for the sort of mass religious gatherings and nationalist pageants that would be barely credible to the 'Tiger Generation'. Yet these events, however they might appear to the modern eye, were of their time and tracing the history of Croke Park is akin partly to tracing the birth of the nation's identity, with all the attendant tragedies, excesses, frustrations and joys.

The new Croke Park is not without its faults. The sponsorship of everything from the scoreboard to the action replays on the big screen suggests a relentless and unhealthy commercialism. The unchallenged proliferation of advertising for burger chains and alcohol producers is surely at odds with the GAA's core values.

Croke Park, though, remains as near to perfection as any sporting organisation can hope to attain in an imperfect world. And as Tim Carey wrote: 'In a country where any major project seems to be ill-conceived, poorly costed, behind schedule and disappointing when completed, the reconstruction of Croke Park represents an almost unique achievement in modern Ireland.'

The Back-Door

The GAA's decision to introduce a qualifier system for the 2001 All-Ireland football championship was one of the most important reforms in the association's history. By the 1990s, the winner-takes-all, knockout championship format had become unacceptable for players and supporters. As teams' championship preparations intensified and attendances soared, it was absurd that an entire season could be reduced to 70 minutes in May or June – and that All-Star quality players could be sidelined for another year. There was always the National League but that was frequently devalued by the apathy of the big powers towards an increasingly secondary competition. Dublin's Brian Stynes articulated the sentiments of the players well after his team's 1–13 to 1–10 exit to Meath in the 1997 Leinster quarter-final: 'The whole system in this country is a disaster. There were 60,000 people here today, we had one of the best games in years but one of the best teams in the country is out of the championship. I think the GAA should get their heads out of their arses.'

From the perspective of September 2005, it seems incredible that the football championship had been circumscribed by the same certainties and limitations for over a century. A 'backdoor' system for beaten provincial finalists was introduced for hurling in 1997 without any lasting damage to the integrity of the Leinster or the holy of holies, the Munster hurling championship. And when the GAA established a National Development Committee for Gaelic football in 1997, it was inevitable that the day of the back-door was on its way for ▶

the big ball code. The more radical campaigners for a reform of the football championship wanted the introduction of a full-blown open draw for the All-Ireland championship, but the provincial championships were weighted with too much significance and lore to be completely abandoned or downgraded. Instead, the GAA opted for a compromise solution that would retain the provincial dramas within a restructured All-Ireland championship. Every team beaten in the first round of the championship would be given a second chance in a series of All-Ireland qualifier matches and the four teams to emerge from that series of games would play the beaten provincial finalists in a final round of qualifiers. The four winners from this round would then advance to play the provincial title winners in the All-Ireland quarter-finals.

There was the usual battalion of nay-sayers but the back-door system was an immediate and unqualified success. By the time the quarter-final stages of the 2001 championship were reached in early August, public interest in Gaelic football was at an all-time high and, by the end of the year, an additional £5 million had been raked in from gate receipts. Saturday evening games gave the championship a new dimension and with three or four live games on television each weekend, the GAA had a summer championship that could rival the Sky Sports bombardment of English soccer during the winter and spring months. Above all, the back-door system enabled the perennial underdogs to escape from the strait-jacket of the provincial system. In 2001, Westmeath embarked on an eight-game odyssey that saw them reach an All-Ireland quarter-final and play eight championship games in one summer. One of the highlights of the entire season was Sligo footballers arriving in Croke Park via the back-door and beating Kildare before falling to Dublin in the last round of qualifier games. Prior to 2001, Sligo had only played two senior championship games in Croke Park in 114 years – the 1928 and 1975 All-Ireland semi-finals.

The new system wasn't perfect. The main flaw was exposed when the draw for the 2001 quarter-finals was made and teams from the same province who had already played each other were drawn to meet again. Tyrone and Derry came out of the hat for one quarter-final. Westmeath were drawn to face Meath who had beaten them by one point in Leinster, and Roscommon weren't too pleased to draw Galway after securing a rare win in Tuam in the Connacht semi-final. The provincial winners also had justified complaints about the GAA's decision to play the quarter-finals in provincial venues rather than Croke Park. Galway had played two games in headquarters since losing to Roscommon in Tuam but Connacht champions Roscommon ended the year without playing a game beyond the Shannon. These flaws in the new system were resolved by 2002, and most of the attention after the 2001 quarter-final draw switched to the clash of Dublin and Kerry which was fixed for the hallowed hurling sod of Semple Stadium.

The evacuation of Hill 16 to Thurles on a Bank Holiday Saturday afternoon was a fraught undertaking and the radio chat shows were busy for days afterwards with complaints from Dubs traumatised by the LA-style gridlock beyond the Pale. There was an outbreak of nostalgia in the week before the game as the great showdowns between the counties in the 1970s were dusted down from the vaults. The first renewal of the 21st century didn't disappoint the capacity crowd assembled in perfect conditions to watch the match. Removed from the familiar surrounds of Croke Park, Dublin appeared tentative in the first half and Kerry took full advantage to lead 1–5 to 0–3 at half-time, Johnny Crowley ▶

the goalscorer. Dublin supporters were aghast in the opening period as first Collie Moran in the 25th minute and then Dessie Farrell
in the 33rd missed clear goal chances. Farrell's shot from a few yards
out ricocheted off the crossbar and, after half-time, Dara Ó
Cinnéide, Crowley and Mike Frank Russell chipped away patiently at the Dublin defence to lead 1–13 to 0–8 with 12 minutes left.

Dublin manager Tommy Carr, normally a restrained character
on the line, kick-started the Dublin revival when he ran on to the
field 15 minutes from time to remonstrate angrily with referee
Michael Curley about a soft free awarded to Kerry. A couple of
minutes later, Carr sent on the redoubtable Vinny Murphy, an
archetypal stocky but skilful Dublin target man, to rescue the situation. In the 62nd minute, Murphy sliced home a goal from a
Jason Sherlock pass and it was game on. Ciaran Whelan, ruling
midfield by now, kicked a point and another from sub Wayne
McCarthy had the margin down to two approaching injury-time.
McCarthy then launched a ball goalwards and Darren Homan
leaped highest and punched it to the net to give Dublin the lead.
The Dublin supporters on the Killanin End were delirious, but
there was one more act to be played out. Three minutes into injury-
time, Kerry were awarded a sideline kick close to the halfway line.
The standard ploy would have been to try and engineer a free or
find a player closer to goal – but Maurice Fitzgerald, only introduced as a substitute in the 64th minute, launched the ball off the
outside of his boot and an entire stadium was rapt as it curved over
the bar. Final score: Kerry 1–14 Dublin 2–11. Dublin celebrated the
draw but there was no second coming for Carr's team. They fought
well in the replay but left themselves with far too much to do after
a poor first half. They were nine points down after 22 minutes and
never recovered and lost by 2–12 to 1–12. Kerry, who had beaten

Cork by three points in a rattling Munster final, remained on course to defend their title.

A couple of hours after Fitzgerald's sorcery, Galway and Roscommon went head-to-head in their quarter-final in front of a full house in McHale Park, Castlebar. Galway supporters were inconsolable leaving Tuam two months earlier as Roscommon celebrated a famous 2-12 to 0-14 Connacht semi-final. Under the management of a former Galway underage prodigy and Tuam man John Tobin, Roscommon had upped the physical intensity and Galway had no answer on the day to the drive and raw endeavour of players such as Conor Connelly, Seamus O'Neill and Francie Grehan and the accuracy of Nigel Dineen and Frankie Dolan. Stephen Lohan had kicked a couple of his trademark points after coming on as a sub to finish off a shell-shocked Galway team. Galway had problems all over the field, particularly in the full-back line where Tomás Mannion took a roasting and centre-back where John Divilly was a shadow of the rollicking figure of 1998.

O'Mahony and his team retreated but had a few weeks to recover and return thanks to the back-door system. The road back began in Aughrim, the fabled stronghold of Wicklow football, but the qualifier game there on 1 July was more of a sparring session than a battle, Galway won 3-12 to 1-9. O'Mahony had reconstructed his defence, introducing a new goalkeeper, Alan Keane, starting an under-21, Kieran Fitzgerald in the corner, and switching Tomás Mannion to centre-back. Necessity may have been the catalyst for change, but the switches proved inspired as the summer progressed. Two weeks later, Galway were back in Croke Park. They looked set for a comfortable passage to the next round when they led Armagh by 0-12 to 0-5 after 53 minutes. But, in a complete turn-around, Armagh kicked seven points without replay to level ▶

the game. They looked the more likely winners until Michael Donnellan blocked down an attempted clearance from Justin McNulty in the 73rd minute and fed the ball to Paul Clancy. A half-time substitute, Clancy kicked the winner from 40 yards and Galway advanced by a point to meet Cork the following Sunday. They won by 1–14 to 1–10 but it was another disconcerting performance. This time they led Cork by 1–7 after 20 minutes, went to sleep for the next 45 minutes and then awoke to score four points in the final five minutes to make the quarter-final draw.

Roscommon had every reason to be wary of Galway the second time around. Apart from the re-jigged defence, Derek Savage and Paul Clancy, who had missed the game in Tuam, were back to full fitness and the two games in Croke Park had restored the team's innate confidence. Roscommon had been idle for a month since snatching the Connacht title from Mayo with a Gerry Lohan goal in the fifth minute of injury-time for an unlikely 2–10 to 1–12 victory in Hyde Park. There were no last-minute reprieves this time as Galway tore into the game with deadly intent. They led by 0–9 to 0–1 at half-time and Joyce, with seven points from frees, along with Donnellan, Savage, Joe Bergin and Declan Meehan, were outstanding as O'Mahony's side produced their most complete performance since the 2000 mauling of Sligo.

The other side of the draw produced the hard-luck story of the year. Westmeath, still chasing a first-ever competitive win over their prosperous neighbours, led Meath by three points before being caught by an Ollie Murphy goal in injury-time. They had led the whole way through but Luke Dempsey's talented group of graduates from All-Ireland minor and Leinster under-21 winning sides froze when victory was theirs and Meath finished them off by 2–10 to 0–11 in the replay. Derry defeated Tyrone in a rematch of the Ulster final and were paired to meet Galway in one semi-final, while Kerry faced Meath in the other.

Kerry's collapse on 2 September was as shocking as it was unexpected. Páidí Ó Sé's team imploded to lose 2–15 to 0–5 and Meath played with such fluency and style that they were immediately installed as favourites to win the All-Ireland title. There was still hope for Kerry at half-time when they trailed 1–6 to 0–4 but they scored just one more point. Long before the final whistle, the Meath supporters were mock-serenading their players' keep-ball antics against an utterly demoralised Kerry – behaviour that came back to haunt them in the final.

The inquests were long and brutal in Kerry. It was the county's worst Croke Park beating but it wasn't so much the margin as the absence of spirit and fight that baffled Kerry supporters and Páidí Ó Sé who described it as 'the hardest kick in the bollox of my career… Didn't see us collapsing like that. Couldn't envisage an early surrender… as the evening passed my emotion changed from disappointment to hurt. I felt let down. We'd dropped our heads early in the game, we didn't win the carpet ball, the difficult stuff on the deck, the breaks. Not Páidí Ó Sé. That upset me. I mean Meath were exceptional but our performance really defies analysis. I was hurt.'

Galway's summer of living dangerously continued in the other semi-final on 26 August. By the 56th minute they were on the brink of surrender when Derry led 1–10 to 0–8 after a sequence of bad Galway wides. One more score from the Ulster team would have decided it. They had the chances in an intense scoreless period of play but it was Seán Óg de Paor raiding from the back who sparked the Galway revival when he kicked a point under severe pressure to pump some life back into his team. The response ▶

Galway win the first 'back-door' football title.

was immediate and stunning. Joyce, Donnellan and Savage finally found their form and along with the two Clancys – Paul and substitute Matthew – ripped Derry apart in the final 14 minutes. Galway scored 1–6 in this period, the goal a fine solo effort from Matthew Clancy, to win by 1–14 to 1–11.

The build-up to the final was like 1998 all over again. As with Kildare that year, Meath were odds-on favourites and O'Mahony was happy as ever to talk up the opposition and plot away in relative silence. But all the pre-match assessments were confounded and in the final minutes Galway did unto Meath as they had done unto Kerry and toyed with possession as their supporters acclaimed every exaggerated pass. The same supporters had their patience tested in the first half when Galway kicked some bad wides and committed a lot of basic errors but, for all that, they still looked the better team, particularly in defence where Declan Meehan, Gary

Fahey, Kieran Fitzgerald and Tomás Mannion had the measure of Ollie Murphy, Trevor Giles and Graham Geraghty. Mannion had grown into the central defensive role and one incident where he emerged from a foul and defiantly bounced the ball off the ground summed up the controlled temper of Galway's best play on the day. They were still level 0–6 to 0–6 at half-time in spite of the missed chances. The doubts were swept away after the break when Pádhraic Joyce, wayward as any of his team-mates in the first half, produced 35 minutes to match Maurice Fitzgerald's in the 1997 decider. Joyce scored 10 points in total, five from play but Meath managed just two more scores. They remained in contention until the final 10 minutes but were in trouble from the 40th minute when they lost their dangerman Murphy to injury. Nigel Nestor was sent off in the 50th and, after Giles missed a penalty in the 58th minute, Galway slipped clear and kicked a sequence of textbook points to claim their second title in three years. Final score: Galway 0–17 Meath 0–8.

It was O'Mahony's crowning achievement and one that elevated him to the ranks of the great managers alongside Boylan, O'Dwyer. He had taken the crocked and beaten squad of June to the pinnacle in September. He had the confidence to reconfigure his team to the extent that only three players – Gary Fahey, Declan Meehan and Seán Óg de Paor – started the All-Ireland final in the same positions they occupied against Roscommon in the Connacht semi-final. The gambles of bringing in Alan Keane as goalkeeper, blooding Fitzgerald and asking Mannion to reinvent himself as a centre-back all came good. Kevin Walsh was given the time to regain enough fitness to make a telling contribution in the final and O'Mahony also resisted the temptation to demand too much from Paul Clancy and Derek Savage before they had fully ▶

recovered from injury. During all the wobbles and journeys to the edge in the Armagh, Cork and Derry matches, O'Mahony was a calm and reassuring presence on the line. He was a class act and his team responded in kind but they never scaled the same heights again. The county won two more Connacht titles and an

Galway manager, John O'Mahony takes another Croke Park bow.

All-Ireland under-21 title in 2002 under O'Mahony but, in 2004, he decided he'd had enough and passed the baton onto another Mayo man, Peter Forde.

The nine-point defeat in an All-Ireland final shocked Meath to the core. They were never the same force again and, while Boylan hung on for another four seasons, it was a melancholic long goodbye for a man who had taken three different Meath teams to All-Ireland titles.

Galway All-Ireland Football Champions 2001

Alan Keane

Kieran Fitzgerald   Gary Fahey   Richie Fahey

Declan Meehan   Tomás Mannion   Sean Óg de Paor

Kevin Walsh   Michael Donnellan

Joe Bergin   Paul Clancy   Jarlath Fallon

Pádhraic Joyce   Derek Savage   Tommy Joyce

SUBS: Alan Kerins for Bergin, Kieran Comer for Tommy Joyce

2002

Clockwork Orange

'It's do or die, yeah. It is do or die. It's do or die as regards
what we feel about the whole thing. We feel you could spend
half your life trying to get to where we are today and maybe
never get back there again. We have to take this chance
because it might never come back.'

Armagh footballer Oisín McConville, September 2002

'When Oisín McConville cut inside and fired that goal to
the net in the second half, the X-factor was unleashed upon
us. A hundred years of oppression, of f**king helicopters,
of jackbooted troops kicking them when they were down
– the lot.'

Kerry manager Páidí Ó Sé, September 2002

IN MAY 2002, two Irish football teams travelled to overseas training resorts. Mick McCarthy and the Republic of Ireland soccer team landed on a South Sea island called Saipan for the first stage of their acclimatisation for the World Cup finals in Japan and Korea. The tragic-comic nature of what happened next – the FAI's farcical training arrangements, the drinking, the rows and Roy Keane's departure from the Irish World Cup squad –

made international headlines. A few weeks earlier, Joe Kernan and the Armagh footballers made local headlines when they flew out to La Manga in Spain to prepare for their Ulster championship first-round clash against Tyrone.

Some Armagh supporters reckoned Big Joe had taken leave of his senses. Spain was hardly a fit place for a gang of lads from Crossmaglen, Cullaville, Dromintee, Mullaghbawn and Killeavey the week before an Ulster championship quarter-final in Clones against cocky Tyrone, the favourites for that year's Ulster title. That deep-rooted Irish dread of becoming a laughing stock because of some extravagant folly was a real possibility for Armagh if Kernan's men didn't deliver against Tyrone. But, unlike Saipan, Armagh's short stay in La Manga was no boozy bonding session – instead it was the improbable starting point for the county's first All-Ireland title and Ulster football's second cycle of All-Ireland dominance.

La Manga had been the Spanish training destination of choice for some of Europe's leading teams since the early 1990s. Galatasaray, Real Madrid and Ajax were all regular visitors and Glenn Hoddle had based his English squad there ahead of the 1998 World Cup finals in Paris. Armagh were the first Gaelic football team to use a facility designed for pre-season, or pre-tournament, physical and psychological fine-tuning. Bringing his players there so close to the championship was a high stakes gamble by Kernan in his first summer managing the county team. An early championship exit would mean ridicule for indulging such a flighty notion as a Spanish training camp; however, beat Tyrone and land an Ulster title and Big Joe would be lauded for his foresight and professionalism.

Kernan was appointed manager the previous autumn when Brian McAlinden and Brian Canavan stepped down after three years of mixed fortunes. In 1999, the two Brians guided Armagh to the county's first Ulster title in 17 years and retained it the following year but hadn't made the breakthrough in Croke Park – although they brought Kerry to a replay in extra-time in the 2000 semi-final and were unlucky not to at least draw their 2001 quarter-final against Galway. While the county team stalled outside of Ulster, Kernan, who played on the Armagh team beaten by Dublin in the 1977 All-Ireland final, led his club Crossmaglen to three All-Ireland club titles and was the logical, and popular, choice for the county job. He appointed Paul Grimley as his assistant and brought in fitness guru John McCluskey, who had worked with the Crossmaglen teams as well as Queen's University Sigerson Cup-winning sides, to develop a new gym-based approach to the physical training.

After a winter and spring spent travelling to venues such as Aughrim and Ruislip, Armagh made a tame exit from the league when they were well-beaten by Mick O'Dwyer's Laois in the Division Two semi-final. Tyrone won the competition outright and were firm favourites to beat Kernan's side when they met in Clones on 19 May. Armagh's obsession with the tactic of bringing 'bodies back behind the ball' and defending, rather than expanding on potential winning positions, had been patented by Brian Canavan and Brian McAlinden and there was no change in tactical direction under the new regime. At times, it was frustrating and negative to watch but, by the 21st-century, aesthetics were a minor consideration for a county obsessed with winning the Sam Maguire. Kernan and his players weren't too bothered if they won ugly but, at times, their preoccupation with defence appeared counter-productive to the point of paranoia considering the calibre of their inside forwards such as Oisín McConville, Diarmaid Marsden, Stevie McDonald and Ronan Clarke.

The Tyrone game was a case in point. Armagh led by 1–11 to 0–10 with 24 minutes left and then retreated, even though their forwards looked to have the beating of the Tyrone full-back line. Teenager Seán Cavanagh scored an equalising goal for Tyrone in the fourth minute of injury-time and Armagh were lucky to escape with the draw when Peter Canavan had a chance to finish the game but passed to team-mate Richard Thornton who scuffed his shot wide as the Armagh keeper Benny Tierney charged off his line. Final score: Armagh 1–12 Tyrone 1–12. The replay, two weeks later, was one of the best games of football seen in Ulster since the early 1990s. This time, spectators were treated to the other, more positive, dimension of northern football. Not even the swarm defensive tactics could negate the natural attacking instincts of both sets of forwards. Tyrone lined out without Peter Canavan but Stephen O'Neill took on the mantle of forward leader, scoring seven points in the second half to leave Tyrone ahead before substitute Barry Duffy clinched the result for Armagh with a 66th-minute goal. Final score: Armagh 2–13 Tyrone 1–13.

Fermanagh provided the opposition in the Ulster semi-final and had high hopes after running in 4–13 against Monaghan, but Armagh had their homework done and completely negated the Erneside dangerman Rory Gallagher as they strolled into the Ulster final on a 0–16 to 1–5 scoreline.

Donegal, managed by Mickey Moran, had been scoring freely on their way to the Ulster decider, with their full-forward line of Adrian Sweeney, Brendan Devenney and Brian Roper amassing 5–27 in three games. Armagh were never likely to allow this trio the same latitude as Antrim, Derry and Down had. A return of just four points from play by their blue-chip forwards was a disappointment for Donegal who conceded a soft goal after just two minutes when John McEntee took full advantage of goalkeeper Tony Blake's difficulties with a wicked bounce. Armagh led 1–6 to 0–6 at half-time and as Donegal squandered

Eamonn O'Hara in action for Sligo against Tyrone.

chances from play and frees, Kernan's team opened a five-point gap and survived the fright of a Jimmy McGuinness goal to win their third Ulster title in four years. Final score: Armagh 1–14 Donegal 1–10.

The debate about the dubious merit of Armagh's tactics gathered more force when they blew a six-point lead and were again fortunate to cling on for a draw in the All-Ireland quarter-final against Sligo on 4 August. As in 2001, Sligo prospered in the back-door qualifiers after losing to Galway in the Connacht final. Their Croke Park victory over Tyrone in the final qualifying round was the shock of the season. There were times in the opening 20 minutes of that game when the Ulster team looked unstoppable as they raced into a 0–8 to 0–2 lead after 20 minutes but, inexplicably, they slowly disintegrated and scored just four points in the remaining 50 minutes. Midfielder Eamonn O'Hara led the Sligo revival and Paul Durcan, Dessie Sloyan, Dara McGarty and Kieran Quinn began to find the target as Sligo narrowed the gap to 0–9 to 0–7 at half-time. In the second half, the Sligo half-back line closed down the supply lines to Peter Canavan and O'Neill and, while Tyrone did enjoy another brief spell of supremacy, Sligo levelled the match at 0–12 each by the 50th minute. Dessie Sloyan's 62nd-minute goal sealed an amazing Sligo comeback. Final score: Sligo 1–14 Tyrone 0–12.

Paul Durcan had a chance to secure an even more implausible victory with the last kick of the quarter-final against Armagh but his shot was wide and Eamonn O'Hara was left to rue not having a pot himself rather than off-loading to his midfield partner. As it was, the 2–9 to 0–15 draw was a sensational result for a Sligo team that had trailed by six points with 16 minutes left and that had then had wing-back David Durkin sent off four minutes later. A Steven McDonnell goal had given the Ulster champions a 1–5 to 0–6 half-time lead and Diarmaid Marsden's goal three minutes after the break should have been the platform for an expansive Armagh performance. Instead, they reverted to type, attempting to suffocate the game by crowding midfield, and retreated into their familiar rearguard cocoon, leaving just two men forward. In contrast, Sligo showed lots of courage to attack relentlessly in the final 15 minutes. Dessie Sloyan, isolated in the full-forward line after Durkin's dismissal, led the comeback and wing-back Brendan Philips and McGarty kicked two great points before substitute Padraig Doohan landed the equaliser. Final score: Armagh 2–9 Sligo 0–15.

While Sligo celebrated their draw, Big Joe harangued his players for 30 minutes in the dressing room and they lived on their wits once more in the quarter-final replay played in Navan where Sligo were furious at having an injury-time claim for a penalty ignored by referee Seamus McCormack. The Connacht team trailed by two points in the 73rd minute when Shaun Davey appeared to be fouled in the square by three Armagh defenders but McCormack waved play on and Armagh progressed to an All-Ireland semi-final against Dublin. They just about deserved the result in a game that turned in a three-minute spell after half-time when Ronan Clarke scored the game's only goal and Armagh added two quick points to lead by seven. Sligo somehow fought their way back but were let down by wayward shooting. Final score: Armagh 1–16 Sligo 0–17.

Meanwhile, the good times dawned again for Dublin and their ebullient new manager Tommy Lyons who was appointed in November 2002. A native of Mayo, Lyons had spent most of his adult life in Dublin and his coaching and management pedigree, including an All-Ireland club title with Kilamcud Crokes and leading Offaly to the 1997 Leinster title, was impressive. His predecessor Tommy Carr was popular with the players during his four seasons in charge but, after seven barren years, Dublin needed a change. In his first summer in charge, Lyons delivered the Leinster title as the capital finally got to share in the GAA's newfound trendiness and feelgood factor. The Armott's jersey was the street fashion trend of the summer as Dublin played some exciting football to steam roll Meath and set up a Leinster decider against Kildare. Lyons had freshened up the mix by introducing some lively new forwards including Alan Brogan and Ray Cosgrove and they poached two goals in the 56th and 57th minutes to win Dublin's first Leinster title since 1995. Final score: Dublin 2–13 Kildare 2–11. Cosgrove was acclaimed as the new King of the Hill after scoring two goals to salvage a draw for Dublin in their All-Ireland quarter-final against Donegal on the Bank Holiday Monday weekend. Donegal had some late chances to win the game but collapsed in the replay six days later and Croke Park was again a sellout for the Dublin– Armagh semi-final on 1 September.

There was an alarming air of hype about the whole Lyons and Dublin bandwagon by this stage and the Dubs didn't endear themselves to neutrals when they embarked on a lap of honour around Croke Park after the quarter-final. The speculation about a possible Dublin–Kerry All-Ireland final had started before the semi-finals.

Tommy Lyons managed Dublin to the 2002 Leinster title.

Instead, Dublin's drive for Sam was halted in the cruellest possible manner right at the death of a tight and exciting game against the Ulster champions. Ray Cosgrove had been scoring goals for fun all summer but his last-minute free kick from 30 yards to the left of the Hill 16 goal to level the game struck the upright and away to safety as referee Michael Collins blew the final whistle. Armagh 1–14 Dublin 1–13.

Another capacity crowd had witnessed a different type of Armagh performance to the cagey, fearful displays against Sligo. They never opened up a substantial enough lead to justify the customary retreat. A Paddy McKeever goal gave Armagh a 1–7 to 0–7 lead after 42 minutes but Ciaran Whelan equalised immediately with one of the goals of the season and Dublin enjoyed a two-point lead on three occasions, forcing Armagh to chase the game. Ironically, this brought the best out of their forwards especially Ronan Clarke, Stevie McDonnell and John McEntee, who scored three second-half points.

On the other side of the draw, Kerry survived three meetings with Cork and the alien terrain of the back-door to book their place in the final and the prospect of atonement for their surrender to Meath in the 2001 semi-final. They drew the Munster semi-final against Cork 0–8 to 0–8 in a game ruined by some terrible weather. Páidí Ó Sé's brother Mike – father of Darragh, Tomás and Marc – died suddenly the following week so Kerry were understandably distracted when they lost the replay 0–15 to 1–9. Kerry dished out hefty defeats to Wicklow, Fermanagh and Kildare in the qualifiers and were flying again by the time they arrived in Croke Park for their quarter-final against reigning All-Ireland champions Galway. O'Mahony's team had limped through Connacht and it was quickly apparent that the efforts of the previous two seasons had drained their will and appetite for more success. Jarlath Fallon, Michael Donnellan, Seán Óg de Paor and Kieran Fitzgerald had all been substituted by the 58th minute as Kerry played exhibition football. Mike Frank Russell and the Kingdom's latest wunderkind Colm 'Gooch' Cooper kicked four points apiece from play. Seán O'Sullivan and Eoin Brosnan ruled midfield and Tomás Ó Sé, Darragh Ó Sé, Dara Ó Cinnéide and Seamus Moynihan had recovered their All-Ireland winning form of 2000.

The underdog story of the championship should have been Tipperary, their 30-year-old manager Thomas McGlinchey and a first Munster senior football title in 67 years. Tipp led well into the second half of a Munster football final played in Semple Stadium with Declan Browne kicking eights points in a performance that secured him Tipp's first football All-Star award. Cork, who brought Diarmuid 'The Rock' O'Sullivan on as a sub with 20 minutes left, retained enough composure to overtake the underlings for a one-point lead but Tipp wing-back Niall Kelly scored a late equaliser to level the match. Final score: Tipperary 1–14 Cork 2–11.

Cork won the replay comfortably but their season ended with an All-Ireland semi-final annihilation by Kerry in Croke Park on 26 August. Cooper, Ó Cinnéide and Russell scored 2–14 between them as Kerry clinically took Cork apart. Darragh Ó Sé produced another virtuoso display at midfield and Seamus Moynihan hounded and frustrated Colin Corkery who was sent off after flinging the ball at referee Brian White. Fionán Murray had already seen red and Kerry, who led by 2–9 to 0–3 at half-time, advanced to a third All-Ireland final in five years. Final score: Kerry 3–19 Cork 2–7.

There are two ways of viewing the outcome of the 2002 All-Ireland football final. For Kerry it was the story of another mystifying loss of concentration and heart by the most gifted group of footballers in the country. And there was no Maurice Fitzgerald around this time to salvage the situation for Páidí and Kerry when some of the Kingdom's marque players went missing when they were most needed. The forwards who had scored 14–90 en route to the decider only kicked three points in the second half of a final that should have been wrapped up with half an hour still to play. The case for Armagh is one of industry, resilience and the often underrated quality of some of their forwards who again proved that there was more to the team than the negativity of the massed defence. Steven McDonnell, Diarmaid Marsden and Ronan Clarke scored three points each from play and Oisín McConville had the vision and class to find a path to goal at a time when Armagh could well have collapsed.

The 'swarm tactics' were rendered meaningless as Kerry powered into a four-point half-time lead 0–11 to 0–7. Armagh had no choice but to chase the game, play football and abandon their ascetic defensive approach. Oisín McConville had missed a penalty three minutes before the break but Marsden's point with the last kick of the half was a critical boost as they headed back into the dressing room to face the wrath of Big Joe. His half-time performance has become part of Armagh mythology. Kernan became euphemistically 'emotional' and flung the trinket he received for his efforts as a losing player in the 1977 All-Ireland

Kieran McGeeney brings Sam to Armagh.

final against Dublin off the dressing room wall to reinforce his call to arms.

It was a symbolic gesture of defiance but Armagh didn't look any more inspired after the break than they had before it. Kerry still owned possession in the first 10 minutes, although their four consecutive wides gave Armagh breathing space to regroup and launch their all-out burst for glory. McGeeney upped his contribution from centre-back and Paul McGrane and John Toal slowly broke even at midfield but Armagh still trailed by 0–14 to 0–10 when Dara Ó Cinnéide pointed a 45 in the 52nd minute. It was Kerry's last score and, from the kick-out, Armagh engineered a goal that turned the game on its head. Diarmaid Marsden raced out of the corner and won Tierney's kick-out. He laid the ball off to wing-back Andy McCann who played it through to McConville. He played a one-two with midfielder McGrane and, on the return ball, McConville powered a low shot from a tight angle past Declan O'Keeffe. Kerry were stunned by the setback and points from Ronan Clarke and Stevie McDonnell put Armagh ahead by one with seven minutes to go. It was then that Armagh's greater familiarity with survival on the defensive tightrope kicked in. Neither side scored in the final 10 minutes. Justin McNulty made some critical interceptions as Kerry, awake at last, sought the winning scores but the All-Ireland was lost when Eoin Brosnan kicked a straightforward 21-yard free wide in the 70th minute.

The usual scenes of joyful pandemonium followed the final whistle, as Kieran McGeeney raised the Sam Maguire and Armagh became the fifth Ulster county to win an All-Ireland title. They surrendered it the following year to Tyrone, their bitterest rivals, as Gaelic football headed into ever more contro-versial territory with Páidí Ó Sé and his Kerry team caught in the eye of the maelstrom.

Armagh All-Ireland Football Champions 2002

Benny Tierney

Enda McNulty   Justin McNulty   Francie Bellew

Aidan O'Rourke   Kieran McGeeney   Andrew McCann

John Toal   Paul McGrane

Paddy McKeever   John McEntee   Oisín McConville

Steven McDonnell   Ronan Clarke   Diarmaid Marsden

Subs: Barry O'Hagan for McEntee,
Tony McEntee for Paddy McKeever

'It's been a difficult year but hopefully, now, it's behind us. Withdrawing our services was the last resort. Without going into negotiations and without withdrawing our services I don't think we'd be where we are now. I don't think we would have got what we got tonight.'

Cork hurler Joe Deane, December 2002

Jimmy Barry Murphy was more than just a manager for the Cork team between 1996 and 2000. Like Jim 'Tough' Barry in 1966, he was a father figure and mentor, in the true sense of the word, to his players and it took Cork hurling two years to recover from his departure. When Jimmy Barry retired, he was replaced by one of his selectors Tom Cashman who, in turn, stepped down after Cork's shock 1–16 to 1–15 defeat to Limerick in the first round of the 2001 Munster championship. Bertie Óg Murphy, who had managed the Cork under-21s to two All-Ireland titles and served as a selector in 2000, was next into the hot seat but, by 2002, revolution was in the air after Cork's dismal collapse against Galway in an All-Ireland qualifier game in Thurles.

Galway won the game 0–21 to 1–9, only their fourth ever victory in 27 championship clashes with the Rebels, and the Cork players' desultory demeanour suggested that there was something seriously amiss in the camp. The Cork squad had no issues with Bertie Óg, who resigned as manager a few months later, but relations between the players and some prominent County Board officials had soured badly since Jimmy Barry's retirement. There was a collective feeling among the players that they were being treated shabbily in comparison with their counterparts in counties such as Tipperary, Clare and Kilkenny.

The players' grievances focused on fundamental issues, such as the provision of adequate training facilities and gear, travelling expenses, compensation for lost earnings and the right to join the fledgling Gaelic Players' Association (GPA). Some players also resented the continued influence and interference of the Cork County secretary Frank Murphy who had been nominated as a team selector by his club, Blackrock, in 2002. Relations between County Board officials and the players nosedived irreparably early in 2002 when the team were told that they would have to travel by bus on a Friday for a Saturday league match in Derry rather than flying to the North as they had done for the corresponding fixture in 2000. The players later claimed that Niall McCarthy, who suffered a head wound in the Derry game, was neglected by board officials and left to arrange his own medical assistance when the team returned to Cork.

The league match in Derry was the point of no return for the players who also claimed that they were pressured not to join the GPA. Mark Landers, team captain in 1999, later revealed that, a few days after attending the 2002 GPA EGM in Portlaoise in April, a Cork official had approached him during a training session in Páirc Uí Chaoimh and warned him to 'take a good look around because you won't be seeing this place again'. Landers was dropped from the panel before being called back into the team for the Munster championship game Cork lost to Waterford.

The Cork players' expressed their growing militancy by staging a symbolic protest during the 2002 National Hurling League final against Kilkenny, a week after the GPA EGM in Portlaoise. During the pre-match parade, they marched around Semple Stadium with their jerseys hanging out and their socks down, an action that, under GAA regulations, would incur a fine for the County Board. The protest had been mooted by the GPA and, while the Kilkenny players had initially agreed to do likewise in sympathy, only one, Andy Comerford, supported the Cork action. War had been declared. Some of the Cork players went public with their grievances after the Galway game in July but there was no sign of the County Board negotiating on any of their demands. If anything, the attitude towards the players hardened in some quarters. While the Cork hurling row was brewing, another Corkman Roy Keane had quit the Irish World Cup squad in Saipan for not dissimilar reasons to those troubling his hurling brothers back home. His 'fail to prepare, prepare to fail' mantra struck a chord with the Cork players and, during the summer months, they moved towards an action, as headline-grabbing as Keane's exit from Saipan.

Talks between the Cork players and the County Board broke down in November. On Friday, 29 November, the players called a press conference in a Cork city hotel and announced that they were withdrawing their services with immediate effect. Cork

Cork hurlers' press conference where they declared a strike in November 2002.

hurlers were on strike. It was a sensational development and the County Board's initial reaction was to go on the offensive. They claimed the players' demand for reimbursement of lost earnings was evidence of creeping professionalism: 'Ignore the smoke-screen; this is about more than tracksuits and travel. We're fighting for one of the most basic principles of the GAA here, the right to run the organisation as an amateur body,' claimed one official. It was a clever but unsuccessful ploy as the public, the GPA and other county teams weighed in behind the players.

The plot thickened when the County Board Executive met the following Tuesday night and played a shrewd political game. It announced that all the existing selectors, had resigned and that the next Cork manager could pick his own selectors. But the executive also went through the players' grievances one by one and gave their, ostensibly reasonable, version of events before empower-ing new County Chairman, Jim Forbes, to reopen negotiations with the players. Led by Donal Óg Cusack, Joe Deane and Seán Óg Ó hAilpín, the players stood firm and while they issued a statement noting the board's actions both 'publicly and privately', the strike remained intact. The players maintained none of their grievances had been clearly addressed and no firm commitments given by the board. To complicate matters, the Cork football squad came out in support of the hurlers the next day.

A truce was declared on Friday, 13 December following a meeting in the Silver Springs Hotel between board officials and representatives from both the hurling and football teams. Sensing that they had lost the propaganda war, the board capitulated completely. Apart from confirming the new system for the appointment of selectors, they agreed to fund gym membership for players, upgrade catering facilities at Páirc Uí Chaoimh and ensure that a team doctor would be present at all Cork games. Because of GAA regulations, the board couldn't give definitive concessions on issue such as mileage, reimbursement and allocation of match tickets, but agreed to forward the players recommendation to Central Council and lobby on their behalf. It was a total victory for the players and a humbling *volte face* for the County Board.

A new manager, Donal O'Grady, was appointed and, under his guidance, Cork hurlers soon reasserted their dominance on the pitch while the Cork County Board established unrivalled standards for player welfare.

The Cork hurlers' successful stand was also a turning point for the GPA and propelled that organisation past its teething difficulties into a respected national voice for the interests of inter-county hurlers and footballers. 'By standing together, the Cork men had proven their power,' wrote GPA Chief Executive Dessie Farrell in his autobiography *Tangled Up in Blue*. 'Images of Joe Deane, Seán Óg Ó hAilpín and Donal Óg Cusack making their public stand sent out a potent message to the GAA. The massive support enjoyed by the players also indicated to officials everywhere how out of touch they were with their own grass-roots. Since our inception, the GPA has been accused of being elitist; only interested in the top counties, only interested in endorsement deals for the star players. However, we had already opened up a can of worms in the weaker hurling counties. We were swamped with complaints from hurlers from nearly every county outside of the top-flight counties. Before the stand taken by Cork's "top players", no one was particularly interested in the plight of the minnows. Now their voice was strengthened and they too would be empowered to speak out against their poor treatment.'

The brainchild of a group of Ulster footballers, the GPA had been formally launched in Belfast in September 1999 followed by a national launch in Dublin in December. The new organisation had gained publicity for its campaigns on issues such as mileage rates but everyone knew that the big battle lay in the area of players getting paid – independently of the GAA – for product endorsements. In August 2000, the GPA had announced a £50,000 sponsorship package with the Marlborough Recruitment Agency involving 10 leading players. This was the start of the process that eventually forced the GAA to concede the right of players to negotiate their own endorsements without any money accruing to county boards or the GAA centrally.

In the meantime, the GPA struggled to attract members even though high-profile figures such as D.J. Carey, Brian Lohan, Kieran McGeeney and Dessie Farrell were on board. Former Armagh footballer Donal O'Neill, the public face of the GPA, was thrown out of GAA's Annual Congress in Galway in 2000 and, later that summer, was chased out of Hyde Park by Roscommon officials when he attempted to recruit some Roscommon players. Forty-five players attended the GPA's first AGM in November

2000 when Clare's Jamesie O'Connor was elected President and Kerry's Seamus Moynihan, Secretary. During 2001, membership increased to 450 players although no players from Meath had come on board and just two Cork hurlers Donal Óg Cusack and Brian Corcoran had joined up.

The GAA remained hostile towards the organisation but the GPA, led by its then chairman Dessie Farrell, slowly bedded down. It negotiated a major sponsorship deal with the Carphone Warehouse, and commissioned an actuary's report that concluded inter-county players suffered an average loss of income of between €100,000 and €180,000 during their playing careers. It upped the ante further by announcing a campaign calling for a flat payment of €127 a week in reimbursement for all inter-county players. This was never likely to happen, but it did force the GAA to address the issue and compensate players adequately for their efforts in the form of improved mileage rates, holiday funds and medical cover.

The first meetings between the GPA and the GAA took place in 2002 but conflict resumed in 2003 when the GPA launched its own Club Energise drink in conjunction with drinks company Cantrell & Cochran. This was a huge deal, worth €10 million over 10 years to the GPA, and has seen the organisation establish scholarship schemes and a benevolent fund. It secured the GPA's future but provoked an angry response from the GAA, which banned all advertising for the product from its grounds and, in 2005, forced RTÉ to ban post-match shots of players swigging from their isotonic drink of choice.

In time, the GAA's stance on the Club Energiser affair will be seen as petty and futile. With 1,400 members, the GPA is here to stay and Dessie Farrell's appointment this season as the players' representative on Central Council represents de facto GAA recognition for the association. The next big battle is likely to be

GPA Chief Executive, Dessie Farrell.

about image rights and the players' entitlement to a percentage of the revenue the GAA earns from RTÉ and other broadcasters. Dessie Farrell believes that, long term, the GAA may have to face the reality of semi-professionalism for the leading players. It's already on the way judging by Tyrone captain Brian Dooher's decision to take several months off work this year to concentrate on football. Whatever the future holds for the GPA, it has ensured that players are no longer viewed as a necessary evil by some officials. Thankfully, the days of the Croke Park post-match voucher for one free pint of beer and hurlers such as D.J. Carey having to run around a dog track in Kilkenny to raise funds for a team holiday are over.

2003

Positively Ruthless

'Deep down, Kerry people don't like to lose. Being a Kerry manager is probably the hardest job in the world because Kerry people, I'd say, are the roughest type of f**kin' animals you could ever deal with… It's a big year for Kerry and Páidí Ó Sé.'

Kerry manager Páidí Ó Sé, January 2003

'Kill or be killed. That's the law of Croke Park.'

Tyrone manager Mickey Harte, *Kicking Down Heaven's Door: Diary of a Football Manager*, 2003

MICHAEL D. HIGGINS, THE LABOUR TD for Galway and poet, isn't noted as a great GAA man but he did hurling and football supporters a lasting service when, in spite of a lot of myopic opposition, he stubbornly forced through government funding for TG4 in 1997. The new station was quick to identify the shortcomings in RTÉ's GAA coverage. Apart from realising that a significant audience existed for live club, league and under-21 matches and women's football, it also did younger generations of GAA followers a serious favour with its reruns of classic matches from the late 1960s onwards. They gave a new generation the opportunity to appreciate the past and reconsider the myths that had accrued around particular teams and matches.

Take the 1977 All-Ireland semi-final between Dublin and Kerry. For years, we were assured ad nauseaum that it was the greatest game of football ever played. Maybe it was for those who were there and caught up in the magic of the Dublin–Kerry cycle between 1975 and 1978 but modern coaches such as John O'Mahony, Mickey Harte or Jack O'Connor would probably dissapprove of the number of missed tackles, bad tackles, mis-kicked passes and wides in the game. In its defence, the second half of the match was exciting and elemental and there were some great exponents of Gaelic football on the field but, while it may have been a classic of its particular era, it doesn't compare favourably with, for example, three games from the 2005 championship – the All-Ireland final between Tyrone and Kerry; the second Tyrone–Armagh replay; and the Laois–Dublin Leinster final.

That is how it should be. Gaelic football, like any healthy sport, should be in a state of continuous revolution. Tactics evolve, the balance of power shifts and what might once have seemed breathtaking and innovative invariably loses its lustre when viewed with a dispassionate modern eye. Evolution in team sports doesn't always equate to improvement especially when the emphasis is on power and speed at the expense of skill or indivi-dual expression. Sports go through peaks and troughs of excellence but an objective evidence of the *All-Ireland Gold* series suggests that Gaelic football in 2005 is faster, more skilful, cleaner and a lot more competitive and interesting than it was in 1995, 1985 or 1975.

After the 2005 All-Ireland final, some commentators were talking about an extended spell of Tyrone supremacy. John O'Mahony, not a man given to exaggeration, suggested they could become one of the greatest teams the game has ever seen after they defeated Kerry with an exhilarating display of athleticism, teamwork, disciplined tackling, point scoring from distance and some transcendent moments from Peter Canavan, Brian McGuigan and Stephen O'Neill. Dick Fitzgerald, a Kerryman who played in eight All-Ireland finals and devised the first Gaelic football coaching manual might have approved. 'Gaelic football fortunately does not tend in the direction of reducing its players to the mere machine level,' he wrote in *How to Play Gaelic Football* published in 1914. 'True it is that combination – and combination of a sufficiently high standard – is much prized. Each player is taught to see the advantage of combining with everybody else on his side and of playing at all times unselfishly. But, such is the genius of the game itself that while combination will always be prominent, the brilliant individual gets his opportunities time out of mind, with the result that, after the match is over, you will generally have a hero or two carried enthusiastically off the field on the shoulders of their admirers.' Nine decades after Fitzgerald defined his ideal of the game, a high standard of combination play, unselfishness and some individual brilliance were the hallmarks of a Tyrone team whose tactics two years earlier against Kerry had been lambasted as the potential ruination of Gaelic football.

❖

Comerford's Cats
Halt Setanta's Glory Quest

He came, he saw and while he didn't quite conquer Croke Park, Setanta Ó hAilpín made a valuable, if fleeting, contribution to Cork hurling's return to the top after their 2002 winter of discontent. If there was such as thing as the prototype 21st-century hurler, Setanta fitted the bill. Everything from the legendary echoes of his Christian name to his eye-catching athleticism and penchant for finding the net marked him out as a potential superstar when he was unveiled by the Donal O'Grady and the Cork selectors for the 2003 championship.

At 6 feet 5 inches and built to match, Setanta was a natural target man and one of the most charismatic characters the GAA had seen since the summer of 1995 and Jason Sherlock's arrival on the big stage. Unfortunately for Cork, and the game of hurling, Setanta only played one season as a senior and, within weeks of the 2003 All-Ireland final, he had flown to Australia to begin a new life as an Australian Rules player with the Carlton club in Melbourne.

Cork went very close to winning Setanta an All-Ireland medal before his departure to Oz but came up short by three points, 1–14 to 1–11, against a more-experienced Kilkenny team. It was a tense and intriguing decider in which Martin Comerford, another young giant, proved to be Kilkenny's match winner. A low-profile character compared to Setanta, Comerford scored 1–4 in a Man of the Match performance ▶

Setanta Ó hAilpín, Cork's young sensation.

on Diarmuid O'Sullivan. Comerford levelled the game for Kilkenny in the 60th minute and, five minutes later, scored the decisive goal after Henry Shefflin created the opening.

With D.J. Carey having another quiet All-Ireland final, Comerford's contribution was vital and his goal cancelled out a similar effort from Setanta in the 54th minute that appeared to have swung the initiative Cork's way. D.J. Carey got to lift the McCarthy Cup as captain for the first time and it was a fitting response to some tabloid newspapers intrusion into his personal life in the weeks leading up to the final.

While Kilkenny celebrated their 28th title, Cork reflected on what had been a dramatic return to form after the chaos and controversy of 2002. Donal O'Grady's rejuvenated side were involved in the two best games of the year – the Munster final against Waterford and the drawn All-Ireland semi-final against Wexford.

The Munster final in Páirc Uí Chaoimh on 30 June was a cracker with Cork edging out Waterford by 3–16 to 3–12. Waterford led by 1–8 to 1–1 after 20 minutes but Cork upped the ante after half-time and led by three points before John Mullane scored his third goal in the 55th minute. Along with Setanta and Martin Comerford, Mullane was one of the players of the year, but not even his heroics could see Waterford hold on to the Munster title they had won in such spellbinding fashion the previous summer.

Waterford never hit the same heights in their qualifier against Wexford and it was the Leinster team, who had been beaten by 11 points by Kilkenny in the Leinster final, that advanced to the All-Ireland semi-final against Cork on 10 August. Apart from the Munster final, it had been a poor enough year of hurling but this match was a real classic as Wexford once again revealed the duality of their hurling nature. The side that had been overwhelmed in the second half of the Leinster final was transformed into a gutsy, tactically aware group of players who picked off some wonderful scores. Veteran campaigners such as Liam Dunne, Larry O'Gorman, Adrian Fenlon and Larry Murphy hurled out of their skins and an early goal from Paul Codd, and some good scores from the two Jacobs, Michael and Rory, saw Wexford take a 1–11 to 0–10 half-time lead.

There were 22 more scores in the second half and Cork looked in serious trouble after 45 minutes when they trailed by six points. Setanta then intervened with one of his trademark fetches and bursts to score a kicked goal and gave Cork a lifeline. They then fired over five points without reply and Joe Deane scored Cork's second goal with 10 minutes left to push the Munster team five clear. Mitch Jordan scored a second Wexford goal with three minutes on the clock but Cork remained three points ahead deep into injury-time until Rory McCarthy ran onto a pass from Jordan and let fly from 30 yards with a shot that rocketed into the top left-hand corner of Donal Cusack's goal at the Hill 16 end. There was time for no more after a game in which hurling had again crossed the line between sport and art. Final score: Cork 2–20 Wexford 3–17. The replay, six days

Martin Comerford of Kilkenny.

later, was a terrible disappointment for Wexford and their supporters. Cork led by five points at half-time and they went to win by 3–17 to 2–7. In the All-Ireland final, the younger Rebels' lack of Croke Park experience and some poor shooting denied the Cork players the ultimate vindication for their strike action the previous November – but honour had been restored and O'Grady and his players made no mistake the second time of asking against Kilkenny in 2004.

THERE HADN'T BEEN AS MUCH ANGST and analysis about 70 minutes of football since the 1996 All-Ireland final replay between Meath and Mayo. The tone of the post-match reaction in the days following 17 August 2003 suggested that Gaelic football was back in the intensive care unit Brendán Ó hEithir had prescribed for the game in 1984. 'House Private,' lamented Con Houlihan. 'Puke football,' spluttered Pat Spillane. 'Time to look at changing the rules,' mused Kerry County Board chairman, Sean Walsh. 'Neutrals in the 58,687 crowd – not to mention the hundreds of thousands watching on television all over the world – were made to suffer through an abomination of a game,' wrote Martin Breheny in the *Irish Independent*. 'One where the pernicious forces of negativity destroyed every flowering instinct quicker than a powerful weedkiller.'

The cause of all the hand-wringing was Tyrone's All-Ireland semi-final mastery of Kerry. Beforehand, the game had been hyped up as a shootout between the two best attacks in the game. Contrary to expectations, it unfolded as a dogmatic clash of cultures where Tyrone's sheer need prevailed over Kerry's belief that the 2002 loss to Armagh was an unfortunate blip and that their cuteness and innate virtuosity would soon restore the natural order. All the pre-match assumptions were scattered by Tyrone's whirlwind first 20 minutes when they blew the Kerry defence open with wave after wave of attack and deprived Páidí Ó Sé's team the most basic of possession. At times, it was hypnotic to watch as Tyrone players, such as Seán Cavanagh, Brian McGuigan, Enda McGinley and Stephen O'Neill, who had starred in the 1998 All-Ireland minor and 2000 and 2001 under-21 victories, came of age as seniors in Croke Park.

The Ulster team lost their playmaker and talisman Peter Canavan to injury after 13 minutes but, such was the seam of quality in the squad, that they were able to replace Canavan

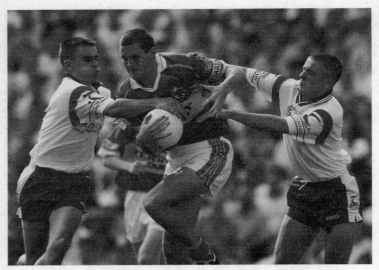

Eoin Brosnan (Kerry) is surrounded by Ryan McMenamin and Ciaran Gourley (Tyrone) in the All-Ireland football semi-final.

with O'Neill without any disruption to the system. Tyrone were six ahead before Colm Cooper scored Kerry's first in the 25th minute and, by then, Kerry were bamboozled by an opposition gameplan that erased conventional notions of backs and forwards, attack and defence. Kerry goalkeeper Declan O'Keeffe remarked afterwards that 'the midfield area was like New York City going down Times Square... It was a weird kind of football.' When a Kerryman won possession, he was surrounded by a phalanx of Tyrone players and either had to surrender possession or commit a foul in an attempt to break free. There was an incident after 15 minutes where Eoin Brosnan slipped in possession and found himself surrounded by eight Tyrone players. Frustration and tempers flared and foul upon foul followed. Referee Gerry Kinneavy played seven minutes of injury-time and, when he blew for half-time, Tyrone led 0–9 to 0–2.

The first 20 minutes were Tyrone at their best; the 30 minutes after half-time reflected their obsession with burying the ghosts of Croke Park past. Instead of pressing on and adding more scores, they defended the lead and were satisfied to kill the game around midfield with persistent fouling, knowing that they had the defensive edge to deprive Kerry's inside-forwards a consistent supply scoring opportunities. Kerry didn't collapse as they had done against Meath in 2001, but they missed some good scoring chances and were a demoralised side before Tyrone finished with another flourish that was a reminder of the depth of footballing talent in the team. The 2001 All-Star Stephen O'Neill and Brian Dooher, one of the older players whose selfless running and work rate was indicative of the team's ethos, scored three points to round off Tyrone's 0–13 to 0–6 passage to the county's third All-Ireland final, the first since 1995.

When the final whistle sounded, a middle-aged Kerryman clambered down to the sideline from the Hogan Stand and attempted to land a haymaker on Páidí Ó Sé. Páidí deflected the punch but his days as Kerry manager were numbered following the county's third successive championship defeat in Croke Park. It was his and Kerry's misfortune that, just as they recovered from the 2001 flop against Meath, they were knocked back again by the second coming of Ulster teams in a decade. The keening in the Kingdom after the game and national condemnation of Tyrone's tactics was over-the-top and simplistic. It didn't give the Ulster team due credit for the football they had played all year or attempt to understand the rationale behind their Armagh-style retreat in the second half of the 2003 semi-final.

The irony wasn't lost on students of the game with long memories who recalled Kerry's controversial 1946 All-Ireland semi-final victory over Antrim. Led by Kevin Armstrong, that Antrim team had pioneered a fast-moving, short-passing game but were unceremoniously halted in their tracks by Joe Keohane and Kerry. There was widespread outrage about Kerry's alleged cynical approach and Antrim appealed the result to Central Council, losing the vote by 21–10. Joe Keohane was unimpressed by the fuss and, years later, surmised that Antrim 'kept coming at us the same way all the time, inviting us to foul them when they should have switched the plan of attack and gone for long-range points. To win an All-Ireland you have to be prepared to hit your opponents hard. We hit them hard that day, within the rules. There's no room for softness or sympathy when you are in there battling to win a place in the All-Ireland final or battling for the title itself.' Kill or be killed. The law of Croke Park.

Tyrone had uncorked plenty of champagne football in the league, beating Cork by 1–17 to 0–14 in the quarter-final, Fermanagh by 4–11 to 1–11 in the semi and Mick O'Dwyer's Laois by 0–21 to 1–8 in the final. They looked fragile and uncertain when trailing by four points to Derry in the Ulster quarter-final, but Canavan and two late subs, Gerald Cavlan and Kevin Hughes, kicked the last four points to level the game. *Sunday Game* analyst and former Derry footballer Joe Brolly labelled their display 'spineless' and Tyrone responded by winning the replay 0–17 to 1–5, with under-21 midfielder Seán Cavanagh scoring three points and Peter Canavan landing eight from frees. Whatever else Tyrone were, they weren't spineless. They conceded four goals against Down in the Ulster final, and were 3–8 to 0–8 down after 45 minutes, but still rallied to draw an Ulster cracker 4–8 to 1–17. Dan Gordon scored Down's fourth goal with five minutes left to cancel Tyrone's comeback, but Harte's team rallied again and levelled the game with points from Owen Mulligan, Ciarán Gourley and a free won and converted by Peter Canavan. Mickey Harte made one of his shrewdest calls of the season when he switched Cormac McAnallen, one of his former underage stars, from midfield to full-back for the replay. This time there were no leaks in the previously suspect Tyrone defence. Dan Gordon, Down's chief plunderer the first day, was held scoreless. He didn't get a touch of the ball in the first 20 minutes as Kevin Hughes and Cavanagh lorded it in midfield. Tyrone led by 0–11 to 0–2 and ran out 0–23 to 1–5 winners, Down's goal coming in injury-time. Peter Canavan scored 11 of his side's total and the presentation of the Anglo-Celt Cup was an emotional experience for the Tyrone captain whose father, Sean, had died two weeks previously.

To understand the tactical logic behind Tyrone's blitzkrieg and sudden retreat against Kerry in the semi-final, you have to appreciate their recent history in Croke Park. They led Kerry by seven points in the second half of the 1986 All-Ireland final but lost by eight. They were denied a legitimate-looking injury-time equaliser against Dublin in the 1995 decider and lost by a point. The following year, they returned home from the All-Ireland semi-final convinced that they had allowed themselves be physically and mentally bullied off the pitch by Meath. Worst of all, in 2002, they led Sligo by 0–9 to 0–2 after 20 minutes but then fell apart and lost by five. Mickey Harte was appointed manager in November 2002, taking over from Art McRory and Eugene McKenna. He realised that, for all the talent and commitment in Tyrone, the mindset had to be changed if they were to fulfil their potential in Croke Park and win the county's first All-Ireland title. He had the same single-mindedness as Ger Loughnane in the pursuit of his goals. Loughnane's gospel was one of 'demonic ferocity' and Harte's vision for his team was that they would be 'positively ruthless'. Harte was determined to set the record straight on Tyrone's 2002 loss to Sligo, the county's other failures in Croke Park and the perception that they were tidy wee footballers who didn't have the bottle for senior success.

Harte kept a diary during the 2003 season which he published at the end of the year (in collaboration with the journalist Kieran Shannon) under the title *Kicking Down Heaven's Door: Diary of a Football Manager*. There are repeated references to Sligo or the 'S-word' and the entry for 3 August, the night of Tyrone's 1–21 to 0–5 victory over Fermanagh in the All-Ireland quarter-final in Croke Park says it all. 'Every one of yesterday's and today's newspapers made some reference to the Sligo game. At last night's meeting, we showed some of the cuttings from the morning papers. They were saying that there was going to be at least one shock from the four games this weekend and that of the four favourites Tyrone had the most temperamental fuse. In every paper, the ghost of Sligo was being shoved into our face as if to make sure it would work again. Today we gave the proper response to that. We were positively ruthless.' Tyrone never let up against Fermanagh even though they led 1–11 to 0–2 at half-time.

In his diary, Harte admitted feeling sorry for Fermanagh manager Martin McElkennon's predicament but he 'didn't feel sorry for what we did today. Last year, Tyrone won their first league, beat Derry in the qualifiers, yet our year was remembered for one game – Sligo. Better that their [Fermanagh's] year be reduced to one game than ours. We're not in the business of being sympathetic, we're in the business of being ruthless.'

Like Clare hurlers and Loughnane, the Tyrone players drive on the field and new-found willingness to go to any lengths to achieve success was a mirror of their manager's personality. Harte had managed Tyrone minors and under-21s to three All-Ireland titles between 1998 and 2001 but there were still people in the county who didn't think he was the right man for the county senior team when he took over. His critics obviously didn't grasp the extent of Harte's preoccupation with Tyrone football and his own personal journey from bearded outcast to stubble-faced prophet.

In the 1980s, Harte lost the best years of his own playing

career when Glencull, his end of Ballygawley parish, seceded from Ballygawley St Ciaran's GAA Club following a dispute in an internal parish league match between the church area of Glencull and the church area of Dunmoyle. Harte, a county player, was Glencull's player manager and he got involved in a fracas that led to his suspension as a player and manager. While his sparring partner from Dunmoyle was allowed to represent Ballygawley at handball, Harte was barred from even standing on the sideline at Glencull's next game. Incensed at what they felt was Ballygawley's harsh treatment of Harte, Glencull – home of the Canavans – decided to break away from Ballygawley and form their own club. Glencull applied for affiliation at the annual county convention six times between 1982 and 1988 and each time the application was rejected, even though the Ulster Council had recommended Glencull be allowed to go their own way. 'For the next six years, Sean Canavan, Peter Quinliven and myself would go there and every time the board would reject the recommendation of the Ulster Council,' recalled Harte. 'I went up to Crossmolina to visit Mick Loftus when he was GAA President but, again, he was powerless. The board was not going to back down to these bearded rebels from Glencull.'

In one of the most unusual GAA splits of all, Glencull, in spite of their non-status within Tyrone GAA, functioned as a de facto club for six years. 'We were like a club in every other way. We ran dances and functions. We held committee meetings, fundraising meetings, we held Irish-language classes. We ran nine-a-side tournaments on our own pitch. We coached underage teams, including some handy young fellas like Eoin Gormley, Seamus Mallon and one wee lad called Peter Canavan. Our adult team would go and play in any and every county in the rest of Ulster. We'd often play in Fermanagh, Armagh and especially teams from South Derry.' But, after seven years in the wilderness, even Harte's enthusiasm was beginning to wane for the phantom GAA club of Glencull. The split was damaging on and off the field for both sides. Ballycawley weren't that far off winning a county championship but needed the Glencull players and the Canavans, especially Stephen and 'the wee lad called Peter'.

Because of the split, the future legend never played any underage club football in his own county and had to register with Killyclogher hurling club to secure legitimate status for selection on the Tyrone minor football team. The arrival of a new priest, Fr Sean Hegarty from Armagh, began the peace process between Glencull and Ballygawley. In 1990, a new united parish club named Errigal Ciaran was formed.

Back in the Tyrone GAA fold, the Glencull men quickly made an impact beyond the parish borders. Peter Canavan led the county to the 1991 All-Ireland under-21 title, scoring 2–5 in the final against Kerry. Harte was appointed manager of the county minor team the same year and, two years later, was a sub when the Tyrone county title returned to Ballygawley for the first time since 1932. Harte was 28 when Glencull seceded from Ballygawley and 36 when the dispute was settled. 'It finished my inter-county career,' he wrote in his 2003 diary. 'But I can live with that because for what I lost on the field, I gained more from what I learned off it. I learned how to lead, how to nurture a cause, I learned that if you create a win–win situation like the birth of Errigal Ciaran, then that's the way to do things. And I learned that there's a stubborn streak in me. That at times, you have to fight, that at times you have to be "wicked wee men".'

Harte managed Tyrone minors from 1991 to 1998 and, during these years, he got to know most of the players who backboned the county's pursuit of the Sam Maguire. Harte's minors went through a lot together on and off the field. In 1997, Paul McGirr died from a punctured liver after a freak accident in an Ulster

Tyrone minors celebrate their Ulster title.

championship game against Down. 'I truly believe that in the days and weeks and months that followed that awful day, boys grew up in a short space of time. Boys learned to face and cope with adversity. Boys grew very close together. They learned to appreciate how precious life is and they learned to appreciate each other. I still feel that bond is with us.'

Paul McGirr's team-mates – including Brian McGuigan, Kevin Hughes, Cormac McAnallen, Mark Harte and Owen Mulligan – battled on and won the Ulster title before drawing the All-Ireland semi-final against Kerry. Two weeks later, they won the replay by 0–23 to 0–21 in one of the all-time great minor matches, though Laois proved a goal too good for Tyrone in the 1997 final. Harte had decided to pack it in after that game but was dissuaded by some of the players including O'Neill and McGuigan and, by August 1998, they were preparing for another All-Ireland semi-final when a Real IRA bomb killed 29 people in Omagh. In his diary entry for 15 August 2003, the fifth anniversary of the bomb, Harte remembered it as 'a horrible, horrible time. We had to go on. Again the circle met and talked about it and from that came strength. The following week, we beat Leitrim. The following month, we beat Laois in the All-Ireland. We had wanted to win anyway for ourselves and the spirit for Paul McGirr but Omagh was there in the background, knowing what the win would do for the people of the county. Now we are back trying to win something else for them. To give a lot of people a reason to go back into Omagh. God knows it's time it had something to celebrate.'

By the time Harte was appointed senior manager, he had guided most of his best minors to two All-Ireland under-21 titles and, along the way, evolved his own ideas about coaching and physical and psychological preparation. He brought in Paddy Tally as the team's physical trainer, Fr Gerard McAleer as a selector and set about making amends for the Sligo defeat and disproving the nay-sayers who argued that Tyrone were too small, had no midfield, weren't doing enough hard training and placed too much emphasis on the league. His intentions were clear from the start. 'I want to win every game, be it league, championship of even the McKenna Cup,' he wrote on 20 November. 'I think that's how you instil confidence and steel. They're the two qualities I feel I have to instil. I feel I can. The boys had to be steely to win those underage titles. Nobody can tell me that Peter Canavan isn't a winner, that he hasn't got steel. Nobody can tell me that Chris Lawn and Brian Dooher aren't winners, that they don't have steel. It just needs to permeate throughout the whole squad.'

Harte looked to a lot of different sources for inspiration. The American motivational guru George Zalucki will probably never know the role he played in Tyrone's first All-Ireland victory. Nor will the Soviet-era scientists whose pioneering systems for measuring the fitness levels of Olympic athletes were procured by the Tyrone management. Peter Canavan's brother-in-law chipped in with state-of-the-art performance-analysis video software. This attention to detail and strategic innovation was nothing new in Ulster football. Down and Joe Lennon had started it in the 1960s when they broke the stranglehold of basic 'catch-and-kick' tactics on the game. In the 1990s, Queen's University Sigerson Cup teams led the way in applying international sports science know-how to Gaelic football and Joe Kernan ranged from Manchester United to La Manga in his efforts to secure an edge for Armagh.

Tyrone's was a scientific approach, focused more on quality rather than quantity of training. The revelation that they only trained collectively two nights a week baffled some southern teams who were still convinced that the path to success lay in masochistic endurance-training regimes. Harte, a life-long tee-totaller, also placed a lot of trust in his players to look after themselves away from the group. They were, and still are, a fairly ascetic, as distinct from dour, group of men. It's one of the paradoxes of modern Ulster football that the values of industry, temperence and personal rectitude that would once have been loosely stereotyped as 'the Protestant work ethic' have been appropriated and taken a stage further by 'the other community' in the quest for All-Ireland success. It's the material of a doctoral thesis for some Ulster academic although due account would also have to be taken of the team's fondness for repeated renditions of 'Amhrán na bhFiann', the eclectic selection of tracks on the squad's match-day CD, and Harte's faith in religious relics, such as the piece of stained cloth from Padre Pio's cloak he produced in the dressing room before the All-Ireland final.

Any account of Tyrone's All-Ireland journey in 2003 has to consider the impact Frank McGuigan's well-publicised struggles with drink had on the collective Tyrone football consciousness. Harte had played minor with McGuigan in 1972 and rates him 'as the most complete footballer I or probably anyone has seen. We all knew Frank drank too much. Even when we were both minors we could all see he was getting drink too easily. It was being poured into him and Frank was too nice and bashful to say no. Frank was a phenomenon at 17 years of age. Everyone wanted a part of him. You're talking about a talent like George Best's, Maradona's, Pele's, genuinely. It's great to read that he's off the drink this past five years, that he's in control of his life, that's he able to cherish and relish these times with [his sons] Brian and Frank junior. I wouldn't be a Tyrone man if I didn't think what would it have been like had he given it up earlier. What if he hadn't gone to the States for those six years? Ireland, let alone Tyrone, didn't get to the chance to really see the quality he had. At least we can be grateful that he came back in 1984 and put on that 11-point exhibition against Armagh. That display inspired Peter Canavan to be the footballer he is today. Peter would have inspired most of our panel... Every Tyrone footballer, not just Brian and Frank, is, in a way, a son of Frank McGuigan. This is all about him too.'

THE ASCENDANCY OF ULSTER FOOTBALL in 2003 was confirmed when Joe Kernan's Armagh progressed to meet Tyrone in the final on 28 September, having defeated Laois in the quarterfinal. Laois, managed by Mick O'Dwyer, had won a first Leinster title in 57 years when they defeated Kildare 2–13 to 1–13 in a terrific Leinster final. Laois had no fear of Ulster opponents. Most of O'Dwyer's team had played in the 1997 and 1998 minor finals against Tyrone, but Armagh's experience and physical strength told in the final 20 minutes when they opened up a four-point gap by the 60th minute and defended the lead against a spirited Laois rally to win by 0–15 to 0–13.

Dublin led Armagh by four points at half-time in the All-

Ireland semi-final that followed but the Dublin management and defence lost the plot before and after the break. Tempers flared before half-time and, when the whistle went for the break, Tommy Lyons called his players back rather than risk a 'tunnel incident' with Armagh. Four minutes into the second half, Armagh's Paddy McKeever was sent off. It should have been advantage Dublin, but their defence conceded four soft frees that allowed Stevie McDonnell to level the game and goalkeeper Stephen Cluxton was red-carded for a rash if harmless off-the-ball swipe on McDonnell. Trying to match Armagh in the machismo stakes was a bad mistake and gifted the initiative to the Ulster team who scored 11 points to Dublin's three in the second half to win 0–15 to 0–11.

As expected, the 2003 All-Ireland final was a hard, sometimes nasty, and tactical battle as Ulster's finest slugged it out in a match that produced 10 yellow cards, and a questionable red card in the second half for Diarmaid Marsden. It was clear from the early exchanges that Armagh were intent on proving their traditional physical superiority and supposed edge in toughness. Seán Cavanagh took some big hits, but Tyrone survived the onslaught and looked the slicker and more skilful team whenever there was a fluent passage of play. They led by 0–5 to 0–3 after 20 minutes. Peter Canavan, who started the game with a badly injured ankle, kicked three points from frees and Ger Cavlan and Brian McGuigan added two good scores from play. Tyrone created several goal chances in the first half, the best falling to Enda McGinley just before half-time. He was clean though on goal but Armagh goalkeeper, Paul Hearty, deflected the shot over the bar to leave Armagh trailing 0–8 to 0–4 at the break.

Kernan's side had relied on Oisín McConville's frees and Stevie McDonnell's points from play to stay in touch and they were boosted by Peter Canavan's non-appearance for the second half. Brian McGuigan, though, was back on. He had been replaced by Stephen O'Neill and, when McGuigan returned to the fray, O'Neill again proved a worthy replacement for Canavan. Armagh slowly ate into Tyrone's lead but were given a taste of their own tactics when Tyrone pulled men back behind the ball, forcing Armagh to shoot from distance or attempt draining passing movements. They had closed the gap to two by the 55th minute, even though they had lost Marsden by that stage, but Tyrone were confident enough to break out and restore a three-point lead thanks to a fine effort from O'Neill. Owen Mulligan could have finished it but blasted a shot off the post.

Armagh had one final throw of the dice when McDonnell, the 'Killeavey sniper', found himself in possession, unmarked and 10 yards from the Tyrone goal two minutes from time. He prepared to shoot but, out of nowhere, Tyrone's right half-back Conor Gormley had tracked back and dived at an angle from behind McDonnell to execute a match-winning block that has entered Tyrone folklore as 'The Block'. Some people are convinced it was the greatest block ever seen in Croke Park and Tyrone survived

Tyrone win the All-Ireland football championship at last, Peter Canavan of Tyrone.

another Armagh attack to finish with a Stephen O'Neill free in injury-time to win their first All-Ireland title by 0–12 to 0–9.

Peter Canavan had been reintroduced by Harte towards the end of the game and, when he accepted the Sam Maguire, the journey from Glencull to Croke Park was complete. Canavan paid tribute to his own father, who had died during the summer, and Paul McGirr. He also acknowledged the contribution Art McRory and Eugene McKenna as well as previous generations of players, such as Frank McGuigan and Iggy Jones, had made to the success. It had been a long and hard trek to the pinnacle for Tyrone and there was a sense that, having made the breakthrough, there were no limits on the potential of this group of players. But four months later, their resolve was tested again by another grievous loss that shocked the entire GAA and Irish sporting world.

Tyrone All-Ireland Football Champions 2003

John Devine

Ciaran Gourley   Cormac McAnallen   Ryan McMenamin

Conor Gormley   Gavin Devlin   Philip Jordan

Seán Cavanagh   Kevin Hughes

Brian Dooher   Brian McGuigan   Ger Cavlan

Enda McGinley   Peter Canavan   Owen Mulligan

SUBS: Stephen O'Neill for Brian McGuigan, Brian McGuigan for Peter Canavan, Colin Holmes for Ciaran Gourley, Peter Canavan for Ger Cavlan, Chris Lawn for Conor Gormley

Cormac McAnallen

Cormac McAnallen's sudden death on the night of 2 March 2004 was another cruel and profound blow to the Tyrone team and a county that had experienced some harrowing losses over the years. He was just 24, but Tyrone had appointed him team captain as they prepared to defend their All-Ireland title and the many eloquent tributes paid to him after his death spoke as much about his leadership qualities, decency and depth of character as they did about his achievements as a footballer.

In Tyrone, they had always known he was special. He played on the two minor teams that reached All-Ireland finals in 1997 and 1998, captaining the 1998 team in their victory over Laois; and he was captain again when Mickey Harte's under-21 sides won their two All-Ireland titles in 2001 and 2002. Along the way, he was named the national Young Footballer of the Year in 2001, won a Sigerson title with Queen's University and also represented Ireland in the International Compromise Rules series tour of Australia in the autumn of 2003. His crowning achievement, of course, was winning an All-Ireland senior medal with Tyrone in 2003 when he reinvented himself as a full-back even though he had little experience of the position. It was when winning the Sam Maguire that McAnallen played three near-perfect games at No 3 to give the team a defensive solidity that had been lacking in their earlier championship games in 2003.

Mickey Harte had switched McAnallen to the edge of the square after Tyrone conceded four goals against Down in the drawn Ulster final and Harte's All-Ireland year diary entry for the first training session after that game makes for moving reading. 'I often say to the players, "You must try and learn something every session. You must strive to be a better player walking of the field than you were walking on to it." Cormac McAnallen is the embodiment of that. His intensity at every drill is a sight to behold. A training session with Cormac McAnallen is a better training session for him being there. It's as simple as that. He's incredibly mature, a real leader in a quiet, unassuming way. We knew he had the right stuff when we played him at centre-half with the minors in 1997 but he really bloomed when we made him captain in 1998. Fr Gerard noticed that when the boys split up into groups to talk about the aftermath of the Omagh bomb, a lot of the other players would say, 'I'll be in Cormac's group,' even though he mightn't say a word. They felt safe around Cormac. I feel safe with him being around the square on Sunday. Cormac McAnallen is gold.'

McAnallen's life beyond football had flowered in many different directions before his death from an undiagnosed heart condition in the small hours of the night at his family home in Eglish. He had started work as a teacher in St Catherine's College and his principal there Margaret Martin, spoke of him as being 'part of the new Ireland. Unafraid to stand up for his language, culture, sport. He just had a deep pride in his country and everything about it.' He had also become engaged in 2003 to his long-time girlfriend Aisling Moore and his life was rich in promise and potential until his sudden death at a time when he appeared to be in robust good health. As long as football is played in Tyrone, the name and life of Cormac McAnallen will never be forgotten.

2004

The Final Frontier

'Members of the British armed forces and police shall not be eligible for membership of the Association. A member of the Association participating in dances, or similar entertainment, promoted by or under the patronage of such bodies shall incur suspension of at least twelve weeks.'

GAA Official Guide 2001, Rule 21

'All property including grounds, Club Houses, Halls, Alleys owned or controlled by the Association shall be used only for the purpose of or in connection with the playing of the Games controlled by the Association, and for such other purposes not in conflict with the Aims and Objects of the Association that may be sanctioned from time to time by the Central Council. Grounds controlled by Association units shall not be used or permitted to be used for Horse Racing, Greyhound Racing or for Field Games other than those sanctioned by Central Council.'

GAA Official Guide 2005, Rule 42

THE GAA'S 2004 ANNUAL CONGRESS in Killarney was the Alamo moment for the forces of stasis and conservatism within the association. Besieged by a grassroots campaign to scrap Rule 42 and examine the option of opening up Croke Park to soccer and rugby, the traditionalists circled the wagons and made one last cunning stand in the weeks leading up to Congress.

Rather than run the risk of another democratic debate on Rule 42 at Congress, those opposed to change played their trump card in the form of the 'Motions Committee'. This committee, previously unknown to most ordinary members of the association, announced in the run-up to Congress that county convention-approved motions calling for the deletion or amendment of Rule 42 had been ruled out of order on 'technical grounds'. It was a clever but patently undemocratic boardroom somersault by the Motions Committee, which comprised 10 past presidents of the GAA and the Director General, Liam Mulvihill. Some of the motions ruled out of order on 'technical grounds' had been approved by the GAA's own Bye-Laws Committee. A motion that didn't satisfy the learned gaze of the Motions Committee had been voted on at a previous Congress. It was a triumph of autocracy and semantics over popular opinion and decency. It was also an embarrassment for the incumbent GAA President Seán Kelly, a long-time advocate for a relaxation of Rule 42.

Kelly had been severely criticised by some GAA figures for publicly voicing his opinion on the controversy in advance of Congress. In Killarney, he rounded on his critics with entertaining venom. 'Some individuals have questioned the right of the Uachtarán to express his personal opinion on this matter. One assumes that these critics are expressing their own personal opinions while wishing to deny me, An tUachtarán, the right to express mine. Wouldn't it be a remarkable state of affairs if everybody in the country was entitled to comment on what changes the country needed except the Taoiseach, or if all could suggest policy changes for the Church except the Pope?' Kelly then questioned how it benefited the GAA that a 'perfectly laudable, well thought-out idea can't be discussed because it's technically out of order'. In a final swipe at some of the past presidents and their supporters, he spoke of knowledge of the GAA's complex rules and bye-laws being the 'preserve of the few'. The past presidents – including Peter Quinn and Joe McDonagh who were understood to support change on Rule 42 – remained silent in the debate.

The King Canutes on the Motions Committee could only hold back the democratic tide so long. On 16 April 2005 at a Special Congress in Croke Park, GAA delegates voted by 227 votes to 97 in favour of a Sligo motion to temporarily relax Rule 42 and give the association's Central Council a mandate to rent Croke Park out to the FAI and the IRFU while Lansdowne Road was being redeveloped. Earlier in the day, there had been fears that the past presidents had struck again when Central Council decided that the vote on the Sligo motion should be decided on a secret ballot rather than a show of hands. Campaigners for a change feared that some delegates, mandated by their county conventions to vote in favour of a relaxation, might vote against change in a secret ballot and that the Sligo motion would fall short of the two-thirds majority required for its approval. 'The view when it went to secret ballot was that there might be considerable slippage when they came to vote but it shows that they obeyed the mandate. I think they reflected the views of grassroots members,' said Tommy Kenoy from Roscommon, a long-time campaigner for change. 'We needed a two-thirds majority and we got a two-thirds majority. It was very clear that the membership stood up and was counted. As a result, we have a truly democratic decision.' An tUachtarán Seán Kelly said delegates 'saw their neighbours were in need and

Some of the members of the Motion Committee: (from top left to right) Liam Mulvihill, Peter Quinn, Con Murphy, Pat Fanning, Joe McDonagh, Seán Kelly, Jack Boothman and Sean McCague.

reached out the hand of friendship to them. I think they have done something that is good for the GAA and also good for Ireland.'

Practical considerations as well as patriotic magnanimity had swayed some previously doubtful delegates towards a change on Rule 42. By the start of 2005, the annual running costs for Croke Park had reached €2.5 million. The GAA revealed the stadium actually ran at a loss for games that attracted crowds of less than 30,000. Rental income from the FAI and IRFU, if they sought the use of the stadium, would go a long way towards covering the running costs and subventing the 'unprofitable' matches. GAA personalities liked to boast about having 'the finest stadium in Europe' and it no longer made any financial sense to have the association's prize asset lying idle for two thirds of the year.

Cork and six Ulster counties – Antrim, Armagh, Down, Derry, Fermanagh and Tyrone – were the only counties to vote against change at the 2005 Special Congress. Prior to the vote, one of the past presidents Con Murphy from Cork declared that the 'association is being put out of existence if the vote goes in favour of all these amendments. If you support the motions you are supporting the formation of a new association which caters for everything and stands for nothing.' Another past president, Pat Fanning from Waterford, said, 'If we open Croke Park, we are abandoning a principle, sacrificing a principle on the altar of expediency. We will double or treble their [FAI and IRFU] income, income to encroach further on our schools. I was told rugby colleges would embrace our games when we removed Rule 27 [the ban on GAA members playing soccer, rugby, hockey or cricket]. Not one did. On the contrary, when we removed Rule 27 they maintained their own severe ban. Of course it will be shameful [if the FAI and IRFU were forced to play internationals in Britain] but no shame must be attached to the GAA. They have created their own problem and it's theirs to solve.'

The relaxation of Rule 42 was a triumph for common sense and the efforts of individuals such as Noel Walsh of Clare, Liam O'Neill of Laois and, in particular, Tommy Kenoy of Kilmore Gaels. Kenoy tabled a Roscommon motion on the opening up of Croke Park at the 2001 GAA Annual Congress and saw it defeated by a famously dubious show of hands – 176 delegates voted in favour and 89 against, two votes short of the required two thirds majority. Forty-five delegates of the 309 present either abstained, including members of the top table, or had their vote overlooked in the show of hands. Kenoy requested a recount, standard practice given the closeness of the vote and margin for human error in the count, but the then GAA President, Sean McCague, refused and moved on to the next item on the agenda declaring, 'The vote is taken and the vote stands.' It was a close shave for the no lobby whose campaign had been boosted by the announcement the evening before the vote of an additional €78 million in government aid for the redevelopment of Croke Park.

In return, the GAA would play a series of games up to and possibly including All-Ireland semi-finals at the proposed new National Stadium in Abbotstown in West Dublin. The National Stadium was a pet project of Taoiseach Bertie Ahern and bringing the GAA on board, along with the FAI, which had dropped its independent plans to develop a new stadium, was seen as a coup for Ahern in his campaign to make the €1 billion 'Bertiebowl' a reality.

The Taoiseach's intervention was manna from heaven for those opposed to opening up Croke Park to soccer and rugby. The FAI and IRFU could continue to play their internationals in Lansdowne Road until the projected opening of the Abbotstown stadium in 2006. The argument that the GAA needed to open up Croke Park to help repay the mounting debt on the redevelopment of the new Hogan Stand was cancelled out by the overnight government windfall.

Before the vote, Cork County Secretary Frank Murphy claimed that a decision to amend Rule 42 could threaten the Abbotstown project, 'We must be conscious that a decision in favour of this motion today will bring, without question, undoubted pressure on the government to change its decision on the building of Stadium Ireland.' Other opponents of change, including three past presidents, were more straight about their objections. 'If it is passed it will be the beginning of a great departure,' warned Pat Fanning. 'Open up Croke Park now and as sure as night follows day, the forces of change will become irresistible... As long as this association stands fast and remains true to itself, so long will the association endure and the ideals which motivates it and for which it was founded. I am asking Congress: maintain this trust, hold fast to the past and everything will be well. Surrender now and we'll be on the rocky road to disaster.'

The campaigners for change were equally eloquent and

impassioned, 'In a multicultural society, exclusivity is not as justifiable as it was in the past. I want us to show that we can be generous, open and welcoming in the best traditions of our nation,' said Liam O'Neill from Laois. One of the most interesting contributions came from Cathal Lynch, the secretary of the GAA's European Board. The Brussels-based Leitrim man questioned the paradox of the GAA saying no to soccer and rugby in Croke Park while its members availed of soccer and rugby grounds abroad for hurling and football. 'This year we're playing in a European league. The first round was held in Rennes, we played it on the grounds of Rennes Rugby Club. The second round was held in Paris last weekend on the grounds of a rugby ground. The third round will be played on a cricket ground in Guernsey, the fourth round will be played in Luxembourg on a soccer ground. The fifth round will be played in Brussels on a cricket ground in, irony of ironies, the British Club in Brussels, and the final round is going to be played on a rugby ground in The Hague. If this motion is defeated here today, if we follow it through, should we still be allowed to play on the grounds given to us by these sports? The world is changing around us. We live in a multicultural society. We should have the self-confidence to go ahead as an association, we have nothing to fear from other sports.'

Despite Lynch's convincing case for a yes to change, the no vote held the day. By the time the 2002 Congress came around, opposition had hardened against any change to Rule 42. After a winter of intense lobbying of the grassroots by the no camp, just one county – Clare – succeeded in even getting a motion on amending Rule 42 onto the Congress agenda. It was defeated by 197 votes to 106, a complete reversal of the previous year's vote. And the 2004 Motions Committee stunt was well signalled when Sean McCague stated, after the vote, that the Clare motion could technically have been ruled out of order. Meanwhile, the GAA's own Strategic Review Committee, including past presidents Quinn and McDonagh, had already recommended that Central Council be given a mandate to decide on opening up Croke Park. But, with the 'Bertiebowl' still a live project and the GAA waiting on the full payment of the promised €78 million, the yes camp had to bide their time. When the Abbotstown proposal was finally abandoned and the IRFU formally committed to demolishing Lansdowne Road, only then could the powerful advocates for change within the GAA's hierarchy emerge and state their case. It should have happened in 2004 but, like the Northern Peace Process, symbolism and nuance and saving face is everything in GAA politics. Having made their last stand in 2004, the no camp had exhausted all possibilities and could accept the 2005 decision to amend Rule 42 while claiming to have done all in their power to halt the march of the Garrison Game into Croke Park.

No one questioned the sincerity or integrity of past presidents Pat Fanning and Con Murphy in their stance on Rule 42 but, by 2005, the idea that soccer and rugby posed a threat to the GAA no longer had any basis in reality. The GAA had survived the era of Jack's Army and Sky Sports intact. It was gaining in profile, prestige and playing numbers with every passing year – and, during the 1990s, had pragmatically sacrificed plenty of other scared cows on the 'altar of expediency'. Few of those opposed to a change on Rule 42 appeared to have any problem with the GAA accepting millions in sponsorship from Guinness or endorsing McDonalds as a sponsor for underage hurling skills competitions in Croke Park even though alcohol abuse and obesity are the two major public health issues in Ireland. It was a case of booze, burgers and Bono, yes; Roy Keane and Brian O'Driscoll, no. By 2005, the entrenched opposition to soccer and rugby and simultaneous embrace of corporate money was an indefensible contradiction in values.

Rule 42 had its roots in the same era as Rule 27 – or 'The Ban' on GAA members playing soccer, rugby, hockey or cricket. 'The Ban' didn't just extend to the playing of 'foreign' – i.e. English – games. GAA players and members could expect a lengthy suspension from hurling or football activity if convicted of even attending a 'foreign' sporting event. Incredible as it might appear to younger readers, the GAA had Stalinist-style Vigilance Committees in place to enforce Rule 27. Vigilance Committee members attended soccer and rugby matches and reported back on any GAA men spotted in attendance. It led to some comical and sad scenarios. The great Limerick hurler Mick Mackey was partial to watching a game of rugby or soccer. So, rather than run the risk of having Mackey suspended, the Limerick County Board appointed him to their Vigilance Committee and he was free to watch whatever he wanted. 'The Ban' and all it stood for reached a nadir in 1938 when Dr Douglas Hyde – the founder of the Gaelic League, the first President of Ireland and a patron of the GAA – was blackballed by the association for attending an international soccer match in his capacity as the nation's President. And even though the Catholic Church had amended it's prohibition on Catholics attending non-Catholic services, there was no official GAA presence at Douglas Hyde's Protestant funeral service in St Patrick's Cathedral in July 1949. The GAA took its lead on this matter of conscience from the coalition government led by Fine Gael's John A. Costello. Neither Costello, nor any member of his cabinet, attended the former Head of State's funeral – the only two Catholics present were the French ambassador and the poet Austin Clarke.

'The Ban', first imposed in 1918, was eventually scrapped at the GAA's 1971 Congress held in Belfast, although it's interesting to note that a motion to abandon it had been moved at Congress as far back as 1923. The campaign to remove 'The Ban' was led by Tom Woulfe, a Kerryman who was a member of the Civil Service Club in Dublin. His club's motion was approved by the Dublin County Board in 1965 but defeated at Congress that year and again in 1968. A Mayo motion that a national referendum of all clubs be held on the issue was successful and the result of the referendum was a massive vote in favour of deleting the ban. By 1971, its removal was a formality. Laois delegate Lar Brady had the distinction of being the last, and only, dissenting voice.

There was also a motion before the 1971 Congress to delete Rule 21 (then known as Rule 15). This was the ban on members of the British army or Northern Irish police forces joining the GAA. 'Amazingly, the Rule 15 motion was not moved at Congress,' Tom Woulfe recalled in *The Irish Times* GAA Centenary Supplement in 1984. 'Had it been put to the meeting, it is likely that it would have been passed in the ecumenical climate of the day.' It took another 20 years for the GAA to remove Rule 21.

The debate on Rule 21 was far more complex and emotive than that on Rule 42. Unlike Rule 42, the thinking behind Rule 21 had a direct and daily relevance for the lives of GAA members in the North. As the Troubles worsened between the early 1970s and 1990s, GAA members were routinely harassed by the British army, the RUC and UDR reservists. GAA clubhouses were frequently attacked and burned out. A section of Crossmaglen Rangers' grounds had been occupied by the British army since the 1970s. In 1988, Aidan McAnespie – a member of the Aghaloo O'Neill's club in Tyrone – was shot dead by British soldiers while crossing the border in Aughnacloy on his way to a football match. Three years later, the UDA declared that GAA members were 'legitimate targets'. Sean Brown, a member of the Bellaghy Wolfe Tones club in Derry, was murdered by loyalist paramilitaries in May 1997 as he left the Bellaghy clubhouse. Like many nationalists, GAA members were convinced that there was British army and RUC collusion in some of the attacks on its members and property. Until the entire political and security climate in Ulster changed, Rule 21 was viewed as a necessary statement of independence and identity in a hostile environment.

In the Republic, political pressure had been growing on the GAA since the early 1990s to remove Rule 21 as a gesture of reconciliation. This intensified after the signing of the Good Friday Agreement on 8 April 1998. Eight days after the agreement, the GAA's progressive new President, Joe McDonagh, attempted a brave if ill-advised coup at the association's Annual

1988

Aiden McAnespie shot dead by British Army as he walked across the Border at Aughnacloy

John McAnespie, the father of Aidan, protesting outside Congress before the debate on repealing Rule 21.

Congress being held at the Burlington Hotel in Dublin. McDonagh, a former Galway senior hurler who gave a famous rendition of 'The West's Awake' in the Hogan Stand after his county's All-Ireland breakthrough in 1980, was a radical by GAA standards. While Sinn Féin held its Ard Fheis less than half a mile away in the RDS, McDonagh proposed a debate and vote on the removal of Rule 21. He was convinced the Taosieach's assurances that the British army was ready to quit Crossmaglen Rangers' property would appease delegates from the North. Successfully pushing through the removal of Rule 21 at his first Congress as President would have silenced many of the association's critics and set the tone for a reforming presidency, but it quickly became apparent that McDonagh's proposal was a step too far for the Ulster delegates, as well as a handful of southern counties, parti-cularly Cork. Four counties – Antrim, Armagh, Derry and Tyrone – opposed a vote, reasonably arguing that they couldn't vote on the proposal without a mandate either way from their clubs. McDonagh could have forced the issue but, rather than risk a walkout and a possible split within the GAA, he backed down and settled for a Special Congress to debate Rule 21 on 30 May 1998.

McDonagh's attempt to remove Rule 21 reflected the post-Good Friday Agreement euphoria and optimism but it was far too soon for Ulster delegates to countenance reaching out the hand of friendship, even if only symbolic, to the security forces. The Special Congress on 30 May didn't vote on removal and instead brokered a compromise that left the way open for change. After a reasoned and even-tempered debate, delegates agreed to the following motion: 'Cumann Luthchleas Gael pledges its intent to delete Rule 21 from its Official Guide when effective steps are taken to implement the amended structures and police arrangements envisaged in the British/Irish Peace Agreement.'

However, it would take three years for the breakthrough to happen. The Patton Report on policing in the North paved the way for the GAA to again tackle Rule 21 and it was finally removed at a Special Congress in Dublin on 14 November 2001. All 26 counties and, crucially, County Down, supported the abolition. The GAA, now led by Sean McCague, had felt it was essential to have at least one of the Six Counties in favour of the motion before it could proceed with the vote. Cork's decision to support change was also critical and the motion was passed by an overwhelming majority.

In practical terms, the removal of Rule 21 has had little immediate effect. The PSNI GAA club's playing activities have been restricted to playing games against An Garda Síochána, the London Met, the NYPD and other Northern Irish civil service teams. Four years after the deletion of Rule 21, no regular club side in the Six Counties has played a match against the PSNI. But, with an increasing number of recruits from the South and a growing nationalist acceptance of the PSNI as an even-handed police service for both communities, there is optimism that in 10 to 20 years time the PSNI may enjoy a similar status in Northern GAA circles as the Garda Síochána does in the South. The GAA announcement at the end of September 2005 that the PSNI training college GAA club been accepted into the Sigerson Cup competition for third-level institutions has moved the rapprochement on further.

KERRY MAY HAVE WON THEIR 33RD TITLE, but the 2004 football championship will be remembered as much for the adventures of Charlie Mulgrew and the Ernesiders and Páidí Ó Sé and the midlanders as the ultimate destination of the Sam

Maguire. The excitement Fermanagh and Westmeath brought to the summer confounded the grave pre-season forecasts about the imminent demise of Gaelic football as we knew it appear hasty and premature.

The 2003 All-Ireland finalists Armagh and Tyrone both exited at the quarter-final stage in Croke Park on Saturday, 7 August. Tyrone had regrouped bravely after the devastating sudden death of their full-back and captain Cormac McAnallen but looked a tired team against rejuvenated Connacht champions Mayo, who played some direct and classy football to advance to the semi-finals. However, that was a minor shock compared to the first quarter-final where lowly Fermanagh ran Armagh off the pitch with a display that restored a lot of people's faith in the game.

Fermanagh were beaten 1–21 to 0–5 by Tyrone in Croke Park

Fermanagh players celebrate at the final whistle of the All-Ireland quarter-final against Armagh.

in the 2003 quarter-final and the internal bickering that followed that defeat saw manager Dominic Corrigan resign and 10 players, including the Gallaghers, Rory and Raymie, leave the panel. Former Donegal player Charlie Mulgrew stepped into the management vacuum and drafted seven under-21s into the team. They lost their opening game in Ulster to Tyrone by four points but beat Meath by 0–19 to 2–12 in an extra-time thriller in Brewster Park.

Instead of massed defence, Mulgrew's team favoured a massed-attack approach based on adventurous and endless running that baffled Cork, Donegal and then an Armagh side who had looked near invincible when beating Donegal 3–15 to 0–11 in the Ulster final, which had been played before 67,000 supporters in Croke Park on 11 July. Fermanagh went within minutes of beating Mayo in the All-Ireland semi-final but John Maughan's side rescued a 0–9 apiece draw with a late point. Mayo scored three points in the last 10 minutes to win the replay by 0–13 to 1–8. Fermanagh again missed a lot of chances but it had been an incredible summer for Mulgrew and players such as such as Barry Owens, Niall Bogue, Martin McGrath, Liam McBarron, James Sherry, Stephen Maguire, Mark Little, Colm Bradley and Tom Brewster. Barry Owens and McGrath won All-Star awards to join Peter McGinnity who won Fermanagh's first – and until 2004 only – All-Star in 1982.

At the beginning of the year, Fermanagh, Wicklow and Westmeath were the only three counties in the country to have never won a senior provincial title. By 24 July, Westmeath, guided by Páidí Ó Sé, had broken their 120-year hoodoo. Ó Sé left Kerry and the bitter memories of Armagh and Tyrone behind him when he was appointed Westmeath manager in October 2003. His predecessor, Luke Dempsey, had laid the groundwork with an exceptional group of players who had come close to the breakthrough in 2001 and Ó Sé and his assistant Tomas

O'Flahartha provided the missing element of championship cuteness and self-belief.

Westmeath's campaign began with a first victory over Offaly in 55 years followed by wins over Dublin and Wexford to set up a Leinster final confrontation with Laois and Mick O'Dwyer. The teams drew 0–13 in an absorbing and high-quality Leinster final where Laois captain Chris Conway scored the equaliser in injury-time. Six days later, Westmeath didn't score for the first 24 minutes but still led 0–7 to 0–5 at half-time, thanks to an extraordinary four-point burst before the break from Dessie Dolan, Denis Glennon and wing-back Michael Ennis. Having diced with disaster and survived, Westmeath were a transformed team for 10 minutes after the restart and points from Feargal Wilson, Dolan, Brian Morley and Mangan left them six ahead, but they didn't score for the final 20 minutes as Laois cut the gap to three. When Laois missed a clear-cut goal opportunity in injury-time, the agony ended for Westmeath and Croke Park experienced another outpouring of tribal rapture. Final score: Westmeath 0–12 Laois 0–10.

Westmeath supporters celebrate their 2004 Leinster title.

Limerick footballers hadn't won a Munster title since 1896 but went close when they drew 1–10 apiece with Kerry in a grim Munster final at the Gaelic Grounds on 11 July. Limerick led a foul-ridden game by three points at half-time and could have ended the 108-year itch if it hadn't been for some spectacular fielding by Darragh Ó Sé. The Gaeltacht man stopped two injury-time frees from Stephen Kelly and Eoin Keating going over the crossbar. There was more sorrow for Limerick in the replay when they again got off to a flying start but were reeled in by two Kerry goals towards half-time. The second came from a controversial penalty scored by Dara Ó Cinnéide and a third goal early in the second half from Tomás Ó Sé wrapped it up for Kerry. Final score: Kerry 3–10 Limerick 2–9.

It was heartbreaking stuff for Limerick manager Liam Kearns and players such as Stephen Lucey, John Galvin, Jason Stokes, Muiris Gavin, Stephen Kelly and John Quane who had been working towards a Munster title for four years.

No other team got as close as Limerick to beating Kerry in 2004. Under the management of Jack O'Connor, Kerry had learned the hard lessons from 2002 and 2003 and were far more focused and better prepared physically as they anticipated another confrontation with either Armagh or Tyrone. Instead, the only Ulster opposition they encountered was a limited Derry team who had a narrow, and fortunate, quarter-final victory over Westmeath. Once they got to grips with Derry's dangerous inside-forwards, Enda Muldoon and Paddy Bradley, Kerry were never troubled and they won their All-Ireland semi-final pulling up by 1–17 to 1–11.

The All-Ireland final was a terrible anti-climax as Mayo again froze and were overwhelmed by Kerry's physical strength, speed of thought and the genius of Gooch Cooper. Alan Dillon's early goal for Mayo was cancelled out by Cooper's 25th-minute strike.

Kerry led by 1–12 to 1–4 at half-time and Mayo supporters had started to leave with 15 minutes remaining as Kerry reclaimed Sam on a 1–20 to 2–9 scoreline. Man of the Match Copper scored 1–4 from play and Dara Ó Cinnéide kicked eight points from frees and play as Kerry amassed the highest All-Ireland final score since the 5–11 they scored when they beat Dublin in 1978.

Kerry All-Ireland Football Champions 2004

Diarmuid Murphy

Aidan O'Mahoney   Michael McCarthy   Tom O'Sullivan

Marc Ó Sé   Eamonn Fitzmaurice   Tomás Ó Sé

William Kirby   Eoin Brosnan

Liam Hassett   Declan O'Sullivan   Paul Galvin

Colm Cooper   Dara Ó Cinnéide   Johnny Crowley

SUBS: Seamus Moynihan for Hassett, Mike Frank Russell for Crowley, Robeird O'Connor for Ó Cinnéide, Paddy Kelly for Galvin, Brian Guiney for Tomás Ó Sé

Cork Mutineers
Come Good at Last

The 2004 hurling championship was decided by another show-down between three-in-a-row chasing Kilkenny and a Cork team smarting from the 2003 defeat and under pressure to justify the new management structures and conditions delivered after the players strike in 2002. Both sides were beaten in their own province with the major shock coming in Leinster where Kilkenny were denied a record seventh consecutive Leinster title by 6/1 outsiders Wexford, who halted the Cats march with an amazing goal in the fourth minute of injury-time. Kilkenny had played poorly but were still two points in front when Michael Jacob blocked down a Peter Barry clearance, collected the sliotar from the break and hammered the winning goal past James McGarry from an acute angle. Kilkenny manager Brian Cody, who had left his customary sideline position to stand behind the Wexford goal collapsed to his knees in shock and despair as Wexford became the first team to beat Kilkenny in Leinster since 1997. Final score: Wexford 2–15 Kilkenny 1–16.

Kilkenny hadn't counted on having to negotiate the back-door in their three-in-a-row quest but they regained their equilibrium and overran Galway by 4–20 to 1–10 in the All-Ireland qualifier in Thurles on 11 July. League champions Galway fancied their chances but were caught up in the hurricane of Kilkenny and Cody's desire to avenge the 2001 All-Ireland semi-final defeat. Cody, normally a calm figure, was lucky to avoid censure for his sideline histrionics and verbal abuse of the referee. The uncharacteristic loss of cool by Cody was all the more unnecessary as Kilkenny were clearly in a different class to a Galway side who conceded 3–7 in the final 20 minutes.

Kilkenny never hit those heights again. Clare, managed by Anthony Daly, weren't going to be intimidated by Kilkenny and they went very close to beating Cody's team in the All-Ireland quarter-final on 25 July, Jamesie O'Connor scoring a late equaliser at the end of a classic display of hard, defensive hurling that finished 1–13 apiece. Clare looked the stronger team at the finish but Kilkenny won the replay in Thurles 1–11 to 0–9 and three first-half goals from Henry Shefflin and John Hoyne saw them defeat Munster champions Waterford by 3–12 to 0–18 in the All-Ireland semi-final on 8 August. It was another disappointing day in Croke Park for a Waterford side that badly missed the menace of John Mullane, who had been sent off in the Munster final. Waterford still edged out Cork by 3–16 to 1–21 in a game rated by some observers as one of the best Munster deciders for decades.

It was an arduous journey to the final for Kilkenny with every game taking a certain toll on a group of players under intense pressure to complete a modern three-in-a-row for the county. Cork, by contrast, cruised through the back-door. Antrim manager Dinny Cahill had the misfortune to publicly question Cork's ability and declare that, 'Brian Corcoran was finished' before the teams' quarter-final clash. The Rebel response was predictably ruthless: Cork 2–26 Antrim 0–10. After three years in retirement, Corcoran had rejoined the Cork squad in April and manager Donal O'Grady reinvented him as a full-forward to replace 2003 hero Setanta Ó hAilpín, who had gone to Australia.

Cork's semi-final opponents were Wexford who had won ▶

After a difficult few years, the Cork players celebrate.

the Leinster final against Offaly by 2–12 to 1–12 thanks to series of superb saves from goalkeeper Damien Fitzhenry. Wexford were optimistic they could reverse their 13-point 2003 semi-final mauling from Cork but, this time, they lost by 15 with Cork looking imperious on a 2–25 to 1–13 scoreline.

Kilkenny's much-vaunted attack failed to deliver in the All-Ireland final on 12 September. D.J. Carey and Eddie Brennan were held scoreless and Henry Shefflin only scored one point from play. Diarmuid O'Sullivan, Wayne Sherlock, John Gardiner, Seán Óg Ó hAilpín and midfielders Tom Kenny and Gerry O'Connor were the key players at the back for Cork who recovered from a bad start to trail by one point, 0–7 to 0–6 at half-time.

Kilkenny could have been four or five points ahead given the amount of quality ball won and delivered by their half-backs, Tommy Walsh, Peter Barry and J.J. Delaney, but their dominance was broken by Niall McCarthy in the second half. The Cork centre-forward scored three points and was a constant menace with his powerful drives at the Kilkenny goal. Kilkenny scored just two points after half-time and failed to score in the final 20 minutes. Corcoran had the final say with a wonderfully angled point in the final minute to seal Cork's 30th All-Ireland title. Final score: Cork 0–19 Kilkenny 0–12.

Cork All-Ireland Hurling Champions 2004

Donal Óg Cusack

Wayne Sherlock   Diarmuid O'Sullivan   Brian Murphy

John Gardiner   Ronan Curran   Seán Óg Ó hAilpín

Tom Kenny   Jerry O'Connor

Ben O'Connor   Niall McCarthy   Timmy McCarthy

Kieran Murphy   Brian Corcoran   Joe Deane

Subs: John Browne for Brian Murphy

2005

Epilogue

'My hurling days are over, but let no one say that the best hurlers belong to the past. They are with us now and better yet to come.'

Christy Ring

'I think Irish society has changed more in the past 10 years than at any time in history.'

Clare hurling selector Fr Harry Bohan, January 2005

THE GAA-RELATED HEADLINES in September and October 2005 painted a vivid portrait of an organisation that never had it so good: 'Spirit of Croke Park gives us all hope and inspiration' (*The Irish Times*, 27 September); 'Cash rich GAA spends €12 million on games development' (*Sunday Independent*, 3 October); 'Finally us GAA muck savages get the credit we deserve' (*Irish Independent*, 10 October); 'Players fume as GAA reaps profits of Playstation game' (*The Sunday Tribune*, 9 October). An association that had once been perceived, in the words of its President Elect Peter Quinn in 1991, as 'negative, defensive and excessively conservative and backward' had embraced and prospered on change.

The serious statistical evidence of the GAA's primacy was provided by an ERSI (Economic and Social Research Institute) report in October that found that 57 per cent of Irish people who attend sporting fixtures go to hurling or Gaelic football matches and that 160,000 people are involved in the GAA as volunteers. The redevelopment of Croke Park is a source of national pride and the envy of the FAI and IRFU. An association that, in the not so distant past, was often accused of being symptomatic of the country's general paralysis is now so hip it almost hurts.

The corporate giants can't get enough of the GAA. Everyone from banks to mobile phone companies, with their live video alerts from Croke Park, wants a slice of the 'branded with tradition' action. It was a sometimes painful and wrenching transition, but the GAA has accommodated change more quickly and astutely than any other sporting or cultural body in the country.

The organisation's evolution has been so comprehensive it's easy to forget how far it has come since the early 1990s. Croke

Ballina players celebrate with fans after winning the All-Ireland club football final.

Park is the obvious beacon of the GAA's new-found confidence and modernity and, while it was being redeveloped, the association had the courage and energy to deal with the divisive relics of its past such as Rule 42 and Rule 21. Other once-sacred cows, such as the prohibition on corporate sponsorship of teams and live television coverage, have also been abandoned. The presence of Dessie Farrell, the chief executive of the Gaelic Players' Association, at a Central Council meeting in October 2005 is also evidence that the GAA is also finally ready to deal with the concerns and demands of its players.

During the summer of 2005, there were other more light-hearted and subtle indications of change at work. The sight of denim-clad Jade, a girl-band from Wexford, belting out 'Amhrán na bhFiann' before the Leinster hurling final was a far cry from the strait-laced days of Pioneer Pins and *fáinnes*. The advertisement for Nivea moisturiser for men on the scoreboard at the All-Ireland hurling final must have perplexed old-school hurling men and the fact that there was barely a whisper of debate about the opening of bars in Croke Park shows how blasé and unquestioning of change GAA people have become.

In tandem with the GAA's political *glasnost*, hurling and football have flourished to an intriguing extent in the face of the fissures that have opened up elsewhere in Irish society over the last two decades. In 2005, Tyrone took Gaelic football to a new level of excellence when they survived some epic tussles with Armagh before beating Kerry in the All-Ireland final. The back-door championship format has revolutionised Gaelic football and enabled counties such as Sligo, Fermanagh and Westmeath to experience previously undreamt of success and exposure in Croke Park.

During the 1990s, there were dire forecasts about the eminent demise of hurling in Cork but, after their victory over Galway in the 2005 final, the Rebels stand on the verge of a three-in-a-row and potential greatness. As ever, 2005 saw plenty of debate about the health of hurling, but Clare's valiant stand against Cork in one semi-final and Galway's 5–18 to 4–18 victory over Kilkenny in the other were two games that could take their place beside the best of any era. The pool of All-Ireland contenders may have narrowed since the halcyon days of Clare, Wexford and Offaly in the mid-1990s but the new structures in the hurling championship should ensure that other counties will emerge in future decades to rattle the game's aristocrats.

Given the GAA's continued lip service to amateur ideals, it's ironic that the corporate sector deserves some of the credit for the upsurge in attendances at Croke Park and elsewhere over the past decade. Slick advertising campaigns from Guinness, Vodafone, the Bank of Ireland, AIB and O$_2$ have opened up new terrain for hurling and football by reawakening the tribal instinct in people and places where it had lain long dormant. The games have been made more accessible and even sexy for audiences, primarily urban, who had been alienated from the GAA for decades.

Right from the beginning of the GAA, Michael Cusack identified the strength of the tribal instinct in Irish people as the rock upon which he would build his association. The parish boundaries that define the GAA are the only native boundaries that survived the Norman Conquest and Cusack recognised that giving ancient rivalries healthy expression in the anarchic energy of the country's native games would give his association a formidable energy and power. And so it has proved.

The GAA derives it real strength and values from its 2,000 plus parish clubs and the tens of thousands of people who work anonymously for the organisation. As Ireland becomes more globalised, the much ridiculed 'pride in the parish' is, if anything, stronger than Cusack could ever have imagined. This

Supporters celebrate James Stephens All-Ireland club hurling championship.

year's club championship finals, won by Ballina footballers and James Stephens hurlers from Kilkenny, drew a crowd in excess of 30,000 to Croke Park and club competitions in general are growing in strength every year.

Even if the finer points of the games are lost on you, the GAA enables you to connect in a meaningful way with the people you grew up with or embraced at some point in your life. More than any other sporting organisation in the country, the GAA also has the potential to be a powerful force for good in accommodating Ireland's changing ethnic mix. How it deals with this challenge will be a defining test of the organisation in the future. The GAA is far from perfect but it remains the closest thing we have to a national organisation of the people for the people.

Permission Acknowledgements

The author and publisher would like to thank the following for allowing the use of their copyrighted material in *GAA: The Glory Years*.

page x, extract from 'Greetings to Our Friends in Brazil' by Paul Durcan, published by Harvill Press. Reprinted by permission of The Random House Group UK.

Inpho Photography: 6; 10; 30; 32; 47; 51; 71; 111; 131; 303; 315 (Jack Boothman) **Inpho/Billy Stickland:** 18; 20; 42; 62; 81; 123; 128; 139; 142; 166; 203; 247; 251; 275 **Inpho/Lorraine O'Sullivan:** 61; 65; 148; 153; 200; 278; 287; 295; 315 (Seán Kelly, Sean McCague) **Inpho/Patrick Bolger:** 87; 91; 101; 160; 194; 211; 229; 240; 272; 283; 310; 315 (Pat Fanning); 329 **Inpho/Tom Honan:** 114; 193; 216; 222; 226; 297; 315 (Joe McDonagh) **Inpho/Keith Heneghan:** 163; 182; 188 **Inpho/James Meehan:** 165; 170 **Inpho/Damien James:** 213 **Inpho/Morgan Treacy:** 232; 253; 258; 292; 315 (Con Murphy); 326; 331 **Inpho/Andrew Paton:** 266; 308; 315 (Liam Mulvihill, Peter Quinn)

Despite our best efforts, the publisher and author were unable to contact all copyright holders prior to the publication *GAA: The Glory Years of Hurling and Football*. However, the publisher will make the usual arrangements with any copyright holders who make contact after publication.

Acknowledgements

Many thanks to Eamonn Sweeney for his good advice and encouragement on this project and almost 20 years of friendship and priceless post-mortems on the GAA and other matters. Dermot Crowe has been a true and constant friend; thanks for the laughs, late nights and the West Clare connection. Michael Clifford has been another rock of friendship and good humour. Special thanks to Clare Taylor and Francesca for the laptop and a welcome non-GAA perspective on the world. Austin Hanna and John Fitzgerald have been real friends during good times and bad as have Cormac Bourke, Patrice Harrington, Fiona Ryan, Eithne Tynan, Mark Keenan and Dave Donnelly.

My brothers Martin, Mike, Seamus and Eugene have always been a great support and special thanks to Martin for all the lifts to matches over the years, Mike for his generosity and keeping the home fires burning in London, Seamus for the accommodation in Dundalk and Eugene for the music. Thanks to Mary Higgins-Bellew for the inside track on Galway and Athenry hurling. Most of all, thanks to my mother for just being herself, for the stories and continuing to prove that good humour does indeed come from the kitchen.

Declan O'Brien, Ken Whelan, Aaron Dunne, Denis Byrne, Liam Hayes, Rebecca Kiernan, Aishling Conway, Eric Haughan, and the rest of the staff at the Gazette Group of newspapers in Lucan have been a great help over the past few months. Gratitude also to Adhamhnan O'Sullivan, Sports Editor of the *Sunday Independent* and Jim Carney in *The Tuam Herald*.

This book wouldn't have been published if it hadn't been for the support, expertise and patience of my publisher Ciara Considine and editor Claire Rourke at Hodder Headline Ireland and the talents of designer Karen Carty at Anú Design. Claire Rourke deserves very special thanks and credit for her faith in the project from start to finish. Finally, I consulted the works of many GAA writers and journalists during the research of this book and it wouldn't have been possible without their efforts and diligence over the years.

Ronnie Bellew
October 2005